The euro

An essential guide

PETER COFFEY

CONTINUUM
London and New York

For Hélène Peters and Charles Thysell,
my loyal and wonderful friends in Minneapolis

Continuum
The Tower Building, 11 York Road, London SE1 7NX
370 Lexington Avenue, New York, NY 10017–6503

First published 2001

British Library Cataloguing-in-Publication Data
A catalogue record for this book is available from the British Library.

ISBN 0–8264–4766–X (hardback)
   0–8264–4767–8 (paperback)

Library of Congress Cataloguing-in-Publication Data
Coffey, Peter.
   The euro: an essential guide/Peter Coffey.
      p. cm.
   Includes bibliographical references and index.
   ISBN 0–8264–4766–X (hardcover)—ISBN 0–8264–4767–8 (pbk.)
   1. Euro. 2. Money—European Union countries. 3. Monetary unions—European
Union countries. I. Title.

HG925 C628 2001
332.4'94—dc21

                                                        2001023518

Typeset by YHT Ltd, London
Printed and bound in Great Britain by Biddles Ltd, Guildford and King's Lynn

CONTENTS

ACKNOWLEDGEMENTS

Although all the opinions expressed in this work are exclusively those of the author, this work would not have been possible without an exchange of views with a number of distinguished friends and colleagues, who, in some cases, provided him with documents. He thus wishes to thank Heino Beckmann of the University of St. Thomas, Pierre-André Buigues of the European Commission, George Hess of the US Bank, Alexis Jacquemin of the European Commission and the University of Louvain–La-Neuve, André Louw, formerly of the European Commission, Ivo Maes of the Belgian Central Bank, André Sapir of the European Commission and the Institut Des Etudes Européennes at the Free University of Brussels, and Andrew Scott of the Europa Institute of the University of Edinburgh.

Every effort has been made to contact copyright holders. The author is very grateful to Lorenzo Riccardi of the Agence Europe S. A. who has kindly allowed him to reproduce most of the documents in the appendices at the end of this book. Similarly, thanks are due to the European Central Bank for permission to reproduce parts of their annual reports.

Last, but absolutely not least, special thanks are due to Tracy Stein, Mike Miklas, Claudia González and Augusto Franco who have so patiently and conscientiously typed the manuscript of this book. Also the author warmly thanks his assistant, Camilo Jaramillo, who has diligently prepared the index as well as obtaining some of the documents used in the preparation of this work. Much of this work was written in the positive environment provided by Kurt Timmer Meister's Café Septième, in Seattle. Also much encouragement was given by the author's friends in Seattle, Dean Bateman and Steven Stinson.

ABBREVIATIONS AND TERMS

BIS	Bank for International Settlements
CDs	certificates of deposit
c.i.f.	Cost, insurance and freight at the importer's border
CPI	Consumer Price Index
ECB	European Central Bank
ECU	European Currency Unit
EMI	European Monetary Institute
ESCB	European Systems of Central Bank
EU	European Union
EURIBOR	Euro Area Interbank offered rate for the euro. This system consists of 57 Prime Banks, grouped in the European Banking Federation (EBF) and the Association Cambiste Internationale (ACI)
GDP	Gross domestic product
HICP	Harmonized Index of Consumer Prices
IMF	International Monetary Fund
Money supply	
M1	Currency in circulation *plus* Current (sight) Accounts with commercial banks and similar institutions
M2	Currency in circulation *plus* Current (sight) Accounts, Deposit Time Accounts.
M3	M2 *plus* Savings Accounts
LIFFE	London Futures and Options Exchange Market
NCBs	National Central Banks
Repos	Repurchase Agreements
Target	Trans-European Automated Gross Settlement. Express System, is the Real-Time Gross (RTGS) system for the euro consisting of 15 national RTGS systems and the ECB payment mechanism

INTRODUCTION

This is indeed a most historic moment in the history of Europe. On the one hand, on 1 January 1999, 11 Member States (the Euro Zone countries are Austria, Belgium, Finland, France, Germany, Ireland, Italy, Luxemburg, Netherlands, Portugal and Spain) of the European Union (EU) entered the final stage of the economic and monetary union (EMU) and created a common currency area, the Euro Zone. Thus, at the latest, by 1 July 2002, the euro will be the sole legal tender for these countries. Until 1 January 2002, however, the national currencies of these countries will co-exist with the euro. This rather long transitional period is a delicate time, an issue discussed in the second half of this work.

On the other hand, the EU is engaged in serious and detailed negotiations with a number of Central and East European countries which wish to become members of the EU. Although I examine the possible implications of the EMU and the euro for these countries, this book is concerned almost exclusively with the EU's (formerly the EEC's) attempts at creating an EMU and a common currency.

In this work I examine the reasons, both economic and political, why the old EEC – as long ago as in 1969(!) – agreed to move along the road to creating an EMU 'provided the political will to do so existed'; the earlier attempts at creating an EMU, and the present situation with all the implications surrounding the creation of the euro.

When examining the euro itself, I assess its qualities as a currency, the institutional arrangements (notably the European Central Bank (ECB) and the European System of Central Banks (ESCB)), the policy choices, and the possible implications for those countries inside the Euro Zone as well as for the outsiders.

In the last but one part of this work, I look at initial developments in the life of the euro – its strengths and weaknesses, the rapid developments in the capital and banking markets and the future international role of the euro.

In the final part of the book, I make a critical assessment of the first eighteen months of the euro. More specifically, I examine

- the performance of the euro vis-à-vis the US Dollar
- the performance of the national economies of the EU Member States
- the practical operations – the Target system
- the European Central Bank in operation
- the economic development of the Euro Zone, taking a new look at this aspect, and
- possible future developments – including the integration and development of capital markets, again making a new assessment.

My conclusions are on the whole positive – despite the relative disappointment with the performance of the euro vis-à-vis the US Dollar. Furthermore, I am optimistic about the future, because whilst, on the whole, the EU Member States have been prudent in their economic management, their economies are now growing. This will encourage capital inflows which, in turn, will strengthen the euro. Finally, when, on 1 July 2002, the euro becomes sole legal tender in the countries of the Euro Zone, it will become a 'real' currency, used for everyday purposes, and less of a phantom-like currency than it might be now.

June and July 2000

As this book was going to press, I received news of a German reaction to the proposal made by the French Finance Minister, Laurent Fabius, that more power be concentrated in the hands of the Euro Zone Finance Ministers vis-à-vis the ECB. Speaking on 17 July 2000, Ernst Welteke, President of the German Bundesbank, flatly rejected this proposal, reaffirming that the independence of the ECB is 'clearly defined' in the EU treaties.

Just prior to this reaction, speaking in Brussels, on 12 July, Commissioner Pedro Solbes expressed his disquiet at the relative lack of preparedness for the introduction of the euro coins and notes. To quote from the *Bulletin Quotidien Europe*, 13 July:

Abandon the national currency units to the benefit of the Euro. On the basis of an assessment made between May and

July, Commissioner Solbes noted that companies were improving their preparations for the introduction of the Euro (in France, he noted, 1,000 companies are converting to the Euro each month), but that the situation nevertheless remains unsatisfactory: 'It will take 200 years at this rate'. The communication therefore notes an 'inadequate level of preparation' in so far as companies are 'preparing themselves rather slowly to the change', not being aware that all the invoices and the accounts in general will have to be established in Euros from 1 January 2002 (with exception of the Netherlands).

As far as the citizens are concerned, Mr Solbes noted that 'the Euro remained "little used" and that "little attention" is given to simultaneous use of Euros and national currency' (he did note, however, that Belgian and French banks are to give their customers' accounts in Euros in July 2001). He also noted with vexation that the public administrations, mainly at the local level, do not sufficiently play the role of instruction in the single currency for citizens. He noted that 'some practical experience should be extended throughout the Union'.

Preparation for introduction of Euro notes and coins. Considering that the transition of the Euro should be carried out 'effectively and rapidly', Commissioner Solbes spoke of the following aspects:

- **Manufacturer of notes and coins.** 50 billion coins are to be minted by 1 January 2002 and 39% had already been minted by end May. Over 14 billion notes will be printed by the same deadline in twelve printers of the Euro Zone, including one in Greece, under the direct control of the ECB and National Banks. There are no less than 120 models of coins to be minted because of the national sides.
- **Quality of coins.** This will be greater than that of national coins and it will be controlled by the ECB.
- **Adaptation for vending machines.** Six testing centres (two in Germany, one in Spain, one in Finland, France and the Netherlands) have been set up since the summer of 1999 and the Member States have been authorized to lend samples so that equipment manufacturers may carry out their tests.

- **Fight against counterfeiting.** Mr Solbes recalled that the mandate of Europol had been extended by the JHA Council in April 1999 and that this council had also, in May 2000, adopted a framework decision aimed at strengthening protection against counterfeiting by using penal sanctions and others. In the wake of this, the Commission will soon present a draft regulation aimed at organizing information flows on counterfeiting and those guilty of this kind of offence.
- **Exchange of notes and coins.** Mr Solbes recalled that this procedure would be broken down into three stages: (a) *Pre-supply before 1 January 2002.* All Member States plan to supply the groups most directly concerned with Euros in advance (banks, traders, fund carriers, manufacturers and operators of vending machines) during the *last four months of 2001.* For the *general public,* advance supplies of Euros will come about during the second half of December 2001 (except for Greece, Ireland and Italy which do not provide for this). (b) *Dual circulation period* (Euro/national currency). The main part of the changeover should be completed by the end of the first two weeks of 2002. Banks should exchange the national currency for the Euros for their customers for up to 500 Euros ('This is the idea we are working on', said Mr Solbes). One question still to be resolved concerns persons who do not have a bank account. National notes and coins will loose their legal value end February, except Germany (1 January), the Netherlands (28 January) and Ireland (9 February). (c) *Later phase of the dual circulation period.* In certain Member States, the exchange of the former national tender may still be carried out by the banks. The question of cash exchange continues to raise some questions to be settled. The Commission will follow-up the situation and, every two months, provide 'information on best practices' as well as 'recommendations'.

In response to questions, Commissioner Solbes noted that the problem encountered with the printing of EUR 100 notes is an 'excellent example of the control carried out by the ECB'.

Part One

The Historical and Theoretical Background

CHAPTER 1

THE EU'S EARLIER ATTEMPTS AT MONETARY UNION

THE BACKGROUND

To some observers, it is sometimes perplexing as to why the original six founder Member States of the then European Economic Community (EEC) – now the European Union (EU) – should have, at the end of 1969, in Den Haag, agreed to embark upon such a hazardous operation as the creation of an economic and monetary union (EMU). Such a commitment, rarely entered into on a voluntary basis, involves a considerable loss of economic and monetary sovereignty. Thus, when an EMU is fully operational, Member States will lose their right to vary the parity of their currencies to counter economic upturns or downturns. Furthermore, at such a stage, balance of payments considerations disappear between partner countries – to be replaced by regional disequilibria. Such a development makes necessary either the creation of a well-endowed regional fund and/or the use of automatic fiscal equalizing mechanisms as found, for example, in the United States and Germany. Thus, we must ask the question why these countries should have embarked upon such an enterprise.

There were, in fact, a number of sound economic and structural reasons why such a decision seemed to be a reasonable one at that time. In the first place, EU Member States are 'open' or 'very open' economies (see Table 1.1) and they thus prefer a régime of stable exchange rates. In the case of the six founder Member States, they had, by 1968, achieved most of the aims as laid down in the Treaty of Rome. Quite simply, ahead of time, the customs union had been achieved. Consequently, the economies of the Member States had become well integrated and they were conducting about half their trade between themselves. Then, there was the position of the Community's

Common Agricultural Policy (CAP). The successful functioning of this policy depended upon stable (preferably fixed) exchange rates. At an international level, the EEC had become the world's most important economic and trading bloc, endowed with the most important reserves of gold and convertible currencies. France had, for a number of years, considered that the Community should consequently be endowed with a 'common international monetary personality'. One of the best ways of demonstrating such a personality would be to create an EMU and a common currency. Finally, it should be borne in mind that up to 1968 the Western world had experienced a full decade of relatively stable exchange rates. It was hoped that this situation would continue, and one of the best ways of ensuring the continuation of this state of affairs would be to create an EMU.

Table 1.1   EC: degree of 'openness' in national economies in 1991 (as a percentage of GNP)

	Exports	Imports
Belgium	74.4	71.3
Denmark	35.8	29.9
France	22.7	22.4
Germany	33.7	27.8
Greece	20.7	30.1
Ireland	63.5	56.3
Italy	20.3	20.1
Luxembourg	97.8	101.4
Netherlands	56.4	50.7
Portugal	32.0	42.2
Spain	17.1	20.2
United Kingdom	23.8	24.2
EC total	28.3	27.1

Source: EC Commission, *European Economy*, No. 50, December 1991

THE EARLIER PLANS FOR AN EMU

In the more recent concern with the Delors Plan and the blueprint Treaty on European Union (the Maastricht Treaty) it is sometimes forgotten that four earlier plans had a tremendous impact on the future evolution of the Community's moves towards an EMU. In fact, during the period 1969–70, until the publication of the compromise (and second) Werner Plan in

October 1970,[1] no fewer than four plans had been submitted to the Council of Ministers. It is to these plans to which we shall now turn.

The aforementioned compromise plan was the result of the fundamental conflict between the two schools of thought, the Economists and the Monetarists. The former school mainly represented the official monetary views of West Germany and the Netherlands and the school's main architect, Carl Schiller. The latter school, the Monetarists, represented the official monetary views of France and Belgium, and the school's main architects were Raymond Barre and Valéry Giscard d'Estaing.

Basically, the differences between these two schools of thought concerned their attitudes to economic coordination and development, the fixing of exchange rates, the provision of credits for countries facing balance of payments problems, the liberalization of capital movements, and the question of supranationality. In turn, these attitudes to a large degree reflected the economic and monetary experiences of the aforementioned countries since the end of the Second World War. Nevertheless, there was some degree of similarity in their attitudes towards budgetary harmonization and coordination within the EEC.

Even thirty years later, it is useful to examine in some detail the plans which represent most clearly the two schools of thought. These are the Schiller and the Second Barre Plans. Both are plans with far-reaching implications for an eventual EMU.

Turning first to the Schiller Plan, one notes that its overriding aim is the coordination of the economic policies within the Community. Unfortunately, nowhere is it possible to find any clear guide as to how such coordination is to be realistically achieved. Also, it is difficult to see how some countries could liberalize capital movements without the provision of a well-endowed monetary fund. Similarly, even in the more heady days of 1969 and 1970, it is hard to see France accepting with equanimity a transfer of sovereignty to central supranational organs of the Community. However, a high degree of economic convergence is a precondition for an EMU.

The Schiller Plan is divided as follows into four stages:

1. The first stage is almost completely devoted to the setting up of a concrete base for the coordination of economic policy.

The principle here is the agreement on medium-term economic aims which should be checked each year by the Medium-Term Economic Policy Committee. In this respect the Commission should recommend to member governments measures which should be adopted where the aims are not being achieved. Here, cyclical weapons should be developed and completed in each Member State, allowing them to have the same effect in each country. To facilitate this process, economic statistics should be improved and coordinated and a communal system of economic signals should be organized.

In the strictly monetary sphere, at this stage, the holding of consultations regarding short-term measures plus the setting up of short-term credits linked with demands in the field of economic policy coordination are proposed. Likewise the coordination of policy regarding rates of interest, under the aegis of the Council of Ministers and the governors of the Central Banks, is envisaged. Finally, at this stage, the capital markets of the Six should be gradually liberalized.

2. Having organized and coordinated economic policy weapons among the Six, Schiller proposed the achievement of more evenly balanced economic development as the main aim during the second stage. This would take the form of recommendations to be made by the Council of Ministers regarding the general economic trend of national budgets and the taking to the Council of more frequent and important decisions concerning economic policy. At the same time, in the monetary field there should be more Cupertino in the cadre of the Committee of the Governors of the Central Banks and of the monetary committee. Equally a system of medium-term monetary aid should be put into effect. By this time, approximately 1974–5, there should no longer exist any fundamental economic disequilibria between the Member States.

3. At the third stage, measures of a supranational nature are proposed. These present an extraordinary volte-face with former German policy and mark a major divergence from the suggestions put forward by the Monetarists, who tend to reject supranational controls and to prefer the discipline of fixed exchange rates as the supreme measure of monetary control.

Schiller proposed an even stricter coordination of national economic priorities. In order to achieve this, the Community should be given powers which it does not yet possess. Thus the rule of the majority should be adopted as regards all important areas of economics, finance and money, e.g. control over national budgets. Hence the following steps should be taken: (a) a federal reserve system should be set up, based on the model of the United States; (b) the margins of exchange fluctuation between the national currencies should be reduced; (c) the exchange rates between the currencies of the Member States should not be modified, except with the agreement of the other partners, using a system of qualified majority voting; (d) lastly, medium-term aid should be increased for members experiencing balance of payments difficulties and a European Reserve Fund should be set up.

4. The final stage would be that of total supranationality when all the necessary powers in the economic, financial and monetary fields would be transferred to the organs of the Community. The Committee of the Governors of the Central Banks would become a European central council of banks using a majority voting system. Fixed and guaranteed exchange rates would be set between the Member States, and at this final stage a single European unit of currency would be introduced.[2]

In contrast, the Second Barre Plan, which represented both the views of the Commission as well as those of the Monetarists, and which was to have such an influence on the old 'snake' system and on the present European Monetary System, was notable because it categorically rejected the principle of fluctuating exchange rates and because it wished to give a unified intenational monetary personality to the European Economic Community. The main reasons given for the rejection of fluctuating exchange rates is that such fluctuations would hinder the creation of a Community capital market and would have negative social and psychological effects on the EEC. As a satisfactory move in the direction of fixing exchange rates, it is proposed that the margin of parity between the national currencies of the Member States of the Common Market should be reduced from 1.5 to 1.0 per cent. Although, like the Schiller

Plan, the Barre Plan does set down a series of stages for the achievement of a full economic and monetary union, it, unwisely, unlike its rival plan, sets down a timetable for this task. Here, again, this was to be a less than happy influence on the definitive Werner Plan.

The stages of the Second Barre Plan are as follows:

1. In the first stage (1970–1) the provision of medium-term aid (using the SDRs), as proposed in the First Plan, is suggested. By the end of 1970 the third economic medium-term plan should be adopted and economic policies should be more effectively coordinated, including medium-term budgetary policy with annual meetings of the Finance Ministers from 1971 onwards. At this stage, moves should also be made to generalize the value added tax (VAT) and plans set up to harmonize its levels throughout the EEC. Similar measures should also be adopted regarding capital movements within the Community. Under the aegis of the governors of the Central Banks, moves should be made towards the harmonization of credit policy. At the international level, the Community should make clear its position in the monetary sphere and establish rules regarding exchange rate fluctuations between the EEC and third parties.

2. During the second phase (1972–5) – the decisive stage – general economic policy directives should be laid down at Community level and its economic evolution should be examined each year on a 'rolling' basis.

   Budgetary and fiscal policies should be harmonized, particularly in the levels of the VAT, and all States should use similar budgetary weapons. Interestingly enough, Barre suggested that the main economic, fiscal and monetary lines should be examined at regular intervals by the Commission in consultation with the social partners and representatives of economic and social life.

   The Community capital market should be organized, thus removing the necessity of its access to the 'international' capital market. Already by the beginning of 1972, exchange fluctuations between the members' currencies should not be greater than one per cent, and in 1972 with the new allocation of SDRs these units should be communally controlled.

3. Thus, after an examination by the Commission of the situation in 1975, the Council could decide whether to move on to the third stage in 1976 or in 1978. At this stage the organs of the Community should be endowed with all the powers which an economic and monetary union would necessitate. A council of governors of the Central Banks should be set up to create a communal banking system. A European Reserve Fund should be set up. In two stages, all fluctuations between currency parities should be irrevocably eliminated.

Capital should be allowed to circulate freely within the Community, taxes should be harmonized, and finally a European unit of currency would be created.[3]

The next plan, the First Werner Report, which was examined by the Community Finance Ministers in Venice in May, 1970, was only concerned with the initial stage of integration, 1971–4. During the course of the examination by the Ministers, there seemed to be some consensus of opinion about the reduction of the margin of fluctuation around the parities of EEC national currencies, but a profound difference of opinion over the setting up of a Reserve Fund during the first stage of the EMU.

It was grave differences of opinion between the representatives of the two schools of thought at Venice in May, and then in Luxembourg in June 1970, which forced Barre to intervene on behalf of the Commission to ask the Ministers to vote on certain points on which they agreed to, and to ask the Werner Commission to prepare a final report for the autumn in which the differences of opinion in other fields would be reduced to a minimum.

Thus, the Second and definitive Werner Plan[4] was the compromise between these two schools of thought and became the blueprint for the first stage of the EMU, better known as the 'Snake' system.

Although the definitive Werner Plan was a compromise between the two schools of thought, it did, nevertheless, err somewhat more on the side of the Monetarists than on that of the Economists. This leaning is shown in a proposal for the narrowing of the margin of fluctuations round the central parity of the national currencies of the participating EEC Member States.

The Report only made detailed proposals for the first stage of the EMU (1971–3), but it did draw the attention of the Ministers to certain problems such as the regional one and the dangerous possibility of certain Central Banks losing out through exchange rate intervention. In the latter case, it was even suggested that compensation should be arranged.

However, the Committee of Governors of Central Banks (Annex No. 5 of the Report) appeared to have been blind to the fact of the crumbling nature of the international monetary edifice since they continued to attach far too great an importance to the role of the US Dollar. Similarly, they were short-sighted in their lack of support for the provision of substantial credits for countries facing balance of payments problems – suggesting that deficits and surpluses would simply balance themselves out!

NOTES

1. A full examination of these plans may be found in Part Two of *European Monetary Integration*, P. Coffey and J.R. Presley, Macmillan, London, 1971.
2. Quoted from Part Two, *European Monetary Integration*, P. Coffey and J.R. Presley, Macmillan, London, 1971.
3. Quoted from Part Two, *European Monetary Integration*, P. Coffey and J.R. Presley, Macmillan, London, 1971.
4. Council–Commission of the European Communities. *Report to the Council and to the Commission on the Realization by Stages of Economic and Monetary Union in the Community*, (The Werner Report), Luxembourg, October, 1970.

CHAPTER 2

THE 'SNAKE' ARRANGEMENT

As noted in the previous chapter, the Werner Plan did, technically speaking, err somewhat on the side of the precepts of the Monetarist school rather than those of the Economic school. This was most evident in the proposal to narrow the margin of fluctuation around the EEC national currencies vis-à-vis a somewhat wider margin of fluctuation for the US Dollar. Thus, the expression coined was the 'Snake in the tunnel' (see Figures 2.1 and 2.2). However, as we shall see, this technical proposal was conceived at a time when exchange rates were still relatively stable. This all changed when, on 21 August 1971, President Nixon unilaterally suspended the conversion of US Dollars against gold (the so-called Gold Exchange Standard). The subsequent floating downwards of the US currency meant that the international monetary environment had changed completely. It also implied that any de facto monetary union did need a much greater degree of economic and monetary coordination than had ever been envisaged by the EEC. Also, it implied that great foreign exchange reserves would be needed to help bolster currencies which came under speculative pressure.

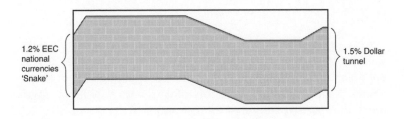

1.2% EEC national currencies 'Snake'

1.5% Dollar tunnel

Figure 2.1 The 'Snake in the tunnel' arrangement as proposed in the Werner Plan in 1970

As has just been noted, the real technical manifestation of the system was to be the 'Snake in the tunnel'. This 'Snake' was to have been a narrow band of fluctuation (of 1.2 per cent) originally planned for central parities of the national currencies of the participating Member States of the EEC – which was to have moved in the wider band of fluctuation (1.5 per cent) formerly allowed for the US Dollar (see Figure 2.1). However, following the major Dollar crisis of 1971, the suspension of the Dollar convertibility against gold and the subsequent Smithsonian Agreement allowing a margin of fluctuation around the Dollar of 4.5 per cent, the EEC had to re-examine the situation. Therefore, in March 1971, it was agreed to introduce, on an experimental basis, before 1 July 1972 (in fact this was introduced in April 1972), a system whereby the margin of fluctuation around the currencies of the participating EEC Member States would be 2.25 per cent – this was to move in a Dollar tunnel of 4.5 per cent (see Figure 2.2). But, with the complete floating of the Dollar in March 1973, the tunnel was dropped and the 'Snake' participants organized a joint float against the Dollar.

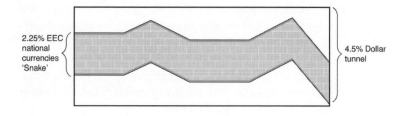

2.25% EEC national currencies 'Snake'

4.5% Dollar tunnel

Figure 2.2 The proposed 'Snake in the tunnel' arrangement following the Smithsonian Agreement in 1971

Although the 'Snake' system did constitute a zone of monetary stability in a sea of considerable international upheavals, it was not a particularly happy experience (see Appendix 1a). Both the United Kingdom and the Republic of Ireland left the arrangement after participating in it for just under two months. Italy left a few months later. France left temporarily, returned and then definitively left the arrangement. At the end of its life (March

1979), the 'Snake' arrangement represented a Deutsche Bank Zone, consisting of Belgium, Denmark, Luxembourg, the Netherlands and West Germany. Many reasons may be advanced for the relative failure of this first attempt at creating an EMU within the EEC. By its very nature, the 'Snake' arrangement, being an attempt at stabilizing exchange rates, was sailing against international economic and monetary winds as symbolized by an international system of floating exchange rates. This situation made a high degree of coordination of national economic and monetary policies among the participating countries absolutely essential. In reality, such coordination was non-existent. In exchange for a greater degree of economic and monetary self-discipline among these States, a much more substantial amount of credits should have been made available to participating countries facing balance of payments problems. The plight of both the United Kingdom and Italy made such a need obvious. In contrast, the technical mechanism was both too rigid and one-sided. When exchange rate adjustments were accepted, they normally came too late. Also, the responsibility for making national economic adjustments – as well as for exchange rate intervention – tended to fall much more heavily on the deficit countries (balance of payments) than on the surplus ones. Nevertheless, the system did represent a rare zone of monetary stability.

As the system was approaching its demise, two very serious developments were making themselves manifest at the international level. One was the inflation-creating element embodied in floating exchange rates. The other was the glaring lack of monetary action by the American administration concerning the US Dollar. Both these developments considerably alarmed governments of EEC Member States – especially those of France and West Germany.

The first semi-official call for united Community action against these two developments came in a speech made by Mr Jenkins (then President of the EEC Commission) at Florence, in October 1977, when he made a proposal for a European Monetary System. This idea was taken up at the Bremen Summit in July 1978 – especially by Chancellor Schmidt and President Giscard D'Estaing. The EMS came into operation on 13 March 1979.

CHAPTER 3

THE EUROPEAN MONETARY SYSTEM

THE BACKGROUND

The background to the creation of the European Monetary System (EMS) is a mixture of economic and political considerations. Thus, at the end of the last chapter, reference was made to the growing disenchantment with the inflationary effects of floating exchange rates and with the alarm at the lack of action in the monetary field by the US administration. This latter point was really important. The economies of the EEC Member States are either open or very open ones, whereas those of both the United States and the Soviet Union are closed ones – then exporting only about five per cent of their gross national product. Therefore, in contrast with the Americans, the West Europeans just cannot afford to ignore volatile and violent exchange rate movements. Consequently, they just had to do something about the lack of American action.

At this point, the question should be asked, why did not the Common Market countries simply organize a joint float against the US Dollar? The answer to this question must be that the West Germans and the French – in the persons of Chancellor Schmidt and President Giscard D'Estaing – wanted something more than a simple arrangement vis-à-vis the United States. They preferred a move towards a greater degree of economic and political integration in the Community. The decision to create a European Monetary System (hereafter called the EMS) was, therefore, much more a political than an economic one.

Italy, although at times in favour of European economic and political integration, had suspicions about the apparent Franco-German cooperation. Eventually, the Italians were placated by the special wide band of fluctuation for the Lira which they obtained. Also, like the Irish, they obtained interest rate subsidies.

The smaller countries, Denmark and the Benelux States, at all times closely linked economically to West Germany and the Deutsche Mark, always tended to follow the movements of that currency.

Even more so than Italy, the United Kingdom was deeply suspicious of the foregone agreement between France and Germany. The British had also never forgotten the trauma of their experience in the old 'Snake' arrangement, when, in the space of less than two months, they lost about 30 per cent of their reserves. Furthermore, since the Pound Sterling was now an oil currency – and tending to appreciate – there were sound scientific reasons why the British should not join the EMS.

At a more profound level, there were reasons linked with the traditions of national economic philosophy which made the planned EMS attractive. France, with the notable exception of the period 1945 to 1957, had, since the beginning of the century, been in favour of stable exchange rates. Thus, any agreement or system which aimed at stabilizing exchange rates should find favour with French governments – especially with a liberal economic one.

West Germany, obsessed with the memories of the dreadful economic and political consequences of the two periods of inflation in the 1920s and the 1930s had made the control of inflation its main postwar economic and monetary aim. Here, any system aiming at controlling inflation would tend to be supported by a West German government. Certain of the smaller countries, notably the Benelux ones, had also, since the end of the Second World War, tended to prone economic and monetary policies aiming at stable exchange rates and the control of inflation. These countries also, at least officially, tended to favour a greater degree of European economic and political integration. Thus, systems which embodied these aims would tend to be supported by these countries.

At this point, it is possible to observe certain economic, monetary, and political trends and preferences among the majority of Community Member States. There is a general alarm at the collapse of the US Dollar and the inaction of the US administration in the monetary field. This alarm is reinforced by the fears (expressed by all EEC countries) of inflation and the desire to combat this danger.

The desire for stable exchange rates and to combat inflation conforms with the basic economic and monetary philosophy of at least five Member States. Some of these countries also desire to see a greater degree of economic and political integration in the EEC. Thus, the stage is set for the construction of a system which has to be superior to the old 'Snake' arrangement.

However, it is important to bear in mind that the EMS is essentially a political decision taken under the impetus of France and West Germany. It obviously has to be more flexible and compulsory than its predecessor. Furthermore, a new failure would tend to bring discredit on any future attempts at economic and monetary integration.

The EMS, which came into being on 13 March 1979, clearly demonstrated – both in the Resolution of the Council of Ministers of 5 December 1978, as well as in the mechanisms used in the System – fundamental economic and monetary aims which had been missing from its predecessor. Thus, the author discerns the following aims in the EMS:

(i) a greater degree of convergence of the economies of the participating Member States;
(ii) the adoption of a common public policy choice for those countries – more specifically the control of levels of inflation – also aiming at convergence;
(iii) exchange rate stability;
(iv) the promotion of a central role for the ECU; and,
(v) hopefully some moves to a greater degree of integration among the Community's Member States.

Clearly, had the old 'Snake' arrangement mechanism of a common band for currency to currency (GRID) fluctuation simply been adopted the EMS would not have differed from its predecessor. However, in view of the aforementioned aims which the author finds to be inherent in the System, then a more sophisticated, effective and responsible mechanism had to be devised. It had to embody these qualities, constraints and indeed flexibility which had been missing from its predecessor.

Equally, it had to attempt to share the responsibilities for exchange rate intervention between both the surplus and the deficit countries. The ECU,[1] then, had, technically at least, to become the kingpin of the mechanism. Equally, for exchange rate intervention purposes, more sophisticated, effective and responsible mechanisms had to be invented. The outcome is two bands of fluctuation, running side by side. The first is indeed the old national currency to national currency (or GRID) mechanism whereby a band of fluctuation (as was formerly the case with the 'Snake' system) of 2.25 per cent (with a band of 6 per cent allowed for Italy) operates (see Figure 3.1). Here, the Commission has introduced a most novel system. This is the 'individualization' of the band of fluctuation for each participating currency (see Table 3.1). This was necessary in order to prevent certain currencies from coming under unwarranted pressure on the exchange markets. At the same time, this mechanism was further refined by the very important introduction of a 'divergence' threshold, the equivalent of 75 per cent of the central part of the 'individualization', at which point, the country concerned should take action to bring its currency into line.

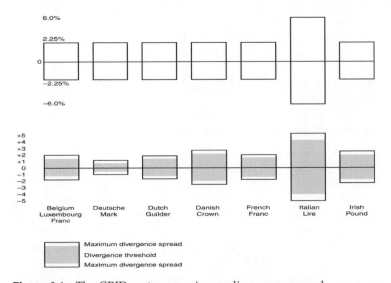

Figure 3.1 The GRID system: maximum divergence spread
Note: Divergence threshold: when a currency reaches the upper or lower limits of this band, the government concerned must intervene in the exchange markets
Source: Reproduced from P. Coffey, 'The European Monetary System – Six Months Later', *Three Banks Review*, December 1979

Table 3.1 The Commission's 'individualization' of Maximum Divergence Spreads and Divergence Thresholds

Currency	Maximum Divergence Threshold Spread vis-à-vis the ECU (as of Nov. 21 1992) %	Divergence Threshold vis-à-vis the ECU (until Sept. 16 1984) %	Divergence Threshold (after Sept. 16 1984) %
Belgian/Luxembourg Franc	2.06	1.52	1.543
Deutsche Mark	1.54	1.13	1.146
Dutch Guilder	–	1.51	1.516
Danish Crown	2.19	1.64	1.642
French Franc	1.80	1.35	1.366
Italian Lira	–	4.07	4.051
Irish Pound	2.22	1.67	1.667
Pound Sterling	–	–	–
Portuguese Escudo	5.95	–	–
Spanish Peseta	5.71	–	–

Here, the responsibilities of the country concerned when the Divergence Indicator is reached vis-à-vis the ECU by its currency are clearly laid down by the Resolution of the Council of Ministers of 5 December 1978. They are:

● diversified intervention;
● monetary measures;
● drawing on credit facilities; and,
● external and domestic policy measures.

Another major innovation of the EMS is the important place given to the ECU.[2] The idea here is that the Community's unit of account (used for all official EEC transactions) should be the kingpin for the future moves towards the implementation of an economic and monetary union. The hoped-for means of achieving this aim was to have been through a transformation of the European Fund for Monetary Cooperation (then a shadow of a legal entity) into a more concrete organ at a second stage in the evolution of the EMS. To this end, the participating Member States, together with the United Kingdom, which is not a member of the EMS, have exchanged 20 per cent of their holdings of gold and dollars against ECUs.

The lack of credits under the old 'Snake' system was one of its more serious defects. This defect has largely been made good under the EMS. Thus, the amount of credits available to Member States – should they face pressures on their currencies and balance of payments problems – are substantially larger. In 1981, the approximate value of these credits[3] was 25 billion units of account compared with 11.45 billion units of account under the former system.

A further refinement of the system was the setting aside each year for a period of five years (until 1983) of 200 million ECUs to provide interest subsidies on EIB or NCI loans for Italy and Ireland.

To the uninitiated outside observer, this sharing of the responsibilities for the management of the EMS may, at first sight, seem to be unduly complex. In reality, this sharing is purely a reflection of the difficult process of economic, monetary and political integration.

The actual responsibility for the day-to-day intervention in the money markets to keep national currencies within the agreed bands of fluctuation naturally lay with the central banks of the participating Member States. However, the overall responsibility for the management of the EMS lay with the Commission. Furthermore, this same body has the right to make recommendations about national economic and monetary policy matters to the same countries. This right emanates from the decision of the Council of Ministers concerning the attainment of a high degree of convergence of the economic policies of the Member States, taken in February 1974.

Officially and legally speaking, the swaps of 20 per cent of national holdings of gold and dollars against ECU on a three-monthly rolling basis,[4] made by nine Member States, were with the European Fund for Monetary Cooperation. However, this institution was only a legal fiction consisting of a name-plate on a building in Luxembourg.[5] Thus, the swaps, like the short- and medium-term credits, were in fact managed by the Bank for International Settlements (BIS), in Basel, Switzerland. The only precondition here is that the two or three officials managing these matters should be Community nationals.

Lastly, whilst short-term credits were accorded to Member States on an automatic basis, such was not the case with medium-term ones. Here, the Council of Ministers (advised by the Commission) makes policy recommendations to the country or the countries receiving aid. Equally, where the Community floats loans on the international market on behalf of Member States, the Council attaches policy conditions to such help. Doubtless, the making of such policy conditions should have provided a possible means of, to some degree at least, coordinating national economic policies – and even of leading to greater integration among Community Member States. However (as was criticized in the Commission's 1983 statement to the Council on Financial Integration), it is precisely such recourse to Community financial support that countries have tried to avoid since 1977. Instead, they preferred to use 'safeguard' clauses and thereby reimpose controls over capital movements wherever they face balance of payments and similar problems. This was clearly not a satisfactory situation and caused the Community to move backwards rather than forwards. Nevertheless, a major change in policy was French recourse in 1983 to a very important Community loan – rather than going to non-EEC sources.

THE EUROPEAN MONETARY SYSTEM – AN ASSESSMENT

The collapse of the old European Monetary System in 1992 and the subsequent replacement of the original 'GRID' band of fluctuation of 2.25 per cent around participating currencies by the much wider one of 15 per cent might lead readers to conclude that the System had been a failure. However, a more detailed and sober examination of the arrangement might lead one to different conclusions. In the author's view, it is necessary to ask four basic questions:

(i) Did the system constitute a zone of relative monetary stability?
(ii) Did adjustments in exchange rates take place easily and discreetly?
(iii) Did inflation rates tend to converge among the participating countries?
(iv) Did participating countries apply rigorous economic and monetary policies which they might not have applied had they not been members of the EMS?

In answering the first question, the record of the EMS should be placed in the context of the steep and rapid changes in the values of the Yen and the US Dollar in the foreign exchange markets. In comparison with these violent movements and pressures, the EMS constituted a zone of monetary stability.

This good record, with the exception of the 1986 adjustment, is also the answer to the second question. Adjustments (see Appendix 2), particularly when compared with the 'Snake' arrangement, have tended to be swift, discreet and relevant. In this sense, the System proved to be a flexible one. In the case of the 1986 adjustment, the pending elections in West Germany and France made a timely change in the exchange rates unacceptable to both countries. Therefore, pressure was allowed to build up on the Deutsche Mark and the French Franc, and, the eventual discussions which took place concerning the degree of adjustment were so heated and protracted that the EMS was, in effect, suspended for a day.

Turning to the third question, that of inflation, after the early years when only the German rate was acceptable, inflation rates (with the exception of Greece) tended to fall quite dramatically. In many cases they also tended to converge (see Table 3.2). In fact, in 1992, the levels for six of the Member States were lower than the German inflation rate. This was a very good record

Table 3.2 Consumer prices: percentage change from previous period

	Average 1971–80	Average 1980–89	1990	1991	1992
Germany (West)	5.1	2.6	2.7	3.5	4.1
France	10.1	6.6	3.4	3.2	2.5
United Kingdom	14.2	6.2	9.5	5.9	6.5
Italy[a]	15.1	10.1	6.1	6.5	5.3
Belgium	7.7	4.6	3.4	3.2	2.4
Denmark	10.3	6.3	2.7	2.4	2.1
Greece	15.6	18.8	20.4	19.5	15.9
Ireland	14.2	8.2	3.3	3.2	3.1
Luxembourg	6.9	4.5	3.7	3.1	3.2
Portugal[b]	19.8	17.5	13.4	11.4	8.9
Spain	16.1	9.6	6.7	5.9	5.9

[a]Index for households of wage and salary earners.
[b]Excluding rent.

indeed. Here, some countries, notably, Belgium and France, but also Italy, had taken very strong steps to control inflation. Thus, the debacle of 1992 was very disappointing indeed for them. The last and fourth question may be answered in the affirmative. All the participating Member States wished to remain in the System. This implied the taking of internal economic and monetary measures as well as exchange rate adjustments. In the case of France, in 1982, the Government made a volte-face with the initial expansionary economic policy of President Mitterand. The severity of these new policies was increased in 1983. In Belgium, the Government, having obtained the right to introduce economic measures by decree, applied severe policies in 1982 which appeared to bear fruit in 1983 when the Belgian Franc was readjusted upwards – having previously been devalued – for the first time in thirty years.

Similar restrictive policies were adopted in Denmark, the Netherlands and in the Republic of Ireland. Even the United Kingdom, which had not been a participant in the EMS, continued to adopt deflationary policies.

Also, in contrast with the old 'Snake' arrangement, by April 1992 all Member States, except Greece, had joined the EMS. This was proof of their desire for monetary and exchange rate stability.

OTHER CONSIDERATIONS – THE ECU

Unexpectedly, pride of place in the EMS's record must go to the expansion in the case of the commercial ECU. At the official level this development has been surprising because it was not planned; indeed there was no place for the private or commercial ECU in the agreement which set up the EMS. Rather, the expansion of the use of the ECU filled a need. For businessmen, engaged in international trade and concerned about volatile exchange rates, the ECU is a model of stability because of its composition. It is a 'risk spreader' and does not represent the economic force of the EEC. Furthermore, at an international level, the rates of interest for ECUs have been particularly reasonable, which has made them particularly attractive to businessmen in countries such as France and Italy.

Also, as the US Dollar came under suspicion, the commercial ECU became attractive to countries outside the EEC – such as

China, Japan and the Commonwealth of Independent States. Thus, the ECU was among the top five currencies or units of account used for international commercial loans. Likewise, there had been an enormous increase in interbank assets and liabilities denominated in ECUs. In September 1991, the total banking sector assets denominated in ECU amounted to 157 billion ECU.

Furthermore, in all EU Member States, citizens may either open a private bank account denominated in ECUs, or open bank accounts to receive credits and/or loans in ECUs. The principal country which had not given these rights to its citizens was West Germany – this was fortunately changed on 17 June 1987.

Since June 1985 it has been possible to purchase traveller's cheques denominated in ECUs. Also, due to the great expansion in business, a clearing union for settling interbank accounts in commercial ECUs was set up at the Bank for International Settlements (BIS).

THE EVENTS OF 1992

The currency upheavals of 1992 which led to the collapse of the EMS in its old form and the departure of the United Kingdom and other countries from the system (though some did subsequently return) have been so well documented (notably, in the *Financial Times*, 11 and 12 December 1992) that it hardly seems worthwhile recapitulating the unfortunate events of that year. Nonetheless, they need never have happened. In the Treaty which created the EMS, the responsibilities of Member States are quite clearly set down. Thus, when their currencies come under pressure, they agreed to undertake the following measures:

(i)   diversified intervention;
(ii) monetary measures;
(iii) drawing on credit facilities;
(iv) external and domestic policy measures.

The first three measures are fairly simple and automatic; the fourth implies swift, discreet and appropriate currency realignments – accompanied by fiscal measures. This last point is clearly an indispensable prerequisite for successful action.

Since these measures had been so successful up to 1992, what caused the breakdown of the system? There is, of course, no single answer to this question. However, the reunification of the two Germanys must be seen as the main cause of the débâcle. Put quite simply, the German government refused to raise taxes to pay for the unification. Consequently, the Bundesbank, the guardian of German currency, had to raise interest rates to safeguard the Deutsche Mark. Other countries, notably France (whose economy was, in fact, strong) had to follow. Subsequently, pressures were put on a number of currencies – especially the British and Italian ones which were overvalued.

The lessons to be learned from these events are that there must, in the future, be a greater coordination of economies and fiscal policies 'a la Nyborg'[6] and that some form of more automatic fiscal transfers between participating countries will have to be organized.

CONCLUSIONS

Despite the collapse of the old version of the EMS in 1992, a recalculation of the composition of the ECU in November of the same year (see Table 3.3) and the subsequent widening of the bands of fluctuation to 15 per cent in August 1993, the EMS was a much greater success than the old 'Snake' arrangement. Furthermore, had Germany raised taxes to finance the union of the two Germanys – in 1991 and in 1992 – the burden of defending the Deutsche Mark would not have fallen so very heavily on the Bundesbank. The subsequent raising of interest

Table 3.3 New composition of the ECU as on 23 November 1992

German Mark	31.69
French Franc	20.16
British Pound	10.90
Dutch Guilder	9.90
Italian Lira	8.98
Belgian Franc*	8.44
Spanish Peseta	4.80
Danish Crown	2.63
Irish Punt	1.16
Portuguese Escudo	0.76
Greek Drachma	0.57

*includes the Luxembourg Franc

rates – linked to the fact that the British and Italian currencies were clearly overvalued – made it difficult and indeed impossible to operate the EMS in its original form.

Despite the disappointments of 1992 and 1993, the ECU (now the euro) did emerge from the crisis relatively unscathed. Also, in the Treaty on the European Union (the Maastricht Treaty) very strict criteria were laid down for Member States wishing to participate in the EMU and the Euro Zone. These are perhaps the real results of the EMS.

NOTES

1. All the EEC Member States participated in the 'swap' operation – exchanging 20 per cent of their holdings of gold and dollars against ECUs.
2. The composition of the ECU, as calculated on 28 June 1974, was as follows:

0.828	Deutsche Mark	3.66	Belgian Francs
0.0885	Pound Sterling	0.14	Luxembourg Francs
1.15	French Francs	0.217	Danish Crown
109.00	Italian Lira	0.00759	Irish Pound
0.286	Dutch Guilders		

3. The new credits were divided as follows: 14 billion ECUs in short-term and 11 billion ECUs in medium-term credit. A short-term credit is available for a maximum period of nine months and a medium-term one for between three and five years.
4. This formula was adopted in order to leave the ownership of these reserves in the hands of the Member States.
5. This situation existed because, in 1983, no decision could be made about the location of the final home for this institution, the contestants being Luxembourg and London.
6. In 1987, in Nyborg, Denmark, the European (EEC) Council of Ministers agreed on greater economic coordination among members of the EMS.

Part Two

Towards the Creation of the euro

CHAPTER 4

FROM THE DELORS PLAN TO MAASTRICHT AND BEYOND

Although the original founder Member States had agreed to move along the road to an EMU as long ago as the end of 1969 and despite the relative success of the EMS, it seems that politicians needed to reaffirm their commitment to an EMU from time to time. Thus, at its meeting in Hanover on 27 and 28 June 1988, the members of the European Council reminded themselves that in adopting the Single Act, the Member States of the Community confirmed the objective of progressive realization of economic and monetary union. A year later, in Madrid, at the meeting of the European Council, the Heads of State and Government decided to entrust to a committee, headed by Jaques Delors, the President of the European Commission, 'the task of studying and proposing concrete steps leading towards this union'. The ensuing report, like its predecessor some twenty years earlier, the Werner Plan, proposed the creation of an EMU in stages. However, unlike its predecessor, in the Delors Plan, which is also a kind of blueprint for an EMU, it was pointed out that a Treaty change (implying, in fact, a new treaty) would be necessary for its implementation. As just mentioned, in the Delors Plan, the implementation of the EMU by stages is laid down.

The First Stage

In this first stage, the emphasis is on economic convergence. In particular, emphasis is placed on the full completion of the Single European Market (SEM). Convergence is thus spelled out in some detail as follows:

> In the economic field the steps would centre on the completion of the internal market and the reduction of existing disparities

through programmes of budgetary consolidation in those countries concerned and more effective structural and regional policies. In particular, there would be action in three directions. Firstly, there would be a complete removal of physical, technical and fiscal barriers within the Community, in line with the internal market programme. The completion of the internal market would be accompanied by a strengthening of Community competition policy. Secondly, the reform of the structural funds and doubling of their resources would be fully implemented in order to enhance the ability of Community policies to promote regional development and to correct imbalances. Thirdly, the 1974 Council Decision on economic convergence would be replaced by a new procedure that would strengthen economic and fiscal policy coordination and would, in addition, provide a comprehensive framework for an assessment of the consequences and consistency of the overall policies of member states. On the basis of this assessment, recommendations would be made aimed at achieving a more effective coordination of economic policies, taking due account of the views of the Committee of Central Bank Governors. The task of economic policy coordination should be the primary responsibility of the Council of Economic and Finance Ministers (ECOFIN). Consistency between monetary and economic policies would be facilitated by the participation of the Chairman of the Committee of Central Bank Governors in appropriate Council meetings. (European Commission, 1989)

Emphasis was also placed on common monetary and exchange rate policies, the opening-up of financial services and the encouragement of the private use of the ECU. Here, there was support for the use of a common currency in the EMU. A number of the Delors Committee similarly advocated the creation of a European Reserve Fund (ERF) that would be the precursor of the future European System of Central Banks.

Stage Two

It is interesting to note that the Report states that this stage could only start once the new Treaty had come into effect. This should require the setting up of the appropriate institutional framework. Furthermore, this second stage is seen as the transitional one on the way to the third and final stage. However, as in the first stage, emphasis is placed on convergence and the opening-up of the internal market.

In the economic field, the European Parliament, the Council of Ministers, the Monetary Committee and the Commission would reinforce their action along three lines. Firstly, in the area of the single market and competition policy the results achieved through the implementation of the single market programme would be reviewed and, whenever necessary, consolidated. Secondly, the performance of structural and regional policies would be evaluated and, if necessary, be adapted in the light of experience. The resources for supporting the structural policies of the member states might have to be enlarged. Community programmes for investment in research and infrastructure would be strengthened. Thirdly, in the area of macroeconomic policy, the procedures set up in the first stage through the revision of the 1974 Decision on convergence would be further strengthened and extended on the basis of the new Treaty. Policy guidelines would be adopted by majority decision. On this basis the Community would:

● Set a medium-term framework for key economic objectives aimed at achieving stable growth, with a follow-up procedure for monitoring performances and intervening when significant deviations occurred;

● Set precise – although not yet binding – rules relating to the size of annual budget deficits and their financing; the Commission should be responsible for bringing any instance of non-compliance by member states to the Council's attention and should propose action as necessary;

● Assume a more active role as a single entity in the discussion of questions arising in the economic and exchange rate field, on the basis of its present representation (through the member states or the Commission) in the various fora for international coordination.

In this stage, equal emphasis is placed on monetary policy because it is during this transitional period when the European System of Central Banks (ESCB) will be set up – absorbing the existing monetary institutions. The work of the ESCB is defined in more general terms.

The key task for the European System of Central Banks during this stage would be to begin the transition from the coordination of independent national monetary policies by the Committee of Central Bank Governors in stage one to the formation and implementation of a common monetary policy by the ESCB itself scheduled to take place in the final stage. The fundamental difficulty inherent in this transition would lie in the organization of a gradual transfer of decision-making power from national authorities to a Community institution. At this juncture, the Committee does not consider it possible to propose a detailed blueprint for accomplishing this transition, as this would depend on the effectiveness of the policy coordination achieved during the first stage on the provisions of the Treaty, and on decisions to be taken by the new institutions. Account would also have to be taken of the continued impact of financial innovation on monetary control techniques (which are at present undergoing radical changes in most industrial countries), of the degree of integration reached in European financial markets, of the constellation of financial and banking centres in Europe and of the development of the private, and in particular banking use of the ECU.

Stage Three

It is this part of the Report which is the most succinct and to the point. It is therefore worth quoting this part in full.

The final stage would commence with the move to irrevocably blocked exchange rates and the attribution to Community institutions of the full monetary and economic competencies described in Part II of this Report. In the course of the final stage the national currencies would be eventually replaced by a single Community currency.
    In the economic field, the transition to this final stage would

be marked by three developments. Firstly, there might need to be further strengthening of Community structural and regional policies. Instruments and resources would be adapted to the needs of the economic and monetary union. Secondly, the rules and procedures of the Community in the macroeconomic and budgetary field would become binding. In particular, the Council of Ministers, in cooperation with the European Parliament, would have the authority to take directly enforceable decisions, i.e.:

● To impose constraints on national budgets to the extent to which this was necessary to prevent imbalances that might threaten monetary stability;

● To make discretionary changes in Community resources (through a procedure to be defined) to supplement structural transfers to member states or to influence the overall policy stance in the Community;

● To apply to existing Community structural policies and to Community loans (as a substitute for the present medium-term financial assistance facility) terms and conditions that would prompt member countries to intensify their adjustment efforts.

Thirdly, the Community would assume its full role in the process of international policy cooperation, and a new form of representation in arrangements for international policy coordination and in international monetary regulations would be adopted.

In the monetary field, the irrevocable locking of exchange rates would come into effect and the transition to a single monetary policy would be made, with the ESCB assuming all its responsibilities as foreseen in the Treaty and described in Part II of this Report. In particular:

● Concurrently with the announcement of the irrevocable fixing of parities between the Community currencies, the responsibility for the formulation and implementation of monetary policy in the Community would be transferred to the ESCB, with its Council and Board exercising their functions;

● Decisions on exchange market interventions in their currencies would be made on the sole responsibility of the ESCB Council in accordance with the Community exchange rate policy; the execution of interventions would be ensured either to national central banks or to the European System of Central Banks;

● Official reserves would be pooled and managed by the ESCB;

● Preparation of a technical or regulatory nature would be made for the transition to a single Community currency.

● The change-over to the single currency would take place during this stage.

OVERVIEW

Like its famous predecessor, the Werner Report, so the Report of the Delors Committee sets down stages for the creation of an EMU. However, the difference in the economic and monetary environment in which the two reports are written are tremendous. In the case of the Werner Report, the original six founder Member States of the EEC had achieved a customs union but not a common market. Furthermore, only Western Germany and the Benelux countries accepted the principle of free capital movements within the EEC.

In comparison, the situation at the end of the 1980s had changed completely. Here, the creation of the SEM meant that a common market was becoming a reality. In turn, this included (internally) the opening-up of banking, financial markets and the insurance services. This greater degree of competition also implied that there should be a much greater degree of economic and monetary convergence between Member States wishing to be part of an EMU. In turn, this meant that the integration process was becoming much deeper than many observers had originally believed possible.

In any moves towards the writing of a new Treaty (as foreseen in the Delors Report), the influence of one Member State would be paramount; this country was Germany. In any moves towards the creation of an EMU with a common currency, Germany had always insisted on three major preconditions:

(i) there should be price stability, i.e. very low levels of inflation;

(ii) any future common European currency should, at least, be

as good as the Deutsche Mark; and,
(iii) any future European Central Bank should, at least, be as
independent as the Deutsche Bank.

Consequently, in the writing of the future Treaty on European
Union (popularly know as the Maastricht Treaty) and the later
Stability Pact, Theo Waigel, the German Finance Minister, was to
play a role.

CHAPTER 5

THE TREATY ON EUROPEAN UNION

THE BACKGROUND

The treaty on European Union (more commonly called the Maastricht Treaty) is a bad treaty. It is a compromise hotchpotch affair: being a kind of rescue attempt made by Luxembourg (based on that country's discussion paper) to salvage an agreement from the wreckage of the misguided Dutch attempt to foist a blueprint for a federation on an unwilling European Community (EC). Inevitably, such a compromise arrangement is full of gaps to which the author will return in a later chapter. However, the Treaty is composed of the three main 'pillars', i.e. (i) the creation of an economic and monetary union (EMU) and a European currency; (ii) the creation of a common foreign defence policy (CFDP) – probably leading to a common security policy; and, (iii) internal cooperation (home affairs). In this work, it is obviously the first pillar which is of concern to us.

THE CONVERGENCE CRITERIA AND THE EUROPEAN CENTRAL BANK

The criterion of price stability is the overriding one in the Treaty. In choosing this criterion, the architects certainly opted for an Optimum Currency Area (OCA), which embodies the quality of what has been called a 'similar propensity to inflate'.[1] We shall return to this criterion later in this chapter. However, the four main criteria about which so much has been written and which have caused some degree of controversy are the following:

1. Government deficit spending (the national budget) shall not exceed three per cent of gross domestic product (GDP) at market prices.
2. Government debt shall not exceed 60 per cent of the GDP at market prices.

3. A country must be a member of the ERM and must n experienced serious upheavals in the two preceding ꜱ. And,

4. In the preceding year, a Member State shall have had an average nominal long-term interest rate that does not exceed by more than two per cent 'that of, at most, the three best performing Member States of price stability'.

These criteria deserve more detailed scrutiny. The first two criteria, which are concerned with the actual or planned budget deficit and the long-term government debt, are those which have lead to the greatest amount of discussion among economists, politicians and observers in general. Two main questions have been raised. The first one concerns the relevance of these criteria. We shall return to this question in a later chapter. The second one refers to the 'definitive' nature of these two criteria. Had they been final and definitive in character, some countries, notably Belgium and Italy, for example, would not have got through the door. Instead, the Treaty is somewhat flexible about 'trends'. Thus, in Article 104 (c), paragraphs 2 and 3, we read,

> the ratio of the planned or actual government deficit to gross domestic product exceeds a reference value (defined in the Protocol as 3% of GDP), unless:
>> either the ratio has declined substantially and continuously and reached a level that comes close to the reference value;
>> or, alternatively, the excess over the reference value is only exceptional and temporary and the ratio remains close to the reference value;
>> (b) the ratio of government debt to gross domestic product exceeds a reference value (defined in the Protocol as 60% of GDP), unless the ratio is sufficiently diminishing and approaching the reference value at a satisfactory pace.

Thus, the key expression is 'substantially and continuously'. There is also the expression of deficit coming 'close to the reference value'.

The third criterion, membership of the Exchange Rate Mechanism (ERM) of the EMS – together with the absence of currency instability in the preceding two years – does reinforce the general umbrella criterion of price stability.

Although the fourth one has not been the object of the attention it probably deserves, it merits more examination, because, like exchange rate stability, it does tend to restrict the freedom of participating countries in the management of their economic and monetary policies. Furthermore, it could have undesirable and even negative effects on a country. Thus, for example, Finland and the Republic of Ireland, in their moves to lowering interest rates, have contributed to a major rise in house prices in the capital cities of both those countries. At this point, it is worth returning to the overriding umbrella criterion in the Treaty, that of price stability. Article 109 J (paragraph 1) of the Treaty clearly stipulates: 'the achievement of a high degree of price stability; this will be apparent from a rate of inflation which is close to that of, at most, the three best-performing Member States in terms of price stability'.

Furthermore, in the first article of Protocol number 6 on the convergence criteria, this criterion is more clearly elucidated:

The criterion on price stability referred to in the first indent of Article 109j (1) of this Treaty shall mean that a Member State has a price performance that is sustainable and an average rate of inflation, observed over a period of one year before the examination, that does not exceed by more than 1½ percentage points that of, at most, the three best-performing Member States in terms of price stability. Inflation shall be measured by means of the consumer price index on a comparable basis, taking into account differences in national definitions.

CONVERGENCE CRITERIA – THE RESULTS

The final results showing to what degree EU Member States fulfilled the Convergence Report of the European Monetary Institute in March 1998 are provided in Table 5.1. Based on this table and the desire of countries to join the Euro Zone and the European System of Central Banks (ESCB), in May 1998, eleven Member States were chosen to join the Euro Zone. These were all countries, except Denmark, Greece, Sweden and the United Kingdom. Denmark, Sweden and the United Kingdom did not

Table 5.1 Economic indicators and the Maastricht Treaty convergence criteria (*excluding the exchange rate criterion*)

		HICP inflation[a]	Long-term interest rate[b]	General government surplus (+) or deficit (−)[c]	General government gross debt[c]
Belgium	1996	1.8	6.5	−3.2	126.9
	1997[d]	1.4	5.7	# −2.1	122.2
	1998[e]	−	−	# −1.7	118.1
Denmark	1996	2.1	7.2	# −0.7	70.6
	1997[d]	1.9	6.2	# 0.7	65.1
	1998[e]	−	−	# 1.1	# 59.5
Germany	1996	1.2	6.2	−3.4	60.4
	1997[d]	1.4	5.6	# −2.7	61.3
	1998[e]	−	−	# −2.5	61.2
Greece	1996	7.9	14.4	−7.5	111.6
	1997[d]	5.2	9.8	−4.0	108.7
	1998[e]	−	−	# −2.2	107.7
Spain	1996	3.6	8.7	−4.6	70.1
	1997[d]	1.8	6.3	# −2.6	68.8
	1998[e]	−	−	# −2.2	67.4
France	1996	2.1	6.3	−4.1	# 55.7
	1997[d]	**1.2	**5.5	# −3.0	# 58.0
	1998[e]	−	−	# −2.9	# 58.1
Ireland	1996	2.2	7.3	# −0.4	72.7
	1997[d]	***1.2	***6.2	# 0.9	66.3
	1998[e]	−	−	# 1.1	# 59.5
Italy	1996	4.0	9.4	−6.7	124.0
	1997[d]	1.8	6.7	# −2.7	121.6
	1998[e]	−	−	# −2.5	118.1
Luxembourg	1996	***1.2	***6.3	# 2.5	# 6.6
	1997[d]	1.4	5.6	# 1.7	# 6.7
	1998[e]	−	−	# 1.0	# 7.1
Netherlands	1996	1.4	6.2	# −2.3	77.2
	1997[d]	1.8	5.5	# −1.4	72.1
	1998[e]	−	−	# −1.6	70.0
Austria	1996	1.8	6.3	−4.0	69.5
	1997[d]	*1.1	*5.6	# −2.5	66.1
	1998[e]	−	−	# −2.3	64.7
Portugal	1996	2.9	8.6	−3.2	65.0
	1997[d]	1.8	6.2	# −2.5	62.0
	1998[e]	−	−	# −2.2	# 60.0
Finland	1996	**1.1	**7.1	−3.3	# 57.6
	1997[d]	1.3	5.9	#−0.9	# 55.8
	1998[e]	−	−	# 0.3	# 53.6
Sweden	1996	*0.8	*8.0	−3.5	76.7
	1997[d]	1.9	6.5	# −0.8	76.6
	1998[e]	−	−	# 0.5	74.1
United Kingdom	1996	2.5	7.9	−4.8	# 54.7
	1997[d]	1.8	7.0	# −1.9	# 53.4
	1998[e]	−	−	# −0.6	# 52.3

Source: EMI, *Convergence Report*, March 1998

* ** *** = first, second and third best performer in terms of price stability.

\# = general government deficit not exceeding 3% of GDP; general government gross debt not exceeding 60% of GDP

(a) Annual percentage changes.

(b) In percentages.

(c) As a percentage of GDP.

(d) Data for HICP inflation and long-term interest rate refer to the twelve-month period ending January 1998. European Commission (Spring 1998 forecasts) for general government surplus or deficit and general government gross debt.

(e) European Commission projections (Spring 1998 forecasts) for general government surplus or deficit and general government gross debt.

want to join, whilst Greece did not meet the criteria. In the case of the former three countries, they were not members of the ERM of the European Monetary System, whilst Sweden's Central Bank had not yet been granted independence. Here, it should be noted that the independence of the national central banks is a further criterion for membership of the Euro Zone.

Looking more closely at the results, it is clear that a number of countries do not meet the criterion of long-term government debt. Among the worst culprits are Belgium and Italy, both members of the Euro Zone. Furthermore, where countries have brought down their current budgetary deficits and/or government debts to reasonable levels, doubts persist as to whether this is the result of 'fudging' or a once and for all phenomenon. Time will clearly tell during the delicate and rather long period between 1 January 1999 and the end of June 2002, when the Euro and the national currencies of the participating countries will co-exist side by side.

THE STABILITY PACT

The Treaty on European Union and its emphasis on price stability and sober government fiscal policies was further reinforced by the so-called 'Stability Pact'. This agreement was almost exclusively the work of Theo Waigel, the then German Finance Minister, who wished to prevent deficit spending by governments. This pact deserves much attention since it is rather rigid in nature and considerably restricts the room for manoeuvre of governments in the field of economics and fiscal policy.

In the 'historic' reports of the ECOFIN Council and the EMI,[2] dated 18 December 1996, and reproduced in Appendix 3 of this book, there are, in clauses 26 to 36 (inclusive), explicit statements describing the sanctions to be imposed on participating Member States which persistently ran up budget deficits. Thus, in clause 32, there is reference to the impositions of a 'non-interest bearing deposit'. If, however (clause 35), two years after the imposition of this deposit the government in question's deficit continues to be excessive, then this deposit may be converted into a fine.

Once again, the author is surprised at the relatively little attention paid by observers to these clauses. This must be one of the very few occasions in post-Second World War history when highly developed countries have voluntarily imposed such Draconian restrictions and penalties upon themselves. And, these clauses are not purely formalities since Professor Wim Duisenberg, the President of the European Central Bank, has threatened to impose just such fines on participating Member States which run up 'excessive' budgetary deficits.

At Dublin, in December 1996, France did nevertheless sense the implicit danger of too blindly accepting the possibility of the impositions of such sanctions. Thus, on French insistence, exceptions to this rule were also included in the pact. Thus, in clause 28, there is reference to an 'economic downturn' as being 'exceptional only if there is an annual fall of real GDP of at least 2 per cent'. Nevertheless, again at the insistence of France, there seems to be a softer approach in clause 37, where we read, 'the Resolution will contain an undertaking by the Member States not to invoke the benefit of the provision in paragraph 30 unless they are in severe recession. In evaluating whether the economic downturn is severe, the Member States will as a rule take as a reference-point an annual fall in real GDP of at least 0.75 per cent.'

Nevertheless, this Stability Pact is a very sobering document. In the negotiations which led to the creation of the compromise Treaty on European Union and the subsequent Stability Pact, little or no attention was paid to the relevance of the convergence criteria and to possible policy options. It is to these questions to which we shall now turn.

NOTES

1. Giovanni Magnifico, *European Monetary Unification*, Macmillan, London, 1973.
2. The 'Historic' Reports of the ECOFIN Council and the EMI that define the Stability Pact, the New Exchange Rate Mechanism (ERM 2) and the Legal Status of the EURO. Europe Documents No. 2015 / 16, Brussels, 18 December 1996.

CHAPTER 6

POLICY CONSIDERATIONS

POLICY CHOICES

Originally, the choice of policy instruments in an EMU was closely identified with the concept of Optimum Currency Areas (OCAs).[1] This concept has, to some degree, influenced the goals, and, eventually, the choice of policy instruments for the Euro Zone.

As has already been observed, the Treaty on European Union (more commonly known as the Maastricht Treaty) is an incomplete treaty since, apart from the attention placed on the question of government debt, all the emphasis is on monetary policy as the means of achieving the goal of price stability and low inflation. Here, as the authors of the European Commission's Economic Paper, Number 124, have observed, 'monetary policy aims to achieve its ultimate goal, price stability, by exerting an influence on price expectations and economic activity'.[2] In this policy area, however, the speed and impact of monetary policy on the behaviour of economic agents does vary between countries. This presents the ECB and the participating EU Member States with a problem.

In clarifying the goal of price stability, the Governing Council of the European Central Bank has, as was reported in the ECB *Monthly Bulletin*, in January 2000, adopted the following clear definition of price stability:

'price stability shall be defined as a year-on-year increase in the Harmonized Index of Consumer Prices (HICP) for the Euro area of below 2%'. Price stability according to this definition 'is to be maintained over the medium term'.

The phrase 'below 2%' clearly delineates the upper bound for the rates of measured inflation in the HICP, which is consistent with price stability. At the same time, the use of the word 'increase' in the definition clearly signals that deflation, i.e. prolonged declines in the level of the HICP index, would not be deemed consistent with price stability.

It should be noted that the Eurosystem's definitions are used by most NCBs in the Euro area prior to the transition to Monetary Union, ensuring an important element of continuity with their successful monetary policy strategies.

The HICP index

The chosen definition identifies the HICP as the price index that should be used in the assessment of whether price stability has been achieved and maintained. This index was initially created for the assessment of developments in the price level.

Among economists in academic, financial and central banking circles, there is a broad consensus that various forms of so-called 'measurement bias' can exist in consumer price indices (CPIs). These biases arise mainly from changing spending patterns and quality improvements in those goods and services that are included in the basket used to define a specific price index. Such biases cannot always be fully corrected in the construction of price indices. The measurement bias typically causes CPIs to overstate slightly the 'true' rate of inflation.

The HICP for the Euro area is a relatively new concept and long runs of back data do not exist. Therefore, studies of the magnitude of the HICP measurement bias are preliminary and inconclusive. Eurostat has expended considerable effort to reduce or eliminate the measurement bias in the HICP. It is therefore probable that the bias in the HICP is smaller than that observed in national CPIs of the countries comprising the Euro area. Moreover, the available empirical evidence suggests that the measurement bias in national CPIs for Euro area countries is smaller than that which has been estimated in a number of prominent studies of consumer price indices in other countries.

The success of these attempts to minimize the measurement bias in the HICP is as yet unknown. Furthermore, the size of the measurement bias is likely to change over time as the structure of the economy evolves and statistical methods change, partly in response to these changes in economic structure. Therefore, the definition has avoided explicitly embodying specific estimates of the HICP measurement bias, while allowing for such bias by not setting the lower bound for measured price level increases at zero.

Finally, the Governing Council explained that, by defining price stability in terms of the HICP for the Euro area, it has made clear that its decisions will be based on an assessment of developments in the Euro area as a whole. With a unified monetary policy, policy decisions must be made in a manner that reflects conditions across the Euro area in its entirety, rather than specific regional or national developments.

Whilst this definition is clear, it was not certain at the outset whether the ECB would use its main policy instrument, control of the monetary supply, or the targeting of inflation. The final choice did – at least, for the time being – consist of a mixture of both instruments.

In the aforementioned European Commission Report, an important section is devoted to the problem of adjustment vis-à-vis economic shocks and cycles. First, the different kinds of shocks are listed. Then, the empirical evidence is examined. Here, the key observation would seem to be that 'studies suggest the existence of a number of EU countries with highly correlated disturbances, and other countries showing more differentiated economic behaviour'. The observation is also made about the detection in some studies of 'core' and 'periphery' regions. This is not, of course, a new phenomenon since for decades, at the regional level in Europe, we have talked about just such a phenomenon. This phenomenon does then lead us to the question of fiscal policy in the so-called adjustment mechanism and the problem of regional disequilibria and related problems. This is indeed a major problem, since, when the final stage of the EMU is reached and a common currency becomes the sole legal tender, then balance of payment considerations between the participating Member States will disappear and be replaced by regional disequilibria (which, of course, were already there but will be intensified).

FISCAL TRANSFERS

There are a number of conflicting views about the use of fiscal transfers and regional disequalibria. The three principal (but, by no means exclusive) schools of thought are the following. The first and arguably the most widely supported is that which has been widely researched by Andrew Hughes-Hallet and Andrew Scott, who warn about the consequences of an EMU in the European Union, where, in contrast with the United States and Germany, for example, there are no automatic fiscal transfers between the regions. In their examination[3] of the relevant case of a monetary union between France and Germany, they concluded that a centralized budget would provide 'a degree of automatic stabilization for one region against another. However, they do question the political willingness of the EU to provide a budget of the magnitude necessitated by such transfers.

The second and quite contrasting view is that held by Asdrubali and others,[4] who, in a study published in 1996, found that financial markets played a much larger role than the Federal Government in the USA as 'channels of interstate risk taking'. Thus, they consider that as capital markets become more integrated in the EU a similar situation could develop to that existing in the United States.

In contrast, the third view, that of this author, is that whilst the private sector is clearly playing a more important role in capital transfers inside the EU (particularly in the United Kingdom) than was the case some ten years ago, there is and will continue to be a heavy reliance on community fiscal transfers to regions and Member States. For example, in 1991 the total EU fiscal transfers received by the Republic of Ireland amounted to some seven per cent of GDP. A few years later, this was five per cent of GDP – still a large figure. Unfortunately, the problem with this kind of transfer is that it is a kind of ad hoc transfer, which is certainly decided for a specific number of years. Thus, this kind of transfer cannot deal with unforeseen shocks and short-run fiscal deficits. This would therefore seem to give support to the call expressed by Andrew Hughes-Hallett and Andrew Scott for the organization of automatic fiscal transfers. Furthermore, whilst it is almost certain that capital markets will become more integrated inside the European Union, it is unlikely that they will emulate the major role played by the same markets in the United States.

The question of regional disequilibria and fiscal transfers is also closely linked with the question of labour mobility as well as with that of capital movements. Here, time and time again, Community, government and other officials and writers have observed that labour is not particularly mobile inside the EU – certainly not when compared with the United States. But does that really matter? Are we not perhaps looking at the wrong side of the problem? If, for example, as was the case in the 1950s and the 1960s, workers moved into the EEC from countries which were not Community Member States, could not the community of workers from the countries of Central and Eastern Europe meet any labour shortages in the EU? The author believes that this question needs to be further researched. Perhaps, however, labour will become more mobile inside the EU when legislation is finally in place allowing workers to transfer their pension rights between Member States as they move between countries.

THE EUROPEAN CENTRAL BANK, AND ITS POLICY CHOICES

Once again, this does place an extra burden on the back of the ECB and it is therefore particularly important that it be right in its choice of monetary policies. As mentioned earlier, there was much discussion about the Bank's choice of monetary policies both before and just after the creation of the ECB. Most recently, the Bank has been more specific in its choice of a 'specific reference rate for monetary growth rather than a reference range'. It did this because it wished to avoid confusion in the minds of the public. Thus, on 1 December 1998, the ECB's Governing Council announced its reference value for M3 growth in the following terms:

The derivation of the reference value was based on the following medium-term assumptions:
● Price stability must be maintained according to the Eurosystem's published definition, so that year-on-year increases in the HICP for the Euro area are below 2%.

- The trend of real gross domestic product (GDP) growth lies in the range 2–2½% per annum.
- Over the medium term, the decline in the velocity of circulation of M3 is in the approximate range ½–1% each year.

In setting the reference value for monetary growth, the Governing Council emphasized that the Eurosystem's published definition of price stability limits increases in the HICP for the Euro area to 'below 2%'. Furthermore, the actual trend decline in velocity is likely to lie somewhat below the upper bound of its ½–1% range. Taking account of these two factors, the Governing Council decided to set its reference value for M3 growth at 4½% per annum.

The Governing Council decided to announce a specific reference rate for monetary growth, rather than a reference range, on the basis that announcing a reference range might be falsely interpreted by the public as implying that interest rates would be changed automatically if monetary growth were to move outside the boundaries of the range, something that would be contrary to the role of the reference value in the overall strategy.

The reference value will help to inform and present interest rate decisions aimed at maintaining price stability over the medium term. Therefore, in the first instance, a deviation of monetary growth from the reference value will prompt further analysis to identify and interpret the economic disturbance that caused the deviation. If this analysis suggests that the disturbance identified indeed points to a threat to price stability, monetary policy would respond in a manner appropriate to counter this risk. The relationship between actual monetary growth and the reference value will therefore be regularly and thoroughly analysed by the Governing Council. The results of this analysis and its impact on monetary policy decisions will be explained to the public. Through this process monetary policy decision-making will be made both clearer and more transparent.

While the presentation of monetary analysis to the public will naturally focus on developments in the 'key' broad monetary aggregate, M3 in relation to the published reference value for monetary growth, developments in other monetary aggregates, in the various components of M3 and in the counterparts to all these aggregates in the consolidated MFI balance sheet will also be thoroughly assessed on an ongoing basis. Such analysis provides useful background information that helps the assessment of developments in M3.

The ECB's definition of M3, as contrasted with M1 and M2, as reproduced from the ECB's *Monthly Bulletin*, February 1999, is explained in the following manner.

Based on conceptual considerations and empirical studies, and in line with international practice, the Eurosystem has defined a narrow (M1), an 'intermediate' (M2) and a broad aggregate (M3). These aggregates differ with respect to the degree of moneyness of the assets included. Table 6.1 shows the definitions of the euro area monetary aggregates using the definition of liabilities issued by the MFI sector (see Table 6.2), as well as by entities belonging to the central government sector (Post Offices, Treasuries) of the euro area. As noted above, these aggregates include only positions of residents of the euro area which are held with MFIs located in the euro area.

MFIs located in the euro area. Holdings by euro area residents of liquid assets denominated in foreign currency can be close substitutes for euro-denominated assets. Therefore, the monetary aggregates include such assets if they are held with MFIs located in the euro area.

Narrow money (M1) includes currency, i.e. banknotes and coins, as well as balances that can immediately be converted into currency or used for cashless payments, i.e. overnight deposits.

Table 6.1 Definitions of euro area monetary aggregates

Liabilities	M1	M2	M3
Currency in circulation	X	X	X
Overnight deposits	X	X	X
Deposits with agreed maturity up to 2 years		X	X
Deposits redeemable at notice up to 3 months		X	X
Repurchase agreements			X
Money market fund (MMF) shares/units and money market paper			X
Debt securities up to 2 years			X

Table 6.2 Schematic consolidated balance sheet of the MFI sector for the euro area*

Assets	Liabilities
1. Loans	1. Currency in circulation
2. Securities other than shares	2. Deposits of central government
3. Shares and other equities	3. Deposits of general governments/other euro area
4. External assets	residents
5. Fixed assets	4. Money market fund shares/units and money market paper
6. Remaining assets	5. Debt securities issued
	6. Capital and reserves
	7. External liabilities
	8. Remaining liabilities

*A detailed description of the instrument categories is provided in Annex 4 of the ECB publication *The single monetary policy in Stage Three: General documentation on ESCB monetary policy instruments and procedures*, September 1998.

'Intermediate' money (M2) comprises narrow money (M1) and, in addition, deposits with maturities of up to two years and deposits redeemable at notice of up to three months. Depending on their degree of moneyness, such deposits can be converted into components of narrow money, but in some cases there may be restrictions involved, such as the need for advance notification, delays, penalties or fees. The definition of M2 reflects the particular interest in analysing and monitoring a monetary aggregate that, in addition to currency, consists of deposits which are liquid.

Broad money (M3) comprises M2 and marketable instruments issued by the MFI sector. Certain money market instruments, in particular money market fund (MMF) shares/units and money market paper, and repurchase agreements are included in this aggregate. A high degree of liquidity and price certainty make these instruments close substitutes for deposits. As a result of their inclusion, M3 is less affected by substitution between various liquid asset categories than narrower definitions of money, and is more stable.

With regard to the components of M3, the following shares have been calculated on the basis of December 1998 data (see Figure 6.1). Overnight deposits account for the largest share,

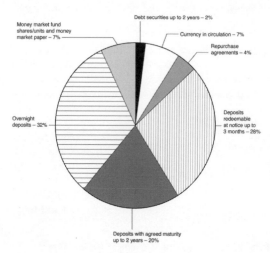

Figure 6.1   Percentage shares of the components of M3, December 1998
Source: ECB *Monthly Bulletin*, February 1999

namely 33 per cent of M3. The share of deposits with agreed maturities up to two years is 20 per cent and that of deposits redeemable at notice up to three months is 28 per cent of M3. The share of currency in circulation is 7 per cent and that of money market paper is also 7 per cent. Finally, the outstanding stock of repurchase agreements accounted for 4 per cent of M3 and that of debt securities issued with maturities up to two years for 2 per cent.

CONCLUSIONS – OVERVIEW

We are thus where we started at the beginning of this chapter. The incomplete nature of the Treaty on European Union has not been rectified. Apart from the strict government budgetary deficit and long-term debt criteria laid down in the Treaty, there has been no progress on the fiscal front. At the Berlin Summit, held in March 2000, agreements (provisional) were made on the amount of finance to be allocated to the Cohesion, Regional and Social Funds for the next six years. The author's opinion is that in view of the impending enlargement of the EU, these sums – without the necessary deep reform of the Common Agricultural Policy (CAP) – are quite inadequate. Thus, as was the case in

Germany with the reunification of the two Germanies where the burden of policy adjustment fell unevenly on the back of the Bundesbank, so in the EU, the burden falls on the ECB. To its credit, the Bank has, in the first months of the existence of the euro, been rather adroit and has made its decisions in a swift and discreet manner. It is, as we shall see, in the next chapter, the manager of the euro.

The starting point for the definition of euro area monetary aggregates is the consolidated balance sheet of the MFI sector (see Table 6.2). In general, the appropriate definition of a monetary aggregate largely depends on the purpose for which the selected aggregate is intended. Given that many different financial assets are substitutable, and that the nature and features of financial assets, transactions and means of payment are changing over time, it is not always clear how money should be defined and which financial assets belong to a certain definition of money. For these reasons, central banks usually define and monitor several monetary aggregates. These range from very narrow aggregates such as central bank money or base money, consisting of currency (i.e. banknotes and coins) and central bank deposits, to broader aggregates, which include currency, bank deposits and certain types of securities.

In defining money, both the microeconomic perspective of the individual holder of money and the empirical properties of monetary aggregates resulting from the joint behaviour of holders of money are relevant.

NOTES

1. G. Magnifico, *European Monetary Unification*, Macmillan, London, 1973. One of the best accounts of the principal earlier contributions to the theories of OCAs may be found in Fabeizio Onida's, *Theory and Policy of Optimum Currency Areas and Their Implications for the European Monetary Union*, Suerf, Tilburg, 1972.

2. European Commission, Director-General II, 'Economic Policy in the EMU', Brussels, November, 1997.

3. Andrew Hughes-Hallett and Andrew Scott, 'The Fiscal Dilemmas of Monetary Union', in Peter Coffey, *Main Economic Policy Areas of the EC after 1992*, Kluwer Academic Publishers, Dordrecht, 1993.

4. P. Asdrubali, B.E. Sorensen and O. Yosha, 'Channels of Interstate Risk Sharing: United States, 1963–1990', *Quarterly Journal of Economics*, No. 111, 1996.

Part Three

The euro

CHAPTER 7

THE EURO – PRACTICAL CONSIDERATIONS

THE BACKGROUND

On 2 May 1998, the Heads of State and Government of the European Union, meeting in Brussels, agreed that the third and final stage of economic and monetary union would begin on 1 January 1999, with eleven Member States participating.[1] Earlier the same day, the ECOFIN Council had decided that the bilateral Exchange Rate Mechanism (ERM) for the euro, to be used as the irrevocable rates for the euro on the first day of Stage Three (1 January 1999) would have to be identical to the value of the ECU as expressed in units of the participating currencies on 31 December 1998.[2] Thus, as agreed, at midnight, on 1 January 1999, the following irrevocable rates were fixed for the national currencies of the participating Member States vis-à-vis the euro. Furthermore, as had already been agreed in Article 2 of the Council Resolution of 17 June 1997, existing ECUs were exchanged on a one-to-one basis with the euro:

1 euro = 13.7603   Austrian Schilling
      = 40.3399   Belgian Franc
      = 2.20371   Dutch Guilder
      = 5.94573   Finnish Markka
      = 6.55957   French Franc
      = 1.95583   German Mark
      = 0.787564   Irish Pound
      = 1936.27   Italian Lira
      = 40.3399   Luxembourg Franc
      = 200.482   Portuguese Escudo
      = 166.386   Spanish Peseta

Writing some years ago, the author suggested the following six qualities which an acceptable currency should embody. These are:

1. A unit of account.
2. A medium of exchange (between individuals).
3. A means of settlement (between institutes, central banks, governments and similar bodies).
4. A store of value. And,
5. A refuge from economic and/or political instability. In this case, individuals and/or institutes may be willing to forego (at least partially and/or temporarily) the attractiveness of the role of the currency or asset as a store value (4) in exchange for enhanced security.
6. Legal tender.

Before examining the degree to which the euro exhibits these qualities, one should note a major proviso. Whilst the euro is 'legal tender' in the eleven participating EU Member States, it co-exists alongside the national currencies of those countries. Furthermore, it is not until 1 January 2002 that national currencies will be exchanged for euro. Equally, it will only be on 1 July of the same year when the euro will be the sole means of 'legal tender' in those countries. Until 1 January 2002 euro coins and notes will not be available to the general public. This fact certainly changes the position of the euro – at least until 2002. Having made this point, we find that the euro does indeed fulfil very well the roles that have just been listed. First, it is most certainly a unit of account for all official transactions of the European Union. It is also heavily used by the European Investment Bank (EIB). Second, it is a medium of exchange between individuals. Indeed, as with its predecessor, the ECU, citizens of EU Member States may open up euro-denominated private bank accounts. They may also settle invoices and bills in euro, though there are no euro coins and notes.

Third, as a means of settlement between institutions, it is a pre-eminent vehicle. Since it is the official unit of account for all EU official transactions, it has the automatic banking of the world's most important trading bloc and source of international capital investment. Similarly, the holding of a part of the official reserves of the EU Member States in euro reinforces its role as a means of settlement. Then, its inherent stability further enhances the role.

Fourth, when we turn to its position as a store of value, we have to be more precise. If we mean a store of value in the sense of stability, it is excellent and is probably equalled by few other currencies. If, however, one wishes to use the euro for speculation, it is probably not a wise choice.

Fifth, in contrast, the euro may not always be seen as a refuge from economic and political instability – particularly if we take the question of economic and political instability together. Here we can look to the case of Kosovo. The crisis in that state has tended to reinforce the role of the US Dollar as a refuge from political instability. Nevertheless, because of the very important economic position of the EU, the euro can be seen as a refuge from economic instability.

Finally, as has already been discussed, whilst the euro is 'legal tender' in the participating EU Member States, it is not the sole currency in those countries. The non-availability of euro coins and notes also tends to reduce its role in this area – until, at least 2002. Thereafter, it will fully play this role and likely to become very important.

In order to place the euro and these criteria in an international context, the author has produced Table 7.1 which shows the position of the euro when compared with other currencies and assets.

Table 7.1 The qualities of the euro and other currencies

	French Franc	Pound Sterling	Gold	Swiss Franc	US Dollar	SDR Special Drawing Rights	Yen	Deutsh Mark	euro
Unit of Account	✓	✓	?	✓	✓	✓	✓	✓	✓
Medium of exchange (between individuals)	✓	✓	✓	✓	✓	×	✓	✓	✓
Means of settlement	✓	✓	✓	✓	✓	✓	✓	✓	✓
Store of value	✓?	✓	×	✓?	✓	×	✓?	✓	✓
Refuge from economic and/or political instability	×	✓?	✓	✓	✓	×	?	?	✓
Legal tender	✓	✓	?	✓	✓	×	✓	✓	✓

OVERVIEW

The euro does then have a legal personality – this is extremely important. The legal basis for the euro is the Treaty on European Union (the Maastricht Treaty) – this is really very important. At a practical level, the Treaty is supplemented by the Council Regulation on the Introduction of the Euro and the Council Regulation on Some Provisions Relating to the Introduction of the Euro.

At a more practical level, it should be noted that the European Commission had issued a number of useful documents,[3] which will facilitate the introduction of the euro in the participating Member States. In these countries themselves, the most detailed, practical plans are already being laid down for the changeover from the national currencies to the euro. In the Netherlands, for example, the government will use the military for this purpose and has already constructed a centre where the national coins and notes will be stored.

Of equal importance, in the opinion of the author, is the degree to which the euro fulfils the roles which one expects a national currency to perform. Success in meeting these criteria will clearly enhance the euro both inside the European Union and at a more international level.

NOTES

1. The participating EU Member States are: Austria, Belgium, Finland, France, Germany, Ireland, Italy, Luxembourg, the Netherlands, Portugal and Spain.
2. The calculation of the value of the national participating currency vis-à-vis the euro takes place in the following three steps:
   (i) *Determination of the EU currencies' concertation exchange rates against the US dollar.* At 11.30 a.m. (CET), the EU central banks, including those with currencies which are not components of the ECU basket, provide to each other (in the context of a teleconference), the US dollar exchange rate for their respective currencies. These exchange rates are recorded as discrete values lying within the market bid–ask spreads. While, as a rule, the discrete values are equal to the mid-points of the bid–ask spreads, the EU central banks, as is allowed by the current concertation procedure, will take into account the need to ascertain exchange rates expressed with six significant digits,

like for the pre-announced rates. The bilateral rates between the euro-area participating currencies obtained by crossing the respective US dollar rates recorded by the EU central banks will be equal to the pre-announced ERM bilateral central, up to the sixth significant digit. The EU central banks participating in the euro area stand ready to ensure equality, if necessary, through the use of appropriate market techniques.

For example, FRF/DEM = FRF/USD:DEM/USD

(ii) *Calculation of the exchange rate of the official ECU against the US dollar.* The rates as recorded by the EU central bank are thereafter communicated by the National Bank of Belgium to the Commission, which uses them to calculate the exchange rates of the official ECU. The USD/ECU exchange rate (expressed as 1 ECU = x USD) is obtained by summing up the US dollar equivalents of national currency amounts that compose the ECU.

(iii) *Calculation of the exchange rate of the official ECU against the EU currencies participating in the EURO area.* The official ECU exchange rates against the EU currencies are calculated by multiplying the USD/ECU exchange rates by their respective US dollar exchange rates. This calculation is performed for all EU currencies, not only the ones which are components of the ECU basket. These ECU exchange rates are rounded to the sixth significant digit. Exactly the same method of calculation, including the rounding convention, will be used in determining the irrevocable conversion rates for the euro for the euro area currencies.

3. The most important documents published by the European Commission for the practical introduction of the euro are:

(i) *Checklist on the Introduction of the Euro for Enterprises and Auditors,* September 1997.

(ii) *Preparations for Changeover of Public Administrations to the Euro,* December 1997.

(iii) *Fact Sheets on the Preparation of National Public Administrations to the Euro* (status 15 May, 1998), July 1998.

(iv) Debt Redenomination and Market Convention in Stage III of EMU. July 1998.

CHAPTER 8

THE EURO – THE INSTITUTIONAL ARRANGEMENTS, THE EUROPEAN SYSTEM OF CENTRAL BANKS AND THE EUROPEAN CENTRAL BANK

THE BACKGROUND

The institutional framework for the euro, as laid down in the Treaty on European Union (the Maastricht Treaty) is the European System of Central Banks which has the European Central Bank at its apex. As has already been observed, Germany had always insisted that a future European Central Bank should be completely independent – rather similar to the Bundesbank. Without the fulfilment of this criterion, it was not possible for Germany to be part of the economic and monetary union with the common European currency. Consequently, this framework is clearly and categorically laid down in the Treaty. Since the overall mission and philosophy of the ECB must be the maintenance of price stability, in Article 105A of the Treaty the ECB is empowered with the 'exclusive right to authorize the issue of bank notes within their Community'.

THE EUROPEAN CENTRAL BANK

To the Germans, then, the independence of the future European Central Bank is of paramount importance – as is the question of price stability and the control of inflation. Recently, André Sapir, Chief Monetary Advisor to the European Commission, has concluded that the future ECB will meet these conditions. Whilst the author would agree with this assessment, he nevertheless finds the division of powers between the different bodies to be somewhat confusing.

For instance, under the Maastricht Treaty, the future ECB shall have the following tasks and responsibilities. In Article 105A of the Treaty, as has already been noted, the ECB is empowered with the 'exclusive right to authorize the issue of bank notes within their Community'. However, interestingly enough, both the ECB and the national central banks share the right to issue these notes. But it is the ECB which shall have the exclusive right to determine the volume of such notes which incidentally will alone have the status of legal tender in the Community.

Furthermore, the sharing of tasks between the future ECB and the existing national central banks is underlined by the fact that they will, together, make up the European System of Central Banks which, in turn, shall be governed by the Governing Council and the Executive Board. According to Article 107 of the Treaty, both the future ECB and the existing national central banks are expected to be totally independent of the Community and the governments of the Member States. This implies a change in the status of some of the present national central banks. In the following Article, Member States are expected to change their national legislation in order to be able to conform to this stipulation. It is, however, the ECB alone that is empowered to issue regulations which shall be binding on the whole Community. But, in Article 109, it is the Council, which acting unanimously, has the right to 'conclude formal arrangements on an exchange rate system for the ECU in relation to non-community currencies'. Hopefully, the implication here is that the ministers concerned will be those in charge of finance! In contrast, the Council only needs to act by a qualified majority to 'adopt, adjust, or abandon the central rates of the ECU within the current exchange rate system'.

Although in both cases the Council is expected to consult with the ECB – though not necessarily to agree with it – it is quite clear that the ministers will have a tremendous degree of authority within the ESCB, and in a number of other areas of exchange rate policy and in relations with international institutions, they only need a qualified majority in order to arrive at their decisions. However, surprisingly perhaps, acting within the EMU framework, 'Member States may negotiate in international bodies and conclude international agreements'.

Article 109a of the Treaty lays down the institutional

provisions (see below) for the ECB. In contrast with the Federal Reserve Board of the United States, their terms of office are relatively short.

Article 109A

1. The Governing Council of the ECB shall comprise the members of the Executive Board of the ECB and the Governors of the national central banks.
2. (a) The Executive Board shall comprise the President, Vice-President and four other members.

   (b) The President, the Vice-President and the other members of the Executive Board shall be appointed from among persons of recognized standing and professional experience in monetary or banking matters by common accord of the Governments of the Member States at the level of Heads of State or of the Government, on a recommendation from the Council of the ECB. Their term of office shall be eight years and shall not be renewable. Only nationals of Member States may be members of the Executive Board.

THE ESCB AND THE ECB – THE ORGANIZATIONAL FRAMEWORK

It is now useful to attempt to analyse the component parts of the ESCB and the ECB. In Figure 8.1, the author has divided the component parts of the ESCB into three parallel columns. In so doing, the aim is to make more clear a system which, at first sight, seems confusing. Also, it is important to note which organs consist of all the fifteen EU Member States and which are made up only of the eleven euro countries. In order to make this difference clear, numbers 11 or 15 are put alongside the different organs.

In the central/middle column, the kingpin is the European Central Bank (ECB), based in Frankfurt. It has the sole privilege of issuing euro, the European currency. It also sets short-term interest rates and manages monetary policy. At the time of writing, it is solely responsible to the European Parliament, to

Figure 8.1 European System of Central Banks (ESCB)

which body it is required to present an annual report.

Immediately below the ECB are the National Central Banks of the (at the time of writing) eleven participating euro EU Member States. They are empowered with operational responsibility for the system. This they do through foreign exchange operations and open-market operations (OMOs). They also have control over financial institutions and markets.

In the left-hand column we have the Council of Ministers of the fifteen EU Member States. It is this body which takes major economic, fiscal, and monetary decisions for the European Union. More precisely, it is the Economic and Financial Council that is entrusted with these decisions.

Below the Council is the European Commission, which is empowered with the implementation and surveillance of policies – most notable the broad convergence outlines of the EMU.

Moving on to the extreme right-hand column, we find two bodies which have and will continue to have tremendous influence over the ECB. At the top there is EURO 11, a committee composed of the Finance Ministers of the eleven participating EU Member States – together with representatives of the Commission and the ECB.

General Council

Governors of Central Banks of all fifteen Member States

● Formulates Opinions

Executive Board

President plus five Members

Governing Council

Executive Board

● Eleven Governors of Central Banks
● A Member of the European Commission
● President of the European Council

Figure 8.2   European Central Bank (ECB)

Below this body is the Economic and Finance Committee which on 1 January 1999 replaced the old, secretive Monetary Committee. This very important and influential body is made up of representatives of National Treasuries and Central Banks and the two European Commissioners.

Turning to the structure of the ECB itself, we note from Figure 8.2 that the umbrella body is the General Council which is composed of the Governors of the Central Banks of all the fifteen Member States. This body simply formulates opinions. In contrast, the real power is wielded by the Executive Board – made up of the President and five members, and the Governing Council which consists of the members of the Executive Board, the Governors of the Central Banks of the eleven participating Member States, a member of the Commission and the President of the European Council.

Although the institutional elements of the ESCB and the ECB would appear to be balanced, recently doubts have been expressed about the equilibrium in the system. These concern the possible rivalry between the national central banks and the ECB. The possibility of such rivalry is based on the fact that whereas the ECB has only a relatively small number of staff members, the national central banks have a veritable army of officials and staff members. Some observers look back to the historic rivalry between the Federal Reserve Board, based in

Washington D.C., and the powerful branches in Chicago and New York.

Disquiet was also expressed by the rivalry between France who supported the candidacy of Jean-Claude Trichet, Governor of the Banque de France, and the other EU Member States who supported Wim Duisenberg of the Netherlands for the Presidency of the ECB. The cloudy outcome of this dispute is that Professor Duisenberg is currently President of the ECB and states that he will serve his full term. In contrast, France declares that the 'gentleman's agreement' was that Professor Duisenberg would serve only half his term before being replaced by Monsieur Trichet. Despite this, it must be said that it would be difficult to find a more competent team of experts who compose the Executive Board of the ECB.

PRUDENTIAL MANAGEMENT

When, in June 1998, the ECB came into operation it was decided that if 15 EU Member States joined the ESCB the Bank's capital would be 5 billion ECUs, whereas, with 11 countries participating, it would be about 4 billion ECUs. In a parallel area, the ECB decided that the level of compulsory reserves which commercial banks must hand over to central banks would be 2 per cent. Regarding the reserves at the Bank's disposal, they are, by any standards, both generous and prudent. Thus, both the BIS and the IMF consider that reserves should cover 3 months' imports. In contrast, the ECB's reserves are the equivalent of about 4.3 months' imports. Between 10 and 15 per cent of these reserves are made up of gold.

In January, this year, the 11 participating countries transferred to the ECB 39.46 billion euros' worth of their foreign reserves. With all 15 countries participating, the value of these reserves would be about 50 billion ECUs.

OVERVIEW

At the time of writing, the ESCB and the ECB will have been in operation for six months. This time has been marked by prudence and by a swiftness of action where needed. Developments have also taken place in integrating the capital markets of the European Union. But there have been complaints about the fees charged by commercial banks for transactions involving changing national currencies into euro. Furthermore, the development of a financial Single European Market (SEM) is in jeopardy. The European Commission has been energetic to maintain the credibility of the euro. Similarly, a positive stance has been taken regarding international institutional representation of the euro.

The international representation of the euro, notably at G7 meetings, had in the second half of 1998 been the subject of intense discussion. In the event, the EU Council of Finance Ministers decided on 2 December 1999 that EURO 11 would be represented by the President of the EURO 11. If he or she comes from a non-G7 state, he or she would attend in addition to the representatives of France, Germany, and Italy. The EURO 11 representative will receive technical assistance from the European Commission. Earlier, the Commission had proposed that EURO 11 be represented by a 'Trinity' consisting of the ECB, the President of EURO 11 and the Commission itself. This proposal was not accepted by the EU Council of Ministers.

Apart from the use of the euro as the parallel currency in the long final transition period leading to full implementation of the EMU, it is necessary that the euro be a vehicle for capital market integration and parallel developments in banking. It is to these developments to which we shall now turn.

CHAPTER 9

THE EURO – CAPITAL MARKETS AND BANKING

THE BACKGROUND

The opening-up and integration of capital and financial markets is an integral part of the process leading to the creation of a Single European Market (SEM). Apart from the basic theoretical considerations (examined below), there are many practical advantages to be gained from such a process – notably in the field of cost savings. For example, in the European Commission's major research project on 'The Cost of Non-EUROpe',[1] we find enormous differences in the prices of standard financial products between different EU Member States. It is therefore clear that the consumer could gain from the opening-up of European financial markets, if, of course, real competition exists in the market.

Some years earlier, the basic advantages of the freeing of capital movements and the creation of a European Capital Market had been examined at some length by, among others, Segré,[2] Magnifico,[3] and Coffey.[4] In particular, if competition and improved access to information prevail among capital markets, banking systems and financial services, then these should lead to:

(i)   an improved allocation of resources;
(ii) increased 'transparency' and efficiency;
(iii) an increase in the welfare of business and citizens through an increase of choice in financial services, and, hopefully, through decreased costs for such services;
(iv) an easier movement of funds from surplus Member States to debtor ones; and,
(v)   the development and/or expansion of specialist centres for financial services.

THE EURO AND RECENT DEVELOPMENTS

In June 1998, the Competitiveness Advisory Group (CAG) made a number of observations and recommendations regarding the euro and the promotion of competitiveness in the European Capital Markets.[5] In their Introduction to their report the CAG almost mirrored the observations made some years ago (see Segré, Magnifico, and Coffey). In particular, they stated,

> A large group of European countries will soon be using a single currency. A substantial increase in the degree of integration of European capital markets will be among the most important consequences of this historical event. The CAG is convinced that the resulting unified competitive market for a much wider range of capital and financial services will greatly enhance efficiency in the allocation of resources and reinforce the competitiveness of the European economy globally. This will mean higher standards of living for European citizens and brighter prospects for their children. It will not, however, come about automatically. Many remaining obstacles to European financial integration will have to be removed, and this even after currency risk disappears.

> Moreover, the CAG warns that the allocative benefits of efficient financial markets and high capital mobility will emerge only if we can also overcome the real distortions, barriers and market imperfections that otherwise channel funds in the wrong directions. It is urgent to complete the Single Market for goods and services, with full implementation of the Commission's directives by all Member States. Only the combination of truly free trade with fully integrated capital markets will lastingly increase the flexibility and competitiveness of Europe, with positive evolution in both its economic and financial geography. Without this combination, clouds may gather and especially then cast their shadow over labour markets.

However, despite, in the author's eyes, the existence of the four following great financial freedoms inside the EU (certainly greater than those existing inside the USA), things are not what they would seem to be. These freedoms are:

(i) freedom of capital movements;
(ii) freedom to set up branches of banks (where legally
     recognized by the host country) in all fifteen EU Member
     States and inside the EFTA countries (with the 'temporary'
     exception of Switzerland);
(iii) freedom to set up branches of insurance companies through
     the EU and most of the EFTA countries (where the company
     is legally accepted in the host country); and,
(iv) freedom to conduct stockbroking activities in all the EU
     Member States and most of the EFTA countries.

Whilst the CAG sees the advent of the euro as an impetus to
greater capital and financial integration inside the EU, this,
despite (also) the existence of the four above-listed freedoms,
does not seem to be happening. Why should this not be so? The
CAG lists four main obstacles to the desired evolution. First, they
note differences in taxation. These differences are clearly visible
in Table 9.1. Despite the Group's awareness of the complexity of
tax harmonization and respect for the principle of subsidiarity,
they nevertheless recommend 'the Union substantially to reduce
the harmful differences in national tax treatment of savings and
investments'. Secondly, they note differences in accounting,
reporting and disclosure. Here, they recommend 'the Union
urgently to pursue, as necessary, the harmonization of accounting, reporting and disclosure rules that govern European
business and capital markets'. Thirdly, they note the existence
(still) of sizeable differences in financial regulation among
Member States. In this area, they make special reference to 'the
different regulation of pension funds, including restrictions on
the type of assets in which they can invest'. Thus, they
recommend 'bridging differences in national regulation of
pension funds, abolishing more or less explicit obstacles to
cross-border marketing of retail financial services'. Likewise,
they recommend a greater harmonization of regulations governing mortgage loans.

Fourthly, they examine 'real distortions'. Here they list the
following six distortions:

Table 9.1 Percentage differences in prices of standard financial products compared with average of the four lowest national prices (The figures show extent to which financial product prices, in each country, are above a low reference level. Each price difference implies a theoretical potential price fall from existing price levels to the low reference level.)

Name of standard service	Description of standard service	Belgium	Germany	Spain	France	Italy	Luxembourg	Netherlands	UK
Banking services									
1. Consumer credit	Annual cost of consumer loan of 500 ECU. Excess interest rate over money market rates.	-41	136	39	n/a	121	-26	31	121
2. Credit cards	Annual cost assuming 500 ECU debit. Excess interest rate over money market rates.	79	60	26	-30	89	-12	43	16
3. Mortgages	Annual cost of home loan of 25,000 ECU. Excess interest rate over money market rates.	31	57	118	78	-4	n/a	-6	-20
4. Letters of credit	Cost of letter of 50,000 ECU for three months.	22	-10	59	-7	9	27	17	8
5. Foreign exchange drafts	Cost to large commercial client of purchasing commercial draft for 30,000 ECU.	6	31	196	56	23	33	-46	16
6. Traveller's cheques	Cost for private consumer purchasing 100 ECU worth of traveller's cheques.	35	-7	30	39	22	-7	33	-7
7. Commercial loans	Annual cost (including commissions, charges) to medium-sized firm of commercial loan of 250,000 ECU.	-5	6	19	-7	9	6	43	46
Insurance services									
1. Life insurance	Average annual cost of term (life) insurance.	78	5	37	33	83	66	-9	-30
2. Home insurance	Annual cost of fire and theft cover for house valued at 70,000 ECU with 28,000 ECU contents.	-16	3	-4	39	81	57	17	90
3. Motor insurance	Annual cost of comprehensive insurance, 1.6 litre car, driver 10 years' experience, no claims bonus.	30	15	100	9	148	77	-7	-17
4. Commercial fire and theft	Annual cover for premises valued at 387, 240 ECU, stock at 232,344 ECU.	-9	43	24	153	245	-15	-1	27
5. Public liability cover	Annual premium for engineering company, 20 employees, annual turnover 1.29 million ECU.	13	47	60	117	77	9	-16	-7
Brokerage services									
1. Private equity transactions	Commission costs of cash bargain of 1440 ECU.	36	7	65	-13	-3	7	114	123
2. Private gilts transaction	Commission costs of cash bargain of 14,000 ECU.	14	90	217	21	-63	27	161	36
3. Institutional equity	Commission costs of cash bargain transactions of 288,000 ECU	26	69	153	-5	47	68	26	-47
4. Institutional gilt	Commission costs of cash bargain transactions of 7.2 million ECU.	284	-4	60	57	92	-36	21	n/a

Source: Paolo Cechini, 'The European Challenge', 1992; *original source:* European Commission, 'The Costs of Non-Europe', Brussels, 1986

(i)   budgetary policies;
(ii) trade distortions;
(iii) the functioning of the labour market;
(iv) decentralized financial supervision, management of bank crises and financial competition policies;
(v)   euro exchange rate strategies and global financial representation; and,
(vi) Public administration and infrastructures.

Thus, it is clear that despite the existence of the four freedoms and the introduction of the euro at the beginning of 1999, it would appear that the European Capital and Financial Market with a highly competitive atmosphere has failed to develop. Consequently, on 11 May 1999, Commissioner Mario Monti unveiled a plan for reforming Europe's financial services with a five-year deadline for fulfilment. In particular, Mr Monti warned that failure to implement the necessary reforms would prevent the Union from reaping the benefits associated with the euro. In particular, he observed, 'It is crucial that the single market for financial services delivers its full potential for consumers, in terms of a broad range of safe, competitive products, and for industry in terms of *inter alia* for easier access to a single deep and liquid market for investment capital.'[6]

It would seem, therefore, that the EU, in the person of the European Commission, is now finally set on enabling European citizens and businesses to reap the many benefits through access to cheaper capital and finance on a pan-European basis. This is, indeed, salutary since several decades have elapsed since the appearance of the Segré Report in 1966! In the author's view, the Action Plan part of this report is of utmost importance for the combined future of the SEM and whole Euro Zone, and it is, therefore, reproduced as Appendix 6 at the end of this book. Also, when looking to the future, logically, reference will be made to this plan.

NOTES

1.   'The Economics of 1992', *European Economy*, No. 35, Brussels, March 1988.
2.   EEC Commission, 'The Development of a European Capital

Market', the Segré Report, Brussels, 1966.

3. Giovanni Magnifico, *European Monetary Unification*, Macmillan, London, 1973.

4. Peter Coffey, *The European Monetary System – Past, Present and Future*, 2nd edn, Kluwer, Dordrecht, 1987.

5. Competitiveness Advisory Group, 'Capital Markets for Competitiveness', Report to the President of the Commission and the Heads of State and Government for the Cardiff European Council, European Commission, Brussels, June 1998.

6. European Commission, 'Financial Services: Implementing the Framework for Financial Markets: Action Plan', Communication of the Commission, Brussels, May 1999.

CHAPTER 10

THE EURO – CAPITAL MARKETS AND BANKING: PRACTICAL DEVELOPMENTS

THE BACKGROUND

Nowhere, it seems, has the arrival of the euro been awaited with such anticipation as by the capital markets and the banking sectors. In particular, two major centres, London and Frankfurt, have expected to gain from the creation of the Euro Zone. In turn, both these centres are rivals and every move made by the one inevitably affects the other.

In the 1970s, all the bankers and economists – whose works have been listed in the preceding chapter – had, rightly or wrongly, anticipated the growth of centres of specialization among the great banking and capital market centres of Europe. Thus, for example, they expected Frankfurt to become a European centre for industrial financing, Paris to become a European centre for short- and medium-term financing, and London to become a centre for financing international trade. Are there then signs of such developments, or what is in fact happening? Furthermore, what is likely to happen? In trying to answer these questions, one major consideration (which was not even mentioned years ago) has to be taken into account ... that is the question of the choice of benchmarks, i.e. LIBOR or EURIBOR.

THE BENCHMARK REFERENCES

Arguably the most famous benchmark in the financial world is LIBOR – the London Interbank Offered Rate – which is a benchmark rate based on the rates of 16 major international banks. LIBOR is the benchmark rate favoured by London and the

United States capital markets. In turn it is used by the LIFFE – the London Interbank Financial Futures and Options Exchange. The benchmark reference rate of the EURIBOR has a much wider European reference spread than is the case for LIBOR since it is based on the reference rate of 57 banks. The EURIBOR is (logically) favoured by the Continental European capital markets. However, the most important continental derivatives exchange, the German one, the Deutsche Terminboese, uses both EURIBOR and LIBOR as reference benchmarks. Nevertheless, LIFFE did announce, in January 1999, that it is to launch a derivative based on the Euro Zone index which is compiled by Morgan Stanley Capital International. It is assumed that this move in the so-called 'battle of the indices' is a reaction to the two main continental competitors, EUREX (Germany and Switzerland) and MATIF (France and associates). Thus, a month later, LIFFE gave the market the opportunity to buy its contract based on LIBOR and to convert its remaining positions into EURIBOR. Despite what at first sight may seem to be a kind of retreat by London, it should be noted that LIFFE did (in February 1999) maintain a 75 per cent share of overall turnover. To the author, this development came as no surprise since, decades ago (in the 1960s), London, at the time when trading in the pound sterling was negligible, demonstrated its flexibility by becoming the main market for Euro-Dollars.

COOPERATION BETWEEN FRANKFURT AND LONDON

Although observers had anticipated much competition between Frankfurt and London, initially, at least, the reverse appeared to be the case. On 6 July 1998 the London Stock Exchange and the Deutsche Boerse formed an alliance to trade in British and German blue-chip stocks. More recently, in March 2000, Frankfurt and London agreed to develop a common clearing and settlement, later in the year, for users of both markets. This would be done via CREST, the system used by the London stock exchange system. It is seen as a step in the direction of creating a pan-European market, which would allow trade in the shares of Europe's top 300 companies.

Naturally, such an alliance is fraught with problems. One concerns the ownership of such a system. Thus, whilst London, we are informed, would prefer ownership to be based on market capitalization of the two exchanges, Frankfurt it seems would prefer it to be based on trading turnover. Another problem is that concerning the harmonization of the rules governing how shares are listed and traded on their respective exchanges. Basically, this second problem refers very much to the quite different stock market cultures in the two centres. But then, these centres are not alone since six other European exchanges have been granted observer status. These exchanges are Amsterdam, Brussels, Madrid, Milan, Paris and Zürich. It would be foolish to imagine that the representatives of these exchanges will not also have their say – particularly if they consider joining the system. Then, one player who has remained relatively silent in this game, should not be ignored. This is MSCI, the leading US index provider which is also moving into the benchmark battle in the European equity markets. Here, it should be noted that the American financial bodies and systems have much experience in their own country and have fabulous financial resources behind them.

THE EURO AND BANKING – THE INTERVENTION OF THE EUROPEAN COMMISSION

Shortly after the birth of the euro, many complaints were made by citizens and enterprises about the exorbitant rates being charged by the commercial banks for conversion from national currencies into euro. This development was both disappointing and unacceptable because, already in April 1999, the Commission had made recommendations for a series of 'principles of good practice' for bank charges for conversion into the euro. The aim was that the conversion must be absolutely transparent, thus allowing citizens and enterprises to choose operations in a competitive environment. Thus, in February 1999, the Commission decided on the following initiatives:

(a) The banks in the Euro Zone are urged to present detailed information by 31 March 1999, comprising an exhaustive state of developments regarding bank charges invoiced for the exchange of banknotes and for cross-border payments (by cheque, by transfer or by card) in the Euro

Zone. The Commission hopes that this exercise will lead to the observation that charges have fallen, with perceptible effects for travellers and tourists from next summer [2000] already;

(b) Users and consumers may notify the Commission of any case of abuse or non-compliance with the Euro's legal framework, by electronic mail or fax at the following numbers: fax: 32–2–295.07–50; e-mail EUROpoint@dg15.cec.be; e-mail EUROsignal@dg24.cec.be;

(c) In the light of information received by banks (through European associations representing the banking sector) and the cases notified by consumers, the Commission will see how to act, and, if need be, envisage new measures, including complementary legislation;

(d) Member States are invited to set up similar instruments by placing at the disposal of the public complaint recording systems and creating 'local observatories of the Euro change-over';

(e) Banks should develop efficient cross-border payment systems, so as to reduce the cost and encourage the generalized use of the Euro (the Euro Banking Association has already taken measures that the Commission welcomes);

(f) In the spring [of 2000], the Commission will publish a communication setting out a framework for achieving the goal of a single payments area. Cross-border payments should become as safe and fast, for a comparable price, as national payments. In addition, the Commission would welcome the creation of a European electronic wallet (an electronic card which stores value and can be used to make low value retail purchases).

OVERVIEW

The creation of the euro has given the European Union a wonderful opportunity to create a pan-European capital market and banking system. In fact, as a result of the process of creating the Single European Market, much of the legal framework is already in place. However, many cultural and technical problems remain. Also, developments may not be those which we would prefer. Thus, for example, the cooperation between the Frankfurt and London Stock Exchanges is surprising since the cultures of both centres are so very different from each other. Then, the mergers between the commercial banks to create European Megabanks (notably for example, the planned merger between the BNP, PARIBAS and the Société Générale) does not bode well for competition and the giving of choice to the consumer. In this respect, it will be remembered that in the study on the 'Costs of Non-EUROpe',[1] it was seen that the costs of financial services differed enormously between different centres. At least the creation of the euro – notably when it becomes legal tender in the 11 participating Member States on 1 July 2002 – will inevitably create the transparency so much desired by the Commission. It may be necessary to wait until that date to obtain the transparency in the euro market which is both desirable and necessary.

NOTES

Although most of the work in this chapter has been devoted to Frankfurt and London, it is the Scandinavians who have (discreetly) been more successful in creating a cross-border equities market. Thus, in June 1999, Europe's first such market, known as NOREX, came on stream. NOREX creates a single market for Denmark and Sweden. NOREX plans to bring in Finland and Norway eventually.

1. Paoto Cechini, 'The Costs of Non-Europe', Wildwood House, 1988.

Part Four

The euro – Initial Experience and the Future

CHAPTER 11

THE FIRST SIX MONTHS

THE BACKGROUND

A few weeks after the surprise simultaneous reduction, in one swoop, of their interest rates by ten of the eleven participating euro Member States, on 3 December 1998, the euro system came into operation on 1 January 1999. This 'historic' event was cemented by the meeting of the ECOFIN Council, the same day, when the ministers accepted the Commission's proposal for the irrevocable fixing of the parities of the national currencies of the participating Member States vis-à-vis the ECU.[1] This then ushered in what in the author's view is a dangerously long period during which time these national currencies will co-exist alongside the euro. It will thus not be until 1 January 2002, when the national currencies will be exchanged for euro, and, only on 1 July of the same year, will the euro be sole legal tender in participating countries. We shall return to this question in the final chapter of this book.

At this point, when considering the second of the first six months of the life of the euro, the following questions should be answered:

A. How smooth, technically speaking, have the first six months been?

B. Has the euro, initially at least, been overvalued?

C. Has the European Central Bank established itself as the effective manager of the ESCB?

D. To what degree, if at all, has the euro possibly contributed to the integration process of the European Union?

A – THE TECHNICAL SMOOTHNESS OF THE FIRST SIX MONTHS

The launch of the euro was surrounded by euphoria on the side of its supporters and by grave misgivings on the side of the critics. Both sides were proved wrong. What, in fact, has the record been?

For a new international monetary system, representing a number of very different countries, the first six months have indeed been remarkably smooth. Technically speaking, things could hardly have been better. In particular, the euro clearing system, the Target system, has worked surprisingly well (see page 108). It has worked to the great satisfaction of the eleven Euro Zone countries and to the equal satisfaction of the 'outsiders'. This is a considerable achievement since the latter was the area about which both supporters and critics of the euro had doubts concerning its success.

B – THE VALUE OF THE EURO

At the outset, the euro was almost certainly overvalued against the US Dollar. Today, it is possibly undervalued. In contrast with the parity of the euro, the euro bond and equity markets have performed surprisingly well ... at times outperforming the American market. Nevertheless, the question of the value of the euro is a tantalizing one. Having stated this, it is true to observe that the value of the euro, in June 1999, was about the same as that of the composite currencies in 1998.

When we consider the value of a currency, it is necessary to take into account so very many variables. At the very least, the following considerations must be taken into account:

(i)   costs and prices compared with the performance of other countries (here, productivity plays a major role);
(ii) fiscal and monetary policies;
(iii) the overall performance of the economy;
(iv) the desire of individuals, institutions and countries to hold a currency; and,
(v)   political and other influences;

In the case of the euro, as also in the case of the US Dollar, these considerations have, in the short space of time under review, influenced the attractiveness of the euro. Overriding these considerations is, nevertheless, the fact that the euro does represent the world's most important trading bloc. This fact should dominate, particularly in the long run, all other considerations.

For classical economists, exchange rates do bring into equilibrium with each other costs and prices in different countries. Here, as has already been mentioned, productivity levels (as well as those of quality and after-sales service) play a great role. In the case of the EU and the USA no major differences during the period under review are to be noted. This area does, nevertheless, deserve much greater in-depth sectoral and country research.

Turning to the fiscal and monetary policies, the performance of the EU could hardly be better. As examined earlier in this work, the author believes that the so-called Maastricht criteria are rather strict. Despite this observation, and with the exception of the recent request by Italy (referred to in the final chapter of this book) for a slight, temporary, exemption in the application of these criteria, fiscal and monetary policies among all EU Member States have been surprisingly well coordinated and inflation levels are consistently very low.

When we turn to the overall performance of the EU economy, we find the picture more varied. In some countries, the economy is expanding and unemployment levels are low. In other countries, the economy is picking up whilst in others the economy is fairly static.

This mixed picture of the overall EU economy contrasts strongly with that of the continuing expanding economy of the USA. To the author, it is the continuous expansion of the American economy that makes the US Dollar so attractive when compared with the euro.

The desire of individuals, institutions and countries to hold currencies is based on a mixture of economic and political considerations. It is also a result of a wish to diversify their portfolios. In the specific case of the euro and the US dollar, one major consideration has tended to overshadow all others ... the search for a refuge from political upheavals. Here, the author is referring specifically to Kosovo. As the hostilities intensified, the euro became less attractive as a refuge currency whilst the US Dollar became extremely attractive.

In conclusion, then, whilst at the outset, the euro was certainly overvalued, today, at the time of writing, it is probably undervalued.

C – THE EUROPEAN CENTRAL BANK

The European Central Bank entered uncharted waters, in January 1999. Not only had the nomination of the Bank's President taken place under the least auspicious of conditions, but many variables, for example the choice of monetary policy, remained undecided. In view of these conditions, the ECB has, in the opinion of the author, performed remarkably well. As should be, the simultaneous reductions of interest rates have been swift and discreet.[2] Naturally, some critics want less secrecy, yet, under the present conditions, some degree of secrecy is surely inevitable.

The choice of monetary policy variables (examined earlier in this work) has been most satisfactory and seems to have been most appropriate for the management of the European System of Central Banks.

One word of criticism may, however, be valid. At least one occasion has been noted when the President, Professor Duisenberg, and a distinguished member of the Board, Heer Tietmeyer, have spoken with different voices … in public. This conduct is untoward and should be avoided.

This said, the author must conclude that in its first six months of active management of the ESCB, the ECB has performed very well indeed.

D – THE INTEGRATION PROCESS

The euro is helping and will continue to facilitate the European integration process. The existence of the euro is helping and will deepen the degree of 'transparency' in the successful achievement of the Single European Market. The comparison of prices in different Member States will thus be easier. In particular, the desired opening-up and integration of financial and capital markets[3] will be facilitated by the use of the euro. It is therefore likely that the EU will, by the year 2005, have an integrated financial market able to rival that of the United States.

CONCLUDING OVERVIEW

Six months is a very, very short time to allow a clear and balanced assessment of such a historic and revolutionary undertaking as the introduction of the euro and the ESCB. This assessment is made more difficult by the challenge presented by the conflict in Kosovo and the rivalry of the booming US economy. This having been said, the euro system, particularly on the technical side, has performed with exemplary smoothness. In particular, it has provided the world with a much-needed zone of monetary stability. This, in itself, is no mean achievement.

NOTES

1. Following a 'historic' meeting of the ECOFIN Council on 1 January 1999, the eleven euro participating Member States accepted the Commission's proposal that their national currencies be 'irrevocably fixed in value vis-à-vis the euro according to the parities listed below:

1 euro	= 13.7603	Austrian Schilling
	= 40.3399	Belgian Franc
	= 2.20371	Dutch Guilder
	= 5.94573	Finnish Markka
	= 6.55957	French Franc
	= 1.95583	German Mark
	= 0.787564	Irish Pound
	= 1936.27	Italian Lira
	= 40.3399	Luxembourg Franc
	= 200.482	Portuguese Escudo
	= 166.386	Spanish Peseta

2. A good example was the cut, on the 8 April 1999, of the benchmark reference rates to five per cent.

3. In this context, it is interesting to note that on 4 May 1999, the London and Frankfurt Stock Exchanges agreed to open-up their bilateral talks to six other bourses.

CHAPTER 12

THE 'INS' AND THE 'OUTS'

THE BACKGROUND

One of the biggest questions concerning the future of the euro is the fate (to use the dramatic expression) of those European countries which have chosen not to join the Euro Zone – or which do not fulfil the Maastricht criteria. In using the expression 'Fate', the author wishes to cover such issues as the future role of such currencies as the Pound Sterling and the Swiss Franc, the rivalry between the London and Frankfurt Stock Exchanges and the possibility of some countries joining the Euro Zone at a later date.

Account must also be taken of the arrangements made by a number of non-Euro Zone countries to link their currencies with the euro. This important question will be examined in the following chapter. It is, however, notable that since the demise of Communism most of the countries of Central and Eastern Europe have become very 'open' and are trading heavily with the EU. Also, in most cases, their levels of inflation are low.

RIVALRY BETWEEN CURRENCIES

One of the most discussed issues during the period leading up to the introduction of the euro was that of the future role of two important European currencies, the Pound Sterling and the Swiss Franc. Basically, there were two points of view: one of doom, the other of a strange kind of euphoria.

In the first case, the protagonists foresaw a situation where the growing strength of the Euro Zone, centred on Frankfurt, would outclass both London and Zürich and diminish the importance of the British and Swiss currencies. In the second case, the proponents argued that London and Zürich would become types of offshore capital centres (as, in fact, had happened in the 1960s and the 1970s when London had become the main international centre for the so-called Euro dollars). In particular, Switzerland feared (and still fears) a massive influx of 'hot' money fleeing the banks in the Euro Zone.

In reality, neither of these scenarios has materialized. As has already been discussed, London has started to establish close links with Frankfurt whilst the much-feared flood of 'hot' money into Zürich has not happened. It is nevertheless true that the importance of Frankfurt has increased. Also, the Pound Sterling would seem to be overvalued, which is not in the interest of Britain's economy. According to the IMF, in 2000, the Pound Sterling was at least 40 per cent overvalued. In another vein, in July 2000, members of the House of Commons Treasury Committee, in London maintained that the Pound Sterling was too volatile for the currency to be able to enter the Euro Zone. This volatility is demonstrated in Figure 12.1.

Many reasons exist why exchange rates should vary. In the specific case of the EU, however, the commitment by members of the ERM of the old EMBS, particularly during the period 1985–91, to keep their exchange rates in line with each other most probably explains the relative stability of the rates of these countries during those years. This relative stability when compared with, for example, the USA, Japan, and the United Kingdom has been graphically shown by the Bank for International Settlements in its *Annual Report* for 1992 (see Figure 12.1).

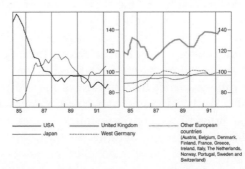

Figure 12.1 Exchange rate variations: real effective exchange rates 1985–91 (1978 = 100)
Note: Real effective exchange rates: nominal effective exchange rates adjusted for movements in relative unit labour costs
Source: BIS *Annual Report*, 1992

FUTURE MEMBERS OF THE EURO ZONE

Discussion about possible future members of the Euro Zone concerns the four 'out' EU Member States (Denmark, Greece, Sweden and the United Kingdom) and the candidate countries for EU membership.

The EU 'Out' Countries

The two 'out' Member States to which most attention has been given are Denmark and the United Kingdom. These two countries do, however, differ quite considerably in their ability to join the Euro Zone. Of these countries, it is Denmark which could, without any discernable problems, joint the club.

Denmark fulfils, admirably it seems, all the so-called 'Maastricht' criteria. Furthermore, unlike the United Kingdom, Denmark is a member of the 'new' EMS and its currency moves in the rather narrow band of 2.25 per cent. So why does Denmark choose not to join the Euro Zone? The reasons are mainly cultural and political. Following the rejection of the Treaty on European Union, in a referendum, by the particularly well-informed Danish citizens, any Danish government would have to have a cast iron case for Euro Zone membership before organizing another referendum.[1]

The case of the United Kingdom could hardly be more different than that of Denmark. Three major factors make Britain's membership in the Euro Zone in the near future extremely unlikely. The author believes it is both dangerous and unfortunate that no British government or major political party (at least in public) makes any reference to these fundamental technical structural problems. First, the structure of British trade is rather different from that of most of her EU partners. Thus, whilst she tends to trade more and more with European countries, Britain still conducts much of her trade with the United States and other countries. In turn, this would always cause tensions for the Pound Sterling vis-à-vis the euro. Secondly, a much more serious problem for British citizens is (when compared with other European countries) that of the exaggerated influence of interest rate changes on mortgage rates. Many British citizens have unpleasant memories of steep hikes in mortgage rates during the last months of British membership

of the old EMS. Consequently, before Britain c
the Euro Zone, this question would have t
researched and the relevant changes made to th
the mortgage market. Thirdly, the most easily rem
for British membership of the Euro Zone is the ᴄᴛ that the
United Kingdom is not a member of the 'new' EMS.

More recently, with the fall in the value of the euro vis-à-vis the US Dollar, support for Britain's entry into the Euro Zone has weakened. Even in the city of London, which, for obvious reasons, has usually been a vocal supporter of the UK joining the club, these voices have, of late, been less shrill.

Turning to the two other EU 'out' countries, they both present a very different picture to that of Denmark and Britain. Surprisingly, perhaps, it is Greece which is the most ardent supporter of euro membership. In that vein, Greece has joined the ERM of the EMS and will join the Euro Zone in January 2001. In contrast, whilst a number of Swedish business interests would like Sweden to join the Euro Zone, the Swedish government does not seem to be in any particular hurry to do so.

The Candidate Countries

We face a very different situation when comparing many of the candidate countries with those of the economically more developed countries of Western Europe. Some of these countries are experiencing difficulties in fulfilling the basic criteria for EU membership. Nevertheless, there are countries in Central and Eastern Europe which wish to join the Euro Zone.

In the negotiations leading to membership of the European Union there are five so-called 'front runners' – Estonia, the Czech Republic, Hungary, Poland and Slovenia. Let us examine the case of these countries.

Among these five countries there is a general agreement that it is little Estonia which is the candidate country most likely to fulfil these criteria. However, at this moment in time, Estonia is not a member of the EMS. Then it is Slovenia which would probably come next in line for membership. Poland has undertaken major economic reforms and is directing its trade more and more towards the EU. The Czech Republic had, at least until recently, undertaken important reforms. Furthermore, unlike 'oland and especially Hungary, that country's external debt position is not important. In contrast, whilst Hungary has undertaken important economic reforms, her external per capita debt is probably the highest in Europe (excluding Russia). It should be noted, however, that as with all other Member States of the EU (except, of course, for the original six founder Member States of the old EEC), negotiations for membership tend to take a long time. Then, once these negotiations are successfully completed there follows a transitional period, which varies in length.

OVERVIEW

In examining the positive of the so-called 'ins' and 'outs' we find a very mixed situation. As already mentioned, it is the position of Denmark and especially Britain about which so much is written and which elicits so much discussion. But, the cases of both countries are very different. Of the two, it is Denmark which could so easily fulfil the criteria for membership. In contrast, the cases of Greece and Sweden[2] are more mixed in quality. Among the candidate countries, at the time of writing, Estonia is most likely to meet all the criteria for membership. However, it is Greece which will join the Euro Zone in January 2001.

NOTES

1. In September 2000, just such a referendum was organized by the Danish government, the people of Denmark rejected Danish participation in the Euro Zone.
2. Whilst some Swedish business leaders favour Swedish membership of the Euro Zone, public opinion appears not to support the view. Also Sweden does not meet all the 'Maastricht criteria' and, like Britain, is not a member of the EMS.

CHAPTER 13

THE EURO – THE FUTURE

The future is never clear. Nevertheless, underlying trends do sometimes indicate in which direction the future may lie. In the specific case of the euro, the author believes that the following main issues should be examined. These are:

(i)   the basic economic and trading strength of the EU;
(ii) the sober economic and monetary policies practised by the EU;
(iii) the delicate transition period between 1 January 1999 and 30 June 2002;
(iv) the questions of structural (notably labour) inflexibility and the possible expansion of the EU's economy;
(v)   the possibility of the euro political government; and,
(vi) the future international role of the euro.

These six issues will influence to varying degrees the future performance and international position of the euro.

THE BASIC ECONOMIC AND TRADING STRENGTH OF THE EU

As was observed in the first chapter of this book, France had always (particularly in the 1960s and 1970s) maintained that the active reserve role of the US Dollar conferred exorbitant privileges on the United States. Furthermore, France maintained that the then European Economic Community, as the world's greatest trading bloc should be endowed with a 'common international monetary personality'. The best way to achieve this would be to have a common currency.

The French observation about the old EEC's position as the world's greatest trading bloc is even more valid today than ever before. The combined strength of the EU and the EFTA is very great indeed. Nearly all the Member States of these combined regional groups have production (with the exception of agriculture) of sophisticated high quality goods. Furthermore, they are nearly all relatively high income countries.

To the author, it is this great trading strength, of which the euro is the symbol, that underpins the long-term prospects of the European currency. This observation is borne out by the ongoing strength of Euro bonds. Linked to this is the fact that the euro is the official unit of account for all official transactions of the EU and is actively promoted by the European Investment Bank.

The Sober Economics and Monetary Policies of the EU

Much has been written and continues to be written about the so-called 'Maastricht Criteria'. These criteria certainly imply sober economic and monetary policies. Some observers believe they are too sober and therefore too restrictive to economic growth – whilst other experts believe they are most appropriate. Linked to these views is the question of a possible structural inflexibility, notably regarding labour. This question is, however, examined later in this chapter.

At this point, let us recap the basic overriding aim and philosophy of the European Union's EMU – that is, price stability. Of this, there can be no doubt. Also, it is possible to have economic growth and low or zero inflation. On the other hand, if prices and inflation do get out of hand, the exchange markets will take care of currencies. This is exactly what happened in 1992 with Britain and Italy, whose currencies were clearly overvalued at that time.

The author does not believe that temporary small deviations in government debt – currently being experienced by France, Germany and Italy – are important, so long as they have negligible effects on levels of inflation. Currently, the inflation record of the EU Member States is satisfactory, as shown in Table 13.1.

A policy area, until relatively recently overlooked by most experts, is the balance of payments record of the EU Member States, compared with that of the United States. Major current account deficits (like the American one) must be covered by the return from overseas investments. Most recently this has not been the case with the United States. This is alarming. In

Table 13.1 EU Member States: inflation rates May 1998–May 1999

	May 1998 – May 1999
Euro Zone	1.0
EU 15	1.1
Sweden	0.3
Germany	0.4
Austria	0.4
France	0.5
Belgium	0.8
Luxembourg	1.3
United Kingdom	1.3
Finland	1.4
Italy	1.5
Denmark	1.6
Spain	2.1
Portugal	2.1
Netherlands	2.1
Greece	2.2
Ireland	2.3

These rates are still partially provisional. *Source*: Eurostat

contrast, the EU shows balance of payments surpluses. This bodes well for the long-term outlook for the euro.

THE DELICATE TRANSITION PERIOD

The author has been deeply concerned by the relatively long transition period between the inauguration of the Euro Zone on 1 January 1999, and the end of June 2002 when, in the Euro Zone countries, the euro will become sole legal tender. This is a very long period of time. The author has long suggested that the transition should take place almost overnight ... like the highly successful West German currency change in 1948. Apparently, for technical reasons, such a swift change was not possible. Nevertheless, there are calls for a quicker move to adopting the euro as sole legal tender in 2002. In response, the Council of Ministers has suggested that an attempt may be made to bring this forward by about two months or so. Most recently, Germany has called for just such a move.

STRUCTURAL FLEXIBILITY

The question of structural (notably labour) inflexibility inside the European Union as a possible impediment to the successful working of the EMU is a burning issue at the present time in Western Europe. It is a complicated and controversial issue which has become deeply politicized. Two recent studies seem to shed new light on this issue. In the first study, by Oliver Blanchard and Justin Wolfers,[1] the authors examine the thesis that Europe's high unemployment levels are due to structural problems. Their detailed research seems, at least partly, to contradict this thesis since some of Europe's unemployment is partly cyclical. Nevertheless, if rigidities exist (as they have done for decades) they do tend to become more profound during the course of cyclical downturns. Equally, labour market rigidities tend to magnify economic shocks. These shocks are mainly falls in annual productivity growth, real levels of interest rates and falls in the demand for labour (due mainly to changes in technology). The two authors are, nevertheless, optimistic about the future.

Most recently, a regular OECD study has set the proverbial cat among the pigeons. This volume is the Jobs Study,[2] produced by the organization's education, employment, labour and social affairs directorate. In the chapter on employment protection and labour market performance, the authors conclude that strong job protection laws 'have little or no effect on overall unemployment'.

From the same organization, the OECD, a group of experts under the direction of Peter Hoeller[3] have come to somewhat different conclusions regarding flexibility, particularly regarding labour. They observe, 'greater overall labour market flexibility would support job mobility and accelerate the pace of wage and price changes at the regional or country level in order to achieve real exchange rate corrections following an adverse shock.' However, these experts also observe that 'there is no guarantee that EMU will set forces in motion that would automatically lead to a better functioning of the labour markets.'

This issue of rigidity and inflexibility is an extremely complicated one, which suggests that a number of other related points must also be taken into account ... apart from job protection. At the outset, the author would make the observation that in a number of EU Member States, i.e. Austria, Denmark, Ireland, the Netherlands, Portugal, Spain and the UK, and in two EFTA countries, Norway and Switzerland, job creation is quite good. In most of these countries (with the possible exception of the United Kingdom), job protection is strong or very strong. So, what do these countries have which sets them apart from their partner countries? The author would suggest that the following issues deserve greater study:

- deregulation;
- consensus between labour and business leaders;
- a more equitable sharing of social security costs between employees and the State.

Deregulation started earliest in the United Kingdom and has therefore gone much further there than in other West European countries. Whilst deregulation is not the panacea for all economic ills, being conducive to the creation of new businesses is an important area. In the United Kingdom (as in the United States) it is relatively easy to start up a new business. Hence, there is an influx of young French businessmen into the south of England who are disenchanted with the bureaucracy of their own country: in much of continental Europe the creation of a new business is a bureaucratic and a legalistic nightmare. This clearly must change. Recent French moves to penalize financially their business leaders who move to England are both stupid and illegal.

Social consensus is very important in Western Europe. Remarkably, nowhere has it gone further than in Denmark, where taxes are high, there are few social inequalities, unemployment is low and just over 1000 citizens reside in prison! The Danes maintain that if all the people living in American jails were counted as being unemployed, US unemployment levels would be very high indeed! Another country where, over the past ten to fifteen years, the social consensus has been good is the Netherlands.

In all countries in the West the issue of the costs and financing of social security is a controversial one. However, it can be stated categorically that three major principles (among others) separate the Europeans from the Americans. As a matter of right, the

European wants:

- free health;
- free education;
- lots of free time.

At stake here is the distinction between social welfare (a level below which no citizen should be allowed to fall – à la Beveridge Plan) and social insurance (where benefits would relate to salary levels and contributions). Also, at stake is the financing of all these benefits. It would seem that in countries such as France and Belgium for example, where the financing falls heavily on the enterprises, there is a disincentive to employment. In contrast, in Denmark, Ireland and the United Kingdom for example, where the costs are more equitably shared between employees, employers and the State, there is an incentive to employment. Equally, much of this social security can be most economical and cost effective. Nowhere is this more true than in the United Kingdom where, as a percentage of GDP, the country spends between one third and one half of the amount spent on health by the United States. However, in Britain, as in other West European countries, all citizens receive health coverage. In contrast, in Britain, job security is not as strong as in most other EU Member States. This is a prickly issue worthy of much more study.

But economists, when looking at the future prospects for the euro, are also concerned with other rigidities … the relative immobility of labour and capital. It has been established for decades that regional labour mobility inside the European Union has never been particularly high. Taking labour mobility first, the author believes that so long as, when necessary, labour continues to enter the EU from non-Member States, all is well. Here, the highly educated and well trained citizens from the countries of Central and Eastern Europe will be a bonanza for the Euro Zone.

In addition, the author believes that the much delayed opening-up and integration of the EU's (and EFTA's, too) capital markets will further strengthen the euro.

Turning to the health of the European economy – when compared with that of the United States – there are at the time of writing distinct signs that the economies of a number of EU Member States are expanding gently. If this expansion is sustained, then the attractiveness of the euro is likely to improve.

An example of a very successful monetary union was that existing since 1921 until the 1980s between the Republic of Ireland and the United Kingdom. Was it so successful because of the freedom of labour and capital movements between the two countries or what? The Irish–British record deserves further study in the interests of the Euro Zone.

EURO POLITICAL GOVERNMENT

Basically, the decision to create a European Monetary Union and a common currency is a political one. This raises the question of how far the creation of the euro, particularly from 1 July 2002 onwards, will lead to the creation of a euro political government inside the European Union. Linked with this question is that of the choice between a confederation and a federation. These are profound and heady issues. Some would argue that a full EMU with a common currency will automatically lead to some form of political union. They imply that countries inside the Euro Zone will be so integrated with each other, and decisions must be taken so swiftly, that political union will become inevitable.

A group of distinguished experts,[4] whose views are endorsed by the author of this book, have tended to give a different and more practical view about the future. Whilst they agree that there will have to be a much greater degree of coordination of national policies, they maintain that this coordination will best and most practically work through pressure among equals and the evaluation of the best practices. This will remove the need for the transfer of more power to the centre. Nevertheless, the author believes that there will always be some countries, notably Germany and the Benelux countries, which will wish to deepen political cooperation in a federalist sense. In contrast, other countries, notably Denmark, France and the United Kingdom, prefer a loose form of political cooperation between Member States, more confederated in nature.

THE EURO'S INTERNATIONAL POSITION AND THE FUTURE

The continued decline in the value of the euro vis-à-vis the US Dollar has caused concern in some circles in Frankfurt and

Brussels. Those European producers who are exporting their goods to the USA are delighted.

As mentioned earlier in this work, the euro bond market (the long-term market) continues to advance and multinational companies trading inside and/or with the EU are very happy to use the euro. Also, more countries are diversifying their portfolios by acquiring euro. Then, as is shown in Appendix 5 at the end of this work, the Euro Zone is represented as one body in international monetary forums, such as the G7 and the IMF. This last organization had already replaced certain national European currencies by the euro in the composition of the Special Drawing Right (SDR).

THE EUROPEAN CENTRAL BANK

The European Central Bank, in its *Monthly Bulletin*, August 1999, stresses the use of the euro as a 'Pegging Currency'. In the first instance, reference is made to those States, which, as a result mainly of former colonial ties, use the euro as their own currency or adopt exchange rate regimes involving the use of the euro.

The Bank then lists around 30 countries, listed in the following categories, which have exchange rate regimes involving the euro. These countries can be divided into four groups.

The first group includes countries the currency of which is pegged to the euro. Excluding the ad hoc monetary agreements mentioned above, this group comprises four countries. Since January 1999 two EU Member States, Denmark and Greece, have been participating in the new exchange rate mechanism (ERM II) that links the currencies of EU Member States to the euro on a bilateral and voluntary basis. Two other countries (Cyprus and Macedonia) unilaterally peg their currency to the euro. A second group (Bosnia-Herzegovina, Bulgaria and Estonia) has adopted euro/Deutsche Mark and these exchange rate regimes are planned to take place at the latest upon the introduction of euro banknotes in 2002. A third group (including Hungary, Iceland and Poland) consists of 17 countries that peg their currency to a basket of currencies including the euro or one of its national denominations. This group also includes, in broad terms, those countries with currencies pegged to the SDR. When it was introduced, the euro automatically replaced the fixed currency amounts of the Deutsche Mark and the French Franc in the SDR basket, which also includes the US Dollar, the Japanese Yen and the Pound Sterling. The weight of the euro in the SDR basket as of 23 July 1999 was 27.3 per cent. Finally, a fourth group of seven countries (including the Czech Republic, the Slovak Republic and Slovenia) has adopted a system of managed floating, with the euro used informally as the reference currency.

Turning to the possibility of the euro replacing the US Dollar, in part as a payment/vehicle currency, the Report suggests the following four factors, which may positively affect this outcome.

First, lower transaction costs are likely to emerge in all markets in which the euro is used as a payment/vehicle currency, thus making it possible that there will be some shift towards the euro. In particular, in order to hedge exchange rate risk, non-residents may increasingly find new euro-denominated instruments in the single euro foreign exchange market. Secondly, more so than in the past, euro area traders may be in a position to demand that the euro be used in their transactions in order to avoid exchange rate risk. In particular, those European exporters that have been willing to use foreign currencies until now may adopt their local currency, the euro, for the invoicing and settlement of exports to other industrialized countries. Thirdly, residents of emerging or transition countries – especially those with less stable domestic monetary conditions at the present juncture in central and eastern Europe – may increasingly resort to the euro as a medium of exchange for their local transactions ('direct currency substitution'). Fourthly, transactions denominated in euro may reach – at some point in time and for reasons different from those related to its functions as a medium of exchange and a unit of account – a threshold above which the propensity of agents to use the euro as a payment/vehicle currency increases. This would further reduce transaction costs and may contribute to furthering the process of internationalization of the euro. A precondition for these four potential factors to produce their effects is that the euro must continue to be associated with price stability.

Whilst the ECB sets out the many benefits for users of the currency, which are of course shared by many supporters of the euro, in the same report it utters a word of warning about the possible costs.

There are also potential microeconomic costs, or risks, related to the internationalization of the euro. As regards the domestic banking sector, there is a drawback to increased foreign holding of short-term euro deposits. At times of sudden changes in exchange rate or interest rate expectations between the major international currencies, these liquid short-term assets might be withdrawn quickly in large amounts by foreign investors. If the domestic banking sector of a country with an international currency is heavily involved in maturity transformation, it can be more exposed to liquidity shocks, in particular during periods of market stress. Other microeconomic costs or risks are related to potential increases in asset price volatility resulting from a growing international role of the euro. In particular, enhanced use of the euro as an investment currency could go hand in hand with more pronounced international portfolio shifts by international investors when uncertainty increased or expectations change. In fact, higher financial market trading volumes seem to be empirically associated with higher short-term volatility. Furthermore, econometric evidence shows that increases in financial market bid–ask spreads are clearly linked to an increase in volatility. This volume–volatility-spread nexus could reduce the beneficial liquidity effects described above, but is unlikely to offset them fully.

The euro will clearly not be a replacement for the US Dollar ... but it will be an alternative. Furthermore, as the EU economy tends to expand (as is currently happening) and as the EU continues to maintain its sober economic and monetary policies and balance of payments surpluses, so, in turn, in the longer run, the euro will become more attractive. Finally, if we can get over this rather long transitional period (until the end of June 2002) without major difficulties, the euro will be competitive internationally. As has been said on many occasions, things will never be quite the same again.

NOTES

1. Oliver Blanchard and Justin Wolfers, 'The Role of Shocks and Institutions in the Rise of European Unemployment: The Aggregate Evidence', MIT and NBER and Harvard, 25 March 1999.
2. OECD, *Annual Employment Study*, Paris, 1999.

3. Peter Hoeller, ed., *'EMU – Facts, Challenges and Policies'*, OECD, Paris, 1999.
4. Kay, John, 'Crisis, What Crisis?', 25 November 1998.

Part Five

The euro in Practice and Political Considerations

CHAPTER 14

THE FIRST EIGHTEEN MONTHS – A CRITICAL ASSESSMENT

THE BACKGROUND

Some disappointment has been experienced with the performance of the euro vis-à-vis the US Dollar, and, in an apparently contradictory vein, satisfaction has been expressed with the current performance of most of the national economies of EU Member States and the outlook for these economies in the coming months and years. This latter satisfaction has been reinforced by the recent decision to admit Greece to the Euro Zone in 2001. Such apparent contradictory developments have encouraged the author to write this part of the book, which is divided as follows:

- the performance of the euro vis-à-vis the US Dollar;
- the performance of the national economies of the EU Member States;
- the euro practical operations – the Target system;
- the European Central Bank in operation;
- a new look at a possible Euro Zone economic government; and,
- a new assessment of possible future developments – including the integration and development of capital markets.

PERFORMANCE OF THE EURO VIS-À-VIS THE US DOLLAR

When, on 8 June 2000, the European Central Bank raised interest rates by a full half of a percentage point and the euro subsequently flopped against the US Dollar, deep concerns were once again expressed about the performance of the euro. This apparent state of depression contrasted with the initial heady months immediately following the launch of the euro, when the European currency was most certainly overvalued against the US Dollar. When, however, the euro fell in value below one Dollar, the euphoria ceased. There seems to be no classical economical explanation for this performance. It is, therefore, necessary to look more closely at the experience of the euro in its first eighteen months in an attempt to establish an explanation for this performance.

The underpinning foundations of the euro system, the so-called 'Maastricht Criteria', have been scrupulously respected. As will be seen in the next section, the Euro Zone is a model of economic sobriety and prudence. As part of this performance, the ECB has, on occasions, raised interest rates when it felt that inflation might be about to increase. Similarly, the balance of payments record of the Euro Zone countries and the EU in general has been positively exemplary and scintillating compared with the grotesque American balance of payments deficits. Last, but not least, unwisely unnoticed and/or mentioned by most observers,[1] is the fact that whilst EU Member States continue to cover any balance of payments deficits on goods with receipts of interest payments and revenue from services, this is no longer the case with the United States. Furthermore, until most recently Americans have tended not to save and the wild and media-fed consumer boom is largely financed by credit. Woe betide the United States when the bills have to be honoured!

The explanation for the strength of the American currency vis-à-vis the euro is most probably to be found in the last sentence of the preceding paragraph. The United States has been experiencing a period of economic expansion of unprecedented duration. In turn, this has encouraged massive inflows of capital from many parts of the world – including Europe. Consequently, the value of the US Dollar has tended, with some variations, to be quite strong. There are, however, signs that Americans are starting to save once again and that their economy is slowing down. The relative slowdown of the American economy coincides with an upturn in the economies of most EU Member States.

Should, as is expected, this European economic expansion be maintained, capital will be attracted back to Europe and the value of the euro is likely to increase vis-à-vis the US Dollar.

PERFORMANCE OF THE NATIONAL ECONOMIES OF EU MEMBER STATES

In this section, we examine all the EU Member States and not just the members of the Euro Zone. This approach is adopted because all Member Sates must respect the so-called 'convergence criteria' – whether or not they are participating in the Euro Zone. It will therefore come as something of a surprise when one reads that the ECOFIN Council, in its assessment of the national economies in late February 2000, was particularly pleased with the performance of the four non-Euro Zone countries in their application of the 'Maastricht Criteria'. The ministers noted that all these countries were enjoying budgetary surpluses with the expectation that their long-term public debt (with the exception of Greece) would fall to below (in some cases well below) the reference level of 60 per cent of GDP. Equally, low inflation levels, satisfactory interest rate levels and growth performance were observed in these countries.

In contrast, the performance of the Euro Zone countries was not quite so consistently satisfactory. Whilst most countries were experiencing low budgetary deficits, and, in some cases, very modest surpluses were experienced – and greater ones were expected – disquiet was nevertheless expressed regarding the future. Questions were raised about the methods of accounting used by Germany in calculating budget surpluses. Similarly, calls were made for a greater restructuring of the Italian economy and the reduction in the public debt. Here, it should be noted that in the cases of Belgium, Greece and Italy, the long-term debt is still well over the 60 per cent of GDP laid down in the Maastricht Treaty.

Regarding inflation levels of the countries of the Euro Zone, whilst in general the situation is satisfactory fears have been expressed recently about a possible increases in inflation in Germany and some other countries, notably France. In this context it should be noted that growth rates differ quite considerably among all the EU Member States. Thus, in the Euro Zone, growth in Finland, Iceland, Portugal and Spain has been much more substantial than in France, Germany and Italy. More recently, however, France has recorded substantial growth.

Outside the Euro Zone, growth in Denmark and the United Kingdom has been good.

Overall, the economic performance of all the EU Member States has tended to be good or very good. This is most important in this long and delicate drawn-out final phase of the EMU. Nevertheless, reservations made by the ECOFIN Council about some countries should be heeded. In the author's view, the position of Italy is still delicate.

THE EURO – PRACTICAL CONSIDERATIONS – THE TARGET SYSTEM

No part of the Euro Zone operations is more important than the Target system, and yet no part of the system has received so little publicity.

The Target or Trans-European Automated Real-Time Gross Settlement Express System enables intra-EU cross-border payments in Europe to be made. As the author observed earlier in this work, before the launch of the euro fears had been expressed by EU Member States which were not members of the Euro Zone that they would not have adequate access to the system. Happily, these fears were not borne out and the system has worked with great ease for all the EU Member States.

According to the European Central Bank, in 1999 the average daily number of payments processed by the system was 163,157, equivalent to 925 billion euro. This sum includes both domestic and cross-border payments. Also, the trend has been, and continues to be, for activities to increase. (See Tables 14.1 and 14.2.) Probably the most important quality of the system is that it has worked extremely smoothly.

The Bank for International Settlements (BIS), in Basel, is most satisfied with this situation, which, in turn, has considerably enhanced the development of the Eurobond Market. Writing in the *Annual Report* (No. 70) of the BIS, the Bank notes:

> The conduct of monetary policy in the framework of EMU requires an efficient mechanism for the allocation of central bank liquidity throughout the single currency zone. The interbank market in unsecured credit has provided this mechanism as it rapidly adapted to the new framework. In this role it has been supported by Target, the large-value

Table 14.1 Payment instructions processed by TARGET and other selected interbank funds transfer Systems: volume of transactions (number of payments)

	Q1	Q2	1999 Q3	Q4	2000 January
TARGET					
All TARGET payments					
Total volume	9,756,845	10,289,259	10,759,496	11,452,184	3,535,001
Daily average	154,871	158,296	163,023	176,187	168,333
Cross-border TARGET payments					
Total volume	1,562,233	1,837,435	1,980,267	2,073,391	712,651
Daily average	24,797	28,268	30,004	31,898	33,936
Domestic TARGET payments					
Total volume	8,194,612	8,451,824	8,779,229	9,378,793	2,822,350
Daily average	130,073	130,028	133,019	144,289	134,398
Other systems					
Euro 1 (EBA)					
Total volume	3,306,689	4,250,282	4,726,750	5,362,563	1,719,422
Daily average	52,487	65,389	71,617	82,501	81,877
Euro Access Frankfurt					
Total volume	2,996,555	2,948,742	3,037,469	3,114,109	989,715
Daily average	47,564	45,365	46,022	47,909	47,129
Paris Net Settlement (PNS)[1]					
Total volume	1,370,755	1,318,159	1,248,698	1,259,603	391,497
Daily average	21,758	20,279	18,920	19,379	18,643
Servicio Español de Pagos Interbancarios (SEPI)					
Total volume	299,860	289,174	260,327	252,381	81,954
Daily average	4,760	4,449	3,944	3,883	3,903

Source: Standard & Poor's DRI, reproduced from BIS *Annual Report*, No. 70, 2000

funds transfer system of the euro area, which quickly overcame minor initial operational problems to become the backbone of the euro area's payment system. The early resolution of all uncertainty relating to the money market reference yield curve also contributed to this successful transition. During the first few months of 1999, the EONIA (euro overnight index average) rate, extended by the EUR-IBOR yield curve and supported by an active derivatives market, emerged as the clear choice of market participants. The establishment of a single money market in euros is clearly evidenced by the convergence of yields across the euro area, and its efficiency demonstrated by the continuing tightening of bid–ask spreads, which are currently about 40 per cent lower than five years ago. (See Table 14.3)

Table 14.2 Payment instructions processed by TARGET and other selected interbank funds transfer Systems: value of transactions (euro billions)

	Q1	Q2	1999 Q3	Q4	2000 January
TARGET					
All TARGET payments					
Total volume	60,704	58,861	58,346	61,651	20,313
Daily average	964	906	884	947	967
Cross-border TARGET payments					
Total volume	21,970	22,838	23,365	25,063	8,138
Daily average	349	351	354	386	388
Domestic TARGET payments					
Total volume	38,734	36,023	34,981	36,498	12,175
Daily average	615	554	530	562	580
Other systems					
Euro 1 (EBA)					
Total volume	1,000	10,777	11,056	11,382	3,469
Daily average	175	166	168	175	165
Euro Access Frankfurt					
Total volume	10,823	9,587	9,331	9,300	3,059
Daily average	172	147	141	143	146
Paris Net Settlement (PNS)[1]					
Total volume	5,767	6,125	5,869	6,280	1,900
Daily average	92	94	89	97	90
Servicio Español de Pagos Interbancarios (SEPI)					
Total volume	340	226	204	171	45
Daily average	5	3	3	3	2

[1] The PNS replaced the System Net Protégé (SNP) in April 1999
Source: ECB *Monthly Bulletin*, March 2000

The emergence of an efficient euro area money market has allowed the treasurers of many large companies to reduce costs by centralizing their cash management operations. Banks have formed a two-tier structure in which larger institutions with a pan-European presence handle the cross-border flow of liquidity and small institutions play a more restricted regional role. The significant increase in cross-border interbank activity between institutions in the euro area after the fourth quarter of 1998 is a direct consequence of this development.

THE EUROPEAN CENTRAL BANK IN OPERATION

Towards the end of 1999 and during the following year the ECB has been the subject of criticism. These criticisms have centred on the tendency, at certain times, of the members of the Governing

Table 14.3 Three-month money market rate bid–ask spreads

		1996	1997	1998	1999	2000
Euro Area	Average	14.4	12.4	9.6	8.9	8.4
	Stand. Dev.	3.0	3.5	1.8	3.4	3.1
Germany	Average	16.5	15.1	8.2	9.2	8.5
	Stand. Dev.	6.3	7.6	2.9	4.1	3.1
France	Average	14.1	11.2	11.3	8.7	8.5
	Stand. Dev.	4.6	2.7	3.0	2.8	3.1
Italy	Average	11.3	9.3	10.1	8.9	8.5
	Stand. Dev.	2.3	2.4	2.8	2.6	3.1
United States	Average	12.5	11.3	8.8	9.0	9.3
	Stand. Dev.	2.9	5.3	4.0	2.9	2.8
Japan	Average	12.0	9.8	11.5	10.5	10.4
	Stand. Dev.	2.0	3.8	3.6	5.9	1.1

Note: Spreads in basis points of euro currency deposit rates, London close.
Source: Standard & Poor's DRI, reproduced from BIS *Annual report*, No. 70, 2000

Board to speak with different voices, an apparent perception of a lack of direction and an apparent lack of transparency in the Bank's operations.

Before examining these criticisms, it is most important to bear in mind that the ECB is a completely new kind of organ in the European context. Furthermore, regarding seniority levels of staff, some of the European national central banks currently appear to have as much or greater influence than the ECB. Here, reference can be made to the early experience of the Federal Reserve Board in the United States when it was rivalled by its branches in Chicago and New York.

In the author's view, of much, much greater practical concern regarding the monetary operations of the ECB was the choice of instruments to be used. As examined in an earlier chapter, fortunately this problem has been very satisfactorily resolved and the Bank has successfully controlled inflation. Equally, in an apparent desire to greatly increase scope for action and to enhance the possibility for intervention in the exchange markets by the ECB, the ECOFIN, in May 2000, agreed to double the Bank's exchange reserves from 50 to 100 billion euro and to double the Bank's capital from five billion euro to a maximum of ten billion – 'if the Governing Council deems it necessary to enable the Bank to have appropriate resources to carry out its operations'.

Turning to the three sets of criticisms to which reference was made at the beginning of this section, the author believes the first one is the most worrying. It is not acceptable for members of the Governing Board to speak with different voices; they should instead settle their differences among themselves and then speak with one voice.

The criticism of a lack of direction is a criticism of a more subjective nature. The ECB is a very young organization and despite its laudable degree of independence it does not function in a vacuum. Although it is responsible for monetary policy, matters of overall economic policy are the province of the ECOFIN Council. Also the eleven euro Finance Ministers are increasingly stressing the importance of their role in managing the economic policy of the Euro Zone. Also it must be stressed that because of the relative newness of the ECB, the public pronouncements of Wim Duisenberg do not, as yet, command the same degree of world attention as those made by his American counterpart, Alan Greenspan.

'Transparency' ... this expression is indeed fashionable in the EU at the present time ... and understandably so. ... The institutions do, alas, appear to be so far removed from the citizens. However, central banks do not usually operate with any degree of 'open-ness' This criticism will not, however, just go away. Thus, on 26 June 2000, Otmar Issing, the ECB's Chief Economist, admitted at a conference in Frankfurt that the 'rather mixed' opinion of the ECB, 'despite its success in the main task of keeping down inflation', does indeed 'indicate a communications problem'. Mr Issing did, however, stress that the Bank and its officials had indeed gone further than its mandate laid down, by publishing a monthly bulletin [much esteemed and praised by the author], by reporting regularly to the European Parliament and by speeches by the Bank's officials.

Overall the author would conclude that the ECB has fulfilled its task very well by controlling inflation. Inevitably, however, a young organization will always face criticisms, particularly, at times, concerning an apparent lack of dynamism. A major example of such a latent criticism caused by expectations that the Bank would intervene in the exchange markets to support the euro was expressed by Portugal's Finance Minister, Mr Joaquin Pina Moura, on 8 May 2000 when at the conclusion of a meeting of the eleven euro Finance Ministers, he mentioned the 'availability' of the instrument of intervention by the ECB to support the euro. It is likely that the euro Ministers will in future more frequently express the political will to intervene to support the value of the euro. Such a possibility will not make the work of the ECB any easier.

A NEW LOOK AT EURO ZONE ECONOMIC GOVERNMENT

Earlier in this work, the author had not given too much credence to the possibility of the evolution of a Euro Zone economic government. More recently, his views have acquired nuances. This partial change of attitude is due mainly to the strongly expressed desire by France to endow the eleven euro Finance Ministers with a greater degree of importance – thus diminishing that of the ECOFIN Council. In turn, this desire by France, together with a French desire for the development of a core group of EU Member States, integrating among themselves more deeply and swiftly than their partners, have reinforced British fears of the development of a 'two tier' Europe. But, much of this had already been proposed by France in 1996 in French proposals for the First Intergovernmental Conference (IGC), which ended so disappointingly in Amsterdam in June 1997. France proposed the development of 'three concentric circles' for Europe ... with, of course, the core countries (mainly, though not exclusively, France and Germany) at the centre. To the author, such a core group of countries does already exist. So, how does a Euro Zone economic government fit into this scenario?

The use of the euro will certainly lead to a greater degree of integration among the Euro Zone Member States. In turn, this will most likely give a greater degree of importance to the role of the eleven euro Finance Ministers. It would, as yet, nevertheless, be a little premature too talk of a euro economic government. It would, also, not yet be possible to assess future institutional developments with any degree of precision until the conclusion of the current IGC.

In the week of 10 July 2000, Laurent Fabius, the French Finance Minister, did however call for the eleven euro Finance Ministers to set inflation targets ... a role hitherto reserved for the ECB! To date, there have been no official reactions to this proposal.

POSSIBLE FUTURE DEVELOPMENTS

In the first part of this chapter, the author expressed optimism about the future strength of the euro vis-à-vis the US Dollar. This optimism will be tempered by the fact that this extended final stage of the EMU is a delicate one, when Euro Zone countries must respect the Maastricht Criteria. When, however, on 1 July 2002, on which date the Euro is the sole legal tender in the Euro Zone countries, the euro will become more important internationally. Equally, economic integration, including the integration of capital markets, will intensify. In the meantime, existing developments in the capital markets will continue. Concerning one particular area, Ivo Maes, of the Belgian Central Bank, has observed a particularly strong development of the Euro Bond market (government bonds). The author believes this is likely to continue with increasing use of the euro.

But the integration of the commercial capital markets is likely to continue. Thus, following the early link-up between London and Frankfurt, these two most import stock exchanges agreed, in May 2000 to merge. Not to be outdone, three stock exchanges, Amsterdam, Brussels and Paris, had, in March, announced plans to merge. Such a merger will place these stock exchanges in a stronger negotiating position vis-à-vis London and Frankfurt. Surprisingly, perhaps, the three Baltic States, Estonia, Latvia and Lithuania, had signed a letter of intent of joining the Scandinavia Norex Alliance by mid-2001. This Scandinavian alliance comprises Copenhagen, Oslo, Stockholm and Iceland.

Finally, Greece's impending membership of the Euro Zone does, yet again, raise the thorny question of Britain's possible membership of this Zone. In June 2000 the British Treasury did conclude that Britain could, technically speaking, be ready to join the Euro Zone in 2002. This echoed similar conclusions reached by the OECD in Paris.

The view of the author is that these developments will not resolve three basic facts or problems, which were examined earlier in this work. First, although most of Britain's trade is with Europe, she still has important trading links with the USA and Commonwealth countries. This fact must cause some tension for the Pound Sterling vis-à-vis the euro. Then, interest rates have, in Britain, disproportionate effects on mortgage rates when compared with other European countries. Thirdly, Britain's interest rates are still very high compared with those of countries in the Euro Zone. Finally, even if all these technical issues can be resolved, the final decision, inside Britain itself, of whether to join or not, is a political one.[2]

NOTES

1. An exception to this rule is the article by Bill Martin and Wynne Godley, 'America's New Era', Philips and Drew, London, October 1999.
2. The British government did, in 1997, list the following five criteria which must be met before Britain could consider joining the Euro Zone:

   1. Are business cycles and economic structures compatible so that we are and others in Europe could live comfortably with euro interest rates on a permanent basis?
   2. If problems do emerge, is there sufficient flexibility to deal with them?
   3. Would joining EMU create better conditions for firms making long-term decisions to invest in the United Kingdom?
   4. Will joining EMU help to promote higher growth, stability and a lasting increase in jobs?
   5. How would adopting the single currency affect our financial services?

   If and when these criteria are met, the British government says it will put the question of membership to a national referendum.

CHAPTER 15

POLITICAL AND RELATED ISSUES

POLITICAL CONSIDERATIONS

At the end of the last chapter the observation was made that the decision whether or not to join the Euro Zone is, for an individual EU Member State, a political one.[1] Thus, whilst Denmark for example clearly fulfils all the Maastricht criteria and is a member of the EMS, with the Danish Kronor moving in the narrow margin of fluctuation of 2.25 per cent, there appears to be a strong political opposition among the Danish people to Denmark's membership of the Euro Zone. Denmark is a small, socially integrated and highly progressive society, fiercely jealous of its unique cultural identity. Rightly on wrongly, it seems that many Danish people fear that membership of the Euro Zone would lead to a watering down of this cultural identity and a loss of national sovereignty.

Consequently, the results of Denmark's referendum of Euro Zone membership have been keenly watched by other EU Member States. At the economic and monetary level, it is clear that the Stability Pact does imply a major (albeit voluntary) loss of national sovereignty. In turn, this does reduce the economic and monetary margin for manoeuvre of countries participating in the Euro Zone.

Again, at the political level, there is a trade-off of political sovereignty between the major European powers. At the centre, nowhere is this more evident than the compromise made between France and Germany. At first sight, it might appear that Germany has given up a great deal. She has given up the Deutsche Mark and the Bundesbank sees its power diminished. As a counterpart the ECB is the independent central bank so much desired by Germany, whilst the Stability Pact does impose monetary sobriety on members of the Euro Zone.[2] A further counterpart, is that France will see the disappearance of the hegemony of the Deutsche Mark in the European Union.

Equally, her voice will be equal to that of Germany's on the Board of the ECB. But France has had to accept the independence of the ECB and the Stability Pact. Both countries see France and Germany integrated (irrevocably, maybe?) in Europe more than at any time since the Second World War. This is itself a considerable economic and political achievement, which may or may not please their partners.

In the political domain, the question of a euro government cannot be ignored. Here, again, the views of France and Germany predominate and are opposed to each other: France would like the euro finance ministers to play a greater role in future, whilst Germany stubbornly (and with the backing of the Treaty on European Union) defends the independence of the ECB.

Despite the existence of these opposite views, the increased economic and monetary integration of the Euro Zone countries after 1 July 2002, when the Euro becomes sole legal tender in these countries, will imply that more decisions will be taken at the centre. Also, at about the same time, the Single European Market in financial services will have been achieved to a large degree.

This critical date of 1 July 2002 raises at least five important questions. First, technically speaking how well prepared is the Euro Zone for this changeover? Second, how might this changeover affect business in Euro Zone countries? Third, how might the changeover affect the citizens of these countries? Fourth, what is likely to be the international status of the euro. Fifth, how close is the United Kingdom to joining the Euro Zone?

THE DEGREE OF PREPAREDNESS FOR THE CHANGEOVER

According to a recent study made by the European Commission,[3] the countries of the Euro Zone are not particularly well-prepared for the technical changeover from national currencies.

Indeed the situation described in their report gives rise to the greatest concern. Speaking in Brussels on 12 July 2000, Commissioner Solbes made the statement, 'Abandon the national currency units to the benefit of the euro'. On the basis of an assessment made between May and July, Commissioner Solbes noted that companies were improving their preparations for the introduction of the euro (in France, he noted, 1000 companies are converting to the euro each month), but that the situation nevertheless remains unsatisfactory: 'It will take 200 years at this rate.' The Commission therefore notes an 'inadequate level of preparation' in so far as companies are 'preparing themselves rather slowly for the change', not being aware that all the invoices and the accounts in general will have to be established in euros from 1 January 2002 (with exception of the Netherlands).

As far as the citizens are concerned, Commissioner Solbes noted that the euro remained 'little used' and that 'little attention' is given to simultaneous use of euros and national currency' (he did note, however, that Belgian and French banks are to give their customers' accounts in euros in July 2001). He also noted with vexation that the public administrations, mainly at the local level, do not sufficiently play a role of instruction in the single currency for citizens. He noted that 'some practical experience should be extended throughout the Union'.

Regarding preparation for the introduction of euro notes and coins, considering that the transition of the euro should be carried out 'effectively and rapidly', Commissioner Solbes spoke of the following aspects:

- *Manufacturer of notes and coins:* 50 billion coins are to be minted by 1 January 2002 and 39 per cent had already been minted by the end May 2000. Over 14 billion notes will be printed by the same deadline in twelve printers of the Euro Zone, including one in Greece under the direct control of the ECB and the national banks. There are no less than 120 models of coins to be minted because of the national sides.
- *Quality of coins:* this will be greater than that of national coins and will be controlled by the ECB.
- *Adaptation for vending machines:* six testing centres (two in Germany, one in Spain, one in Finland, France and the Netherlands) have been set up since the summer of 1999 and the Member States have been authorized to lend samples so that equipment manufacturers may carry out tests.
- *Fight against counterfeiting:* Mr Solbes recalled that the mandate of Europol had been extended by the JHA Council

in April 1999 and that this Council had also, in May 2000, adopted a framework decision aimed a strengthening protection against counterfeiting by using penal and other sanctions.

– *Exchange of notes and coins:* Mr. Solbes recalled that this procedure would be broken down into three stages: (a) *Pre-supply before 1 January 2002.* All members states plan to supply the groups most directly concerned with euros in advance (banks, traders, fund carriers, manufacturers and operators of vending machines) during the *last four months of 2001.* For the *general public,* advance supplies of euros will come about during the second half of December 2001 (except for Greece, Ireland and Italy which do not provide for this). (b) *Dual circulation period* (euro/national currency). The main part of the changeover should be completed by the end of the first two weeks of 2002. Banks should exchange the national currency for euro for their customers for up to 500 euro ('This is the idea we are working on,' said Mr Solbes). One question still to be resolved concerns persons who do not have a bank account. National notes and coins will loose their legal value at the end of February, except Germany (1 January), the Netherlands (28 January) and Ireland (9 February). (c) *Later phase of the dual circulation period.* In certain Member States, the exchange of the former national tender may still be carried out by the banks. The question of cash exchange continues to raise some questions to be settled. The Commission will follow up the situation and every two months provide 'information on best practices as well as recommendations'.

In response to questions, Commissioner Solbes noted that the problem encountered with the printing of 100 euro notes is an 'excellent example of the control carried out by the ECB'.

EFFECTS ON BUSINESS

Theo Waigel, the then German Finance Minister, in his statement in which he proposed the later-accepted Stability Pact, [4] put the advantages for businesses in a proverbial nutshell. He stated: 'A stable unified currency area brings important economic advantages. The potential of the internal market can be utilized fully. There are no transaction costs for business and consumers and the financial markets are provided with reliable points of reference for their activities.' To this, the author would stress that the transaction costs are particularly important for small- and medium-sized businesses.

In view of this statement, the European Commission's first 'Quarterly Note' on 'Use of the Euro' makes disappointing reading. According to this report,[5] the use of the euro by private individuals is very low.

Similarly, the euro is not widely used by companies at the national level. In contrast, however, it is more widely used for international payments and in invoicing. More disappointingly, perhaps, the use of the euro by national administrations is low ... but it is increasing.

THE CITIZENS

In the final analysis, it is the reaction of the citizens that really matters: thus, what are the likely implications for citizens of the Euro Zone of the date of 1 July 2002, and what will be the attitudes of European citizens to the euro in the summers of 2002?

Without the use of a crystal ball, the author would suggest the following as being the likely implications for the citizens of the Euro Zone when the euro becomes the sole legal tender in those countries. First, logically, the euro will be their sole monetary reference.

Secondly, they will, with complete ease, be able to compare the prices of goods and services in the different countries of the Euro Zone. In turn, this should make access to financial services much easier. Similarly, this increased 'transparence' should lead to an increase in competition, and, and, hopefully, to a fall in prices. In contrast, however, the room for economic and monetary manoeuvre by their governments will be restricted.

So, what will they think about the euro in the summer of 2000? According to the most recent survey[6] the popularity of the euro among European citizens is declining. Accordingly to this survey, part of this decline in popularity seems to be due to the relative decline in value of the euro vis-à-vis the US Dollar.

The author's view, however, is that part of the trouble seems to lie with the relatively long transitional period between the launch of the euro in January 1999 and the moment, 1 July 2002, when the currency becomes sole legal tender in the Euro Zone countries. Although, in many Euro Zone countries, bills and statements in banks, shops and restaurants are quoted in both the local national currency and the euro, the European currency still appears to be a phantom one. At this level, at least, the situation should change on 1 July 2002.

THE EURO – ITS INTERNATIONAL STATUS

Since its launch in January 1999 most attention has been focused on the position of the euro vis-à-vis the US Dollar. In the previous chapter, the author sought to explain the reasons for the continuing popularity of the US currency. The suggestion was also made that if and when the economies of the countries of the Euro Zone expand (which started to happen in 2000) then the euro will become more attractive. If this is accompanied by some degree of inflation, it is almost certain that the ECB will be forced to raise interest rates which in turn would make the euro more attractive.

However, again in the view of the author, one of the most important considerations is that to some degree the euro is still a kind of phantom currency. But, as has just been mentioned, this will change at the end of June 2002. Therefore, what might be the international status of the euro?

The euro represents one of the world's most important economic and trading blocks. As it replaces the national currencies of the Euro Zone countries its international status will automatically increase since it will be the sole currency reference for those countries. Consequently, it will be used to a greater degree in international trade than has been the case hitherto.

In an allied sense, its importance will increase as more countries join the Euro Zone. Greece is about to join and will be almost certainly joined by a number of new EU Member States from Central and Eastern Europe.

The example of the European Union is also influencing regional groupings in other parts of the world. Thus, the countries of the MERCOSUR group intend to create an EMU and a common currency. Even the countries of the ASEAN groups desire some form of monetary union. Where, therefore, will this leave the euro?

The author believes that after the end of June 2002 there will be three major international currencies in the world: the US Dollar, the euro and the Japanese Yen. Then, as more regional groupings create their own currencies, more currencies of an international status will develop. In the meantime, the international status of the euro is likely to be reinforced.

THE UNITED KINGDOM AND THE EURO

The debate about Britain's possible future membership of the Euro Zone continues unabated. At this point, therefore, it worth making reference to a poll organized by *The Economist* in 1999, when a number of British economists were asked whether it would be in Britain's economic interests to join the European single currency within the next five years. The verdict among the 164 economists who replied was overwhelmingly positive (almost two-thirds said yes). It is useful to examine the main reasons why so many economists replied positively.

High on the list was the importance of the stable exchange rate within Europe. This argument is reinforced by the destablizing influence of rapid and massive internal movements of capital. Membership of the Euro Zone would counteract such movements.

Of almost equal importance was the likelihood of Britain maintaining its attractive record as a recipient of direct foreign investment if she should join the single currency.

Then, if Britains joins the Euro Zone, she would have influence on economic and monetary policies. This influence would, for example, be equal to that of France and Germany.

Finally, the increased 'transparency' of and competitiveness in the Euro Zone would benefit British citizens.

Although in the minority, the opponents of Britain's membership of the Euro Zone made a number of important points. High on their list is the relative lack of accountability of the ECB. Here, reference was made to the Bundesbank, which, though independent, is accountable.

Of equal importance, two other points were strongly voiced by the 'No' camp. First, they stated that the EMU had imposed a 'one-size-fits-all' monetary policy on the Euro Zone – with alarming and contrasting consequences. They used booming Ireland and slumping Germany as examples.

Secondly, they maintain that the labour and product markets are too inflexible to deal with the strains that will be put upon them in the Euro Zone.

It is particularly interesting to note that both sides do agree that the European labour market is rigid and that there are differences in the economic cycles. However, the two sides agree that this situation will change over time, the 'No' camp believing, however, that change will be slow.

So where does this leave us? At this point, whilst agreeing with many of the different views just examined, the author would underline some of the observations he made earlier in this work.

Apart from the obvious importance of the difference in economic cycles between countries, it is necessary to stress the importance of the geographical direction of Britain's trade. Whilst most of this trade is with EU partner countries, the United Kingdom still conducts a substantial amount of her trade with the United States and with Commonwealth countries. This does place some strain on the Pound Sterling.

Then, the importance of the exaggerated influence of changes in interest rates on mortgage rates in Britain must be emphasized. Something would certainly have to be done in this field before Britain could join.

In contrast with other EU Member States, the author finds that British labour is relatively flexible.

However, he does not think the source of labour to be too important provided that it is allowed to move freely within the EU. This, he suggests, would/should lead us to redefine the concept of an Optimum Currency Area where the movement of factors of production is concerned.

But even if these problems are solved, there remains the vexed question of the value of the Pound Sterling vis-à-vis the euro. Britain has had a somewhat traumatic experience with membership of both the Snake arrangement and the end of the EMS, when her currency was overvalued. In July 2000, the influential

British Parliamentary Treasury Committee stated that, while the conditions of British membership of the Euro Zone had been met, currency swings made it 'difficult to join the euro'. This is a critical factor because at times the Pound Sterling would seem to be overvalued and at other times to be undervalued. Part of the solution might be for Britain to emulate both Denmark and Greece in joining the ERM and to 'shadow' the euro. In this way it might be possible to arrive at the 'right' value for the Pound Sterling vis-à-vis the euro.

In conclusion then, it seems that most of Britain's academic experts and business leaders are in favour of British membership of the Euro Zone but the majority of British citizens strongly oppose such a move.

CONCLUDING OBSERVATIONS

In this work, the author has traced the historical, theoretical, economic and political background to the momentous moves made by the old EEC, now the EU, towards the establishment of an EMU and the creation of a common currency. We now find ourselves in the final stage of the EMU, and the common currency, the euro, has been created.

In the final assessment, eleven EU Member States have joined the Euro Zone and Greece will join on 1 January 2001. In September 2000, in a referendum, Denmark rejected membership of the Euro Zone. A number of candidate countries of Central and Eastern Europe have expressed a desire to join the EMU and to accept the common currency. In this sense, the euro is a success story.

In contrast, there is a concern at the continuing weakness of the euro vis-à-vis the US Dollar. This is due to a continued expansion of the American economy and America's consequent attractiveness as a magnet for capital flows. Therefore, when (as seems to be happening) the European economies expand, capital is likely to start to move back to Europe and the euro will become stronger.

In the long run, however, the prudent economic, fiscal and monetary management of EU Member States, and their balance of payments surpluses and/or low deficits, will prove to be attractive. Also, on 1 July 2002, when the Euro becomes sole legal tender in the Euro Zone countries, it will cease to be a kind of phantom currency. In turn, this will lead to increased 'transparency' among the economies of these countries, increased competition and more integration. These factors should strenghten the euro, making it more attractive to both the citizens of Europe and outside investors.

NOTES

1. This was clearly reconfirmed in the *Monthly Report*, February 1992, of the German Bundesbank.

   The question of whether an EMU is to be established is a political decision. This decision is within the competence and responsibility of the government and Parliament. As part of its advisory function, the Bundesbank pointed out at an early stage that the implications of monetary policy pursued in a monetary union at Community level – in particular the implications for the value of money – will be crucially influenced by the economic and fiscal policies of and by the behaviour of management and labour in all the participating countries. It also drew attention to the fact that a monetary union is 'an irrevocable joint and several community which, in the light of past experience, requires a more far-reaching association, in the form of a comprehensive political union, if it is to prove durable' (statement by the Central Bank council of September 1990). The Maastricht decisions do not yet reveal an agreement on the future structure of the envisaged political union and on the required parallelism with monetary union. Future developments in the fields of the political union will be of key importance for the permanent success of the monetary union.

2. This is explained in the publication *Les Cartes de la France*, Hubert Vedrine (together with Dominique Moisi), Fayard, 2000.

3. Pedro Solbes, *Bulletin Quotidien Europe*, Brussels, 13 July 2000.

4. The Stability Pact for Europe, proposed by German Finance Minister Theo Waigel, Europe Documents No. 1962, Agence Europe, Brussels, 25 November 1995.

5. *Bulletin Quotidien Europe*, No. 7624, 30 December 1999.

6. European Commission Opinion Poll, Brussels, April and May, 2000.

INTRODUCTION TO THE APPENDICES

THE BACKGROUND

A feature of the author's previous books is appendices containing important documents many of which are frequently difficult to obtain. This book is no exception. In fact, in view of the topical and somewhat technical nature of the subject examined, there is even greater need to include important and relatively inaccessible documents. As the author stresses in the Acknowledgements, he is particularly grateful to Ferdinando Riccardi, Editor-in-Chief of the Agence Europe S. A., in Brussels, who once again has so kindly allowed him to reproduce documents originally published by the Agency.

'HISTORIC' REPORTS OF THE ECOFIN COUNCIL AND THE EMI

These documents are probably the most important working documents concerning the euro because they contain not only the very far-reaching obligations for both Euro Zone and non-Euro-Zone EU Member States but also define the legal basis of the euro.

The logical complement of these reports is the Special Edition of the European Council and the European Parliament Sessions on 1 and 2 May 1998. At these sessions, the Heads of State and Government approved the list of eleven Member States, which would constitute the Euro Zone and the appointment of Professor Duisenberg as the first President of the ECB, as well as the Bank's Board Members.

Europe Document, Number 2099, of 9 October 1998, on the next logical step in the creation of the Euro Zone, is a paper presented by France. It sets down the contributions to be made by the EU and its Member States in reorganizing the international monetary system. It is supplemented by a paper, presented by Belgium concerning representation outside the Euro Zone.

At a more practical level, the Commission's Action Plan, 'Financial Services: implementing the Framework for Financial Markets', of May 1999, sets down the modalities for, finally, creating the Single European Market in financial services.

Finally, a most up-to-date and critical document is included in the appendices. The report on 'Co-ordinating Public Debt Issuance in the Euro Area', the Report of the Giovanni Group, raises so many critical issues. It notes the almost complete lack of integration in the field of co-ordinating public debt and notes that some 'smaller Member States with limited financing needs have seen increased competition from non-sovereign borrowers such as large corporate and "pfandbriefe" issuers'.

It should be noted that these small countries are not credit risks. Thus, the Group proposes four hypotheses to solve this problem. These range from a calendar for making issues to the Community going into the market on behalf of the sovereign borrower.

APPENDIX 1A: THE 'SNAKE' SYSTEM RECORD

Source: Commission of the European Communities

1971

August 15	Suspension of dollar convertibility to gold.
December 19	Smithsonian Agreement: Return to fixed parities for IMF currencies; band of 4.5 per cent allowed for the dollar.

1972

March 21	Resolution of the Council of the European Communities proposing the 'Snake' of the Community currencies (a band of fluctuation of 2.25%) in the dollar tunnel (a band of 4.5%).
April 10	Basel Agreement between EEC central banks to implement the Resolution of March 21.
April 24	Implementation of Basel Agreement. Participating countries: Belgium, France, West Germany, Italy, Luxembourg, and the Netherlands.
May 1	Pound Sterling, Irish Pound and the Danish Krone join the 'Snake'.
May 23	The Norwegian Krone is associated with the 'Snake'.
June 23	Britain and Ireland leave the 'Snake'.
June 27	Denmark leaves the 'Snake'.
October 10	Denmark rejoins the 'Snake'.

1973

February 13	Italy leaves the 'Snake'.

March 12	The Deutsche Mark is revalued 3 per cent vis-à-vis the European Monetary Unit of Account (EMUA). The participating Member States in the 'Snake' organize a joint float against the US Dollar.
March 14	The Swedish Krona is associated with the 'Snake'.
June 29	The Deutsche Mark is revalued 5.5 per cent against the EUMA.
September 17	The Dutch Guilder is revalued 5 per cent against the EUMA.
November 16	The Norwegian Krone is revalued 5 per cent against the EUMA.

1974

| January 19 | France leaves the 'Snake'. |

1975

| July 10 | France returns to the 'Snake'. |

1976

| March 15 | France again leaves the 'Snake'. |
| October 17 | Special Realignment (the Frankfurt one) of the exchange rates against the EUMA. Deutsche Mark revalued 2 per cent; Danish Krone devalued 4 per cent; Norwegian Krone and Swedish Krona devalued 1 per cent. |

1977

| April 1 | Devaluations against the EMUA: Swedish Krona – 6 per cent, Danish and Norwegian Kroner – 3 per cent. |
| August 28 | Sweden leaves the 'Snake'. Devaluations against the EMUA of 5 per cent for the Danish and Norwegian Kroner. |

1978

| February 13 | Devaluation of 8 per cent of the Norwegian Krone against the EMUA. |
| October 17 | Revaluations against the EMUA: Deutsche Mark – 4 per cent, Dutch Guilder and Belgian France – 2 per cent. |

| December 4, 5 | Meeting of the Council of Ministers in Brussels: adoption of Resolution establishing the EMS. |
| December 12 | Norway leaves the 'Snake'. |

1979

| March 13 | Governors of Central Banks and Board of Governors of EFMC sign instruments implementing the EMS. |

APPENDIX 1B: THE RECORD OF THE EUROPEAN MONETARY SYSTEM

Source: Commission of the European Communities

13 March 1979
Introduction of the EMS

23 September 1979
Adjustments within the EMS

(1) 5 per cent re-evaluation of the Deutsche Mark vis-à-vis the Danish Krone
(2) 2 per cent re-evaluation of the Deutsche Mark vis-à-vis the Belgain, French and Luxembourg Francs, Dutch Guilder, Italian Lira and the Irish Punt

27 November 1980
5 per cent devaluation of the Danish Krone

23 March 1981
6 per cent devaluation of the Italian Lira

4 October 1981
5.5 per cent revaluation of the Deutsche Mark and the Dutch Guilder
1.5 per cent devaluation of the French Franc and the Italian Lira

21 February 1982
8.5 per cent devaluation of the Belgian Franc
3 per cent devaluation of the Danish Krone

12 June 1982
4.25 per cent revaluation of the Deutsche Mark and the Dutch Guilder
5.75 per cent devaluation of the French Franc
2.75 per cent devaluation of the Italian Lira

21 March 1983
5.5 per cent revaluation of the Deutsche Mark
3.5 per cent revaluation of the Dutch Guilder
2.5 per cent revaluation of the Danish Krone
1.5 per cent revaluation of the Belgian/Luxembourg Franc
2.5 per cent devaluation of the French Franc and the Italian Lira
3.5 per cent devaluation of the Irish Punt

21 July 1985
6 per cent devaluation of the Italian Lira
2 per cent revaluation of the Deutsche Mark, the Dutch Guilder, the Danish Krone, the Belgain/Luxembourg Franc and the French Franc and the Irish Punt

7 April 1986
3 per cent revaluation of the Deutsche Mark and the Dutch Guilder
1 per cent revaluation of the Belgian/Luxembourg Franc and the Danish Krone
3 per cent devaluation of the French Franc

4 August 1986
8 per cent devaluation of the Irish Punt

12 January 1987
3 per cent revaluation of the Deutsche Mark and Dutch Guilder
2 per cent revaluation of the Belgian/Luxembourg Franc

19 June 1989
Spanish Peseta enters the EMS under the wide band of ± 6 per cent

5 January 1990
Italian Lira moves to the narrow band of ± 2.25 per cent
3.5 per cent devaluation of the Italian Lira

5 October 1990
British Pound enter the EMS under the wide band of ± 6 per cent

6 April 1992
Portuguese Escudo enters the EMS under the wide band of ± 6 per cent

13 September 1992
7 per cent devaluation of the Italian Lira
Italian Lira membership is suspended

16 September 1992
British Pound membership is suspended

17 September 1992
5 per cent devaluation of the Spanish Peseta

22 November 1992
6 per cent devaluation of the Spanish Peseta
6 per cent devaluation of the Portuguese Escudo

1 February 1993
10 per cent devaluation of the Irish Punt

13 May 1993
8 per cent devaluation of the Spanish Peseta
6.5 per cent devaluation of the Portuguese Escudo

August 1993
All ERM currencies allowed to fluctuate by 15 per cent
Drachma, Lira and Sterling still floating

APPENDIX 2: CHRONOLOGY OF MONETARY POLICY MEASURES OF THE EUROSYSTEM

Source: ECB *Monthly Bulletin*, February 2000

22 DECEMBER 1998

The Governing Council of the ECB decides that the first main refinancing operation of the Eurosystem will be a fixed rate tender offered at an interest rate of 3.0%, a level which it intends to maintain for the foreseeable future. This operation will be initiated on 4 January 1999, while the allotment decision will be taken on 5 January 1999 and settlement will take place on 7 January 1999. In addition, the first longer-term refinancing operation will be announced on 12 January 1999 (with a settlement date of 14 January 1999) and will be conducted through a variable rate tender using the single rate allotment procedure.

The Governing Council furthermore decides that the interest rate for the marginal lending facility will be set at a level of 4.5% and the interest rate for the deposit facility at a level of 2.0% for the start of Stage Three, i.e. 1 January 1999. As a transitional measure, between 4 and 21 January 1999,

the interest rate for the marginal lending facility will be set at a level of 3.25% and the interest rate for the deposit facility at a level of 2.75%. The Governing Council intends to terminate this transitional measure following its meeting on 21 January 1999.

31 DECEMBER 1998

In accordance with Article 109(4) of the Treaty establishing the European Community, the EU Council, acting with the unanimity of the Member States of the European Community without a derogation, upon a proposal from the European Commission and after consultation of the ECB, adopts the irrevocable conversion rates for the euro, with effect from 1 January 1999, 0.00 a.m. (local time).

The ministers of the euro area Member States, the ECB and the ministers and central bank governors of Denmark and Greece decide, in a common procedure involving the European Commission and after consultation of the

Monetary Committee, to fix the central rates against the euro for the currencies participating in the exchange rate mechanism which comes into operation on 1 January 1999. Further to this decision on the euro central rates, the ECB, Denmark's Nationalbank and the Bank of Greece establish by common accord the compulsory intervention rates for the Danish krone and the Greek drachma. A fluctuation band of ±2.25% will be observed around the euro central rate for the Danish krone. The standard fluctuation band of ±15% will be observed around the euro central rate for the Greek drachma.

7 JANUARY 1999

The Governing Council of the ECB decides that for the two main refinancing operations to be announced on 11 and 18 January 1999 respectively the same conditions will apply as for the first such operation, which was settled on 7 January 1999, i.e. they will be fixed rate tenders conducted at an interest rate of 3.0%.

12 JANUARY 1999

Following the decision of the Governing Council of the ECB on 22 December 1998, the ECB announces that the first longer-term refinancing operations of the Eurosystem will be conducted as variable rate tenders using the single rate method of allotment. With a view to phasing in the longer-term

refinancing operations, the first such operation is conducted through three parallel tenders with three different maturities, namely 25 February, 25 March and 29 April 1999. The ECB also announces that the intention is to allot an amount of €15 billion in each of these parallel tenders. For the subsequent longer-term refinancing operations in the first three months of 1999, the intention is to allot an unchanged amount of €15 billion per operation.

21 JANUARY 1999

The Governing Council of the ECB decides to revert to the interest rates on the Eurosystem's two standing facilities which it had set for the start of Stage Three, i.e. to set the interest rate for the marginal lending facility at a level of 4.5% and that for the deposit facility at a level of 2.0% with effect from 22 January 1999. Furthermore, it decides that for the two main refinancing operations to be settled on 27 January and 3 February 1999 respectively the same conditions will apply as for the first three such operations settled earlier in January, i.e. they will be fixed rate tenders conducted at an interest rate of 3.0%.

4 FEBRUARY 1999

The Governing Council of the ECB decides that for the main refinancing operations to be settled on 10 and 17 February 1999 the same conditions will apply as for the first such operations settled earlier in the year, i.e. they will be fixed rate tenders conducted at an interest rate of 3.0%. In addition, the interest rate on the marginal lending facility continues to be 4.5% and the interest rate on the deposit facility remains 2.0%.

18 FEBRUARY 1999

The Governing Council of the ECB decides that for the main refinancing operations to be settled on 24 February and 3 March 1999 the same conditions will apply as for the previous such operations settled earlier in the year, i.e. they will be fixed rate tenders conducted at an interest rate of 3.0%. In addition, the interest rate on the marginal lending facility continues to be 4.5% and the interest rate on the deposit facility remains 2.0%.

4 MARCH 1999

The Governing Council of the ECB decides that for the main refinancing operations to be settled on 10 and 17 March 1999 the same conditions will apply as for the previous such operations settled earlier in the year, i.e. they will be fixed rate tenders conducted at an interest rate of 3.0%. In addition, the interest rate on the marginal lending facility continues to be 4.5% and the interest rate on the deposit facility remains 2.0%. The Governing Council also decides that for forthcoming longer-term refinancing operations of the

Eurosystem the multiple rate method of allotment will be applied (starting from the operation with a settlement date of 25 March 1999) until otherwise indicated.

18 MARCH 1999

The Governing Council of the ECB decides that for the main refinancing operations to be settled on 24 and 31 March and 7 April 1999 the same conditions will apply as for the previous such operations settled earlier in the year, i.e. they will be fixed rate tenders conducted at an interest rate of 3.0%. In addition, the interest rate on the marginal lending facility continues to be 4.5% and the interest rate on the deposit facility remains 2.0%.

8 APRIL 1999

The Governing Council of the ECB decides to reduce the interest rate on the main refinancing operations by 0.5 percentage point to 2.5%, starting with the operation to be settled on 14 April 1999. In addition, it decides to lower the interest rate on the marginal lending facility by 1 percentage point to 3.5% and the interest rate on the deposit facility by 0.5 percentage point to 1.5%, both with effect from 9 April 1999.

22 APRIL 1999

The Governing Council of the ECB decides that the interest rates on the main refinancing operations, the marginal lending facility and the deposit facility will remain unchanged at 2.5%, 3.5% and 1.5% respectively. In addition, the Governing Council announces that for the longer-term refinancing operations to be settled during the next six months, the intention is to continue to allot an amount of €15 billion per operation.

6 MAY 1999

The Governing Council of the ECB decides that the interest rates on the main refinancing operations, the marginal lending facility and the deposit facility will remain unchanged at 2.5%, 3.5% and 1.5% respectively.

20 MAY 1999

The Governing Council of the ECB decides that the interest rates on the main refinancing operations, the marginal lending facility and the deposit facility will remain unchanged at 2.5%, 3.5% and 1.5% respectively. The Governing Council also decides to change the maturity of the longer-term refinancing operation scheduled to be settled on 30 September 1999. The redemption date of this operation will be brought forward from 30 December to 23 December 1999. Correspondingly, the longer-term refinancing operation which was originally scheduled to be announced on 27 December 1999 and to be allotted and settled on 30 December 1999 will be an-

nounced on 21 December, allotted on 22 December and settled on 23 December 1999. The rescheduling of operations is intended to alleviate the working procedures for financial market participants at the turn of the year.

2 JUNE, 17 JUNE, 1 JULY, 15 JULY, 29 JULY, 26 AUGUST, 9 SEPTEMBER 1999

The Governing Council of the ECB decides that the interest rates on the main refinancing operations, the marginal lending facility and the deposit facility will remain unchanged at 2.5%, 3.5% and 1.5% respectively.

23 SEPTEMBER 1999

The Governing Council of the ECB decides that the interest rates on the main refinancing operations, the marginal lending facility and the deposit facility will remain unchanged at 2.5%, 3.5% and 1.5% respectively.

The ECB releases to the public the indicative calendar for the Eurosystem's tender operations in 2000, it also announces that no new main refinancing operation will be initiated in the first week of the year 2000, and that no such operation will mature during that week. For this reason the maturity of the main refinancing operation of 21 December 1999 will be lengthened exceptionally to three weeks. To avoid two main refinancing operations maturing on 12 January 2000, the maturity of the operation of 30 December 1999 will also be lengthened to three weeks. These steps are taken to minimize any potential problem for counterparties and for the financial market which could result from the conduct and settlement of a large operation directly after the transition to the new century.

7 OCTOBER 1999

The Governing Council of the ECB decides that the interest rates on the main refinancing operations, the marginal lending facility and the deposit facility will remain unchanged at 2.5%, 3.5% and 1.5% respectively.

21 OCTOBER 1999

The Governing Council of the ECB decides that the interest rates on the main refinancing operations, the marginal lending facility and the deposit facility will remain unchanged at 2.5%, 3.5% and 1.5% respectively.

It also decides that for the longer-term refinancing operations to be settled on 28 October 1999, 25 November 1999 and 23 December 1999, the intention is to allot an amount of €25 billion per operation. This amount is higher than the amount of €15 billion allotted for all previous longer-term refinancing operations conducted in 1999. This decision takes into account the intention of the ECB to contribute to a smooth transition to the year 2000.

4 NOVEMBER 1999

The Governing Council of the ECB decides to raise the interest rate on the main refinancing operations of the Eurosystem by 0.5 percentage point to 3.0%, with effect from the operation to be settled on 10 November 1999. In addition, it decides to increase the interest rates on both the marginal lending facility and the deposit facility by 0.5 percentage point to 4.0% and 2.0% respectively, both with effect from 5 November 1999.

18 NOVEMBER 1999

The Governing Council of the ECB decides that the interest rates on the main refinancing operations, the marginal lending facility and the deposit facility will remain unchanged at 3.0%, 4.0% and 2.0% respectively.

2 DECEMBER 1999

The Governing Council of the ECB decides that the interest rates on the main refinancing operations, the marginal lending facility and the deposit facility will remain unchanged at 3.0%, 4.0% and 2.0% respectively.

The Governing Council also decides to confirm the reference value for monetary growth, namely an annual growth rate of 4½% for the broad monetary aggregate M3. This decision is taken on the grounds that the components underlying the derivation of the reference value, namely the Eurosystem's definition of price stability (an annual increase in the HICP for the euro area of below 2%), the estimate for the trend of real GDP growth (2% to 2½% per annum) and that for the trend decline in M3 income velocity (½% to 1% per annum), have basically remained unchanged. As before, the Governing Council will assess monetary developments in relation to the reference value on the basis of a three-month moving average of annual growth rates. The Governing Council also decides to review the reference value henceforth on a regular annual basis. The next review will take place in December 2000.

With regard to the minimum reserve system of the Eurosystem, the Governing Council, after reviewing new statistical evidence, decides to increase from 10% to 30% the standardized deduction from the reserve base to be applied to debt securities issued with an agreed maturity of up to two years and to money market paper. This decision shall take effect as from the determination of the reserve requirement to be fulfilled in the maintenance period starting on 24 January 2000.

15 DECEMBER 1999

The Governing Council of the ECB decides that the interest rates on the main refinancing operations, the marginal lending facility and the deposit facility will remain unchanged at 3.0%, 4.0% and 2.0% respectively.

4 JANUARY 2000

The ECB announces that on 5 January 2000 the Eurosystem will conduct a liquidity-absorbing fine-tuning operation with same-day settlement. This measure aims at restoring normal liquidity conditions in the money market after the successful transition to the year 2000.

5 JANUARY 2000

The Governing Council of the ECB decides that the interest rates on the main refinancing operations, the marginal lending facility and the deposit facility will remain unchanged at 3.0%, 4.0% and 2.0% respectively.

15 JANUARY 2000

At the request of the Greek authorities, the ministers of the euro area Member States, the ECB and the ministers and central bank governors of Denmark and Greece decide, following a common procedure, to revalue the central rate of the Greek drachma in the exchange rate mechanism (ERM II) by 3½%, with effect from 17 January 2000.

20 JANUARY 2000

The Governing Council of the ECB decides that the interest rates on the main refinancing operations, the marginal lending facility and the deposit facility will remain unchanged at 3.0%, 4.0% and 2.0% respectively.

It also announces that the Euro-system intends to allot an amount of €20 billion for each of the longer-term refinancing opera-tions to be conducted in the first half of 2000. This amount takes into consideration the expected liquidity needs of the banking system of the euro area in the first half of 2000 and the desire of the Eurosystem to continue to provide the bulk of its refinancing of the financial sector through its main refinancing operations.

3 FEBRUARY 2000

The Governing Council of the ECB decides to raise the interest rate on the main refinancing operations of the Eurosystem by 0.25 percentage point to 3.25%, starting from the operation to be settled on 9 Feb-ruary 2000. In addition, it decides to increase the interest rates on both the marginal lending facility and the deposit facility by 0.25 percentage point, to 4.25% and 2.25% respectively, both with ef-fect from 4 February 2000.

Source: ECB *Monthly Bulletin,* May 2000 (The chronology of monetary policy measures of the Eurosystem taken in 1999 can be found on pages 176 to 179 of the ECB Annual Report 1999)

4 JANUARY 2000

The ECB announces that on 5 January 2000 the Eurosystem will conduct a liquidity-absorbing fine-tuning operation with same-day settlement. This measure aims at restoring normal liquidity condi-tions in the money market after the successful transition to the year 2000.

5 JANUARY 2000

The Governing Council of the ECB decides that the interest rates on the main refinancing operations, the marginal lending facility and the deposit facility will remain unchanged at 3.0%, 4.0% and 2.0% respectively.

15 JANUARY 2000

At the request of the Greek autho-rities, the ministers of the euro

area Member States, the ECB and the ministers and central bank governors of Denmark and Greece decide, following a common pro-cedure, to revalue the central rate of the Greek drachma in the exchange rate mechanism (ERM II) by 3½%, with effect from 17 January 2000.

20 JANUARY 2000

The Governing Council of the ECB decides that the interest rates on the main refinancing operations, the marginal lending facility and the deposit facility will remain unchanged at 3.0%, 4.0% and 2.0% respectively.

It also announces that the Euro-system intends to allot an amount of €20 billion for each of the longer-term refinancing operations to be conducted in the first half of 2000. This amount takes into consideration the expected liquidity needs of the banking system of the euro area in the first half of 2000 and the desire of the Eurosystem to continue to provide the bulk of its refinancing of the financial sector through its main refinancing operations.

3 FEBRUARY 2000

The Governing Council of the ECB decides to raise the interest rate on the main refinancing operations of the Eurosystem by 0.25 percentage point to 3.25%, starting from the operation to be settled on 9 February 2000. In addition, it decides to increase the interest rates on both the marginal lending facility and the deposit facility by 0.25 percentage point, to 4.25% and 2.25% respectively, both with effect from 4 February 2000.

17 FEBRUARY, 2 MARCH 2000

The Governing Council of the ECB decides that the interest rates on the main refinancing operations, the marginal lending facility and the deposit facility will remain unchanged at 3.25%, 4.25% and 2.25% respectively.

16 MARCH 2000

The Governing Council of the ECB decides to raise the interest rate on the main refinancing operations of the Eurosystem by 0.25 percentage point to 3.5%, starting from the operation to be settled on 22 March 2000. In addition, it decides to increase the interest rates on both the marginal lending facility and the deposit facility by 0.25 percentage point, to 4.5% and 2.5% respectively, with effect from 17 March 2000.

30 MARCH, 13 APRIL 2000

The Governing Council of the ECB decides that the interest rates on the main refinancing operations, the marginal lending facility and the deposit facility will remain unchanged at 3.5%, 4.5% and 2.5% respectively.

27 APRIL 2000

The Governing Council of the ECB decides to raise the interest rate on the main refinancing operations of the Eurosystem by 0.25 percentage point to 3.75%, starting from the operation to be settled on 4 May 2000. In addition, it decides to increase the interest rates on both the marginal lending facility and the deposit facility by 0.25 percentage point, to 4.75% and 2.75% respectively, both with effect from 28 April 2000.

11 MAY 2000

The Governing Council of the ECB decides that the interest rates on the main refinancing operations, the marginal lending facility and the deposit facility will remain unchanged at 3.75%, 4.75% and 2.75% respectively.

APPENDIX 3: EUROPE DOCUMENT, NO. 2015/16, THE 'HISTORIC' REPORTS OF THE ECOFIN COUNCIL AND THE EMI THAT DEFINE THE STABILITY PACT, THE NEW EXCHANGE RATE MECHANISM (ERM 2) AND THE LEGAL STATUS OF THE EURO, AGENCE EUROPE, BRUSSELS, 18 DECEMBER 1996

THE 'HISTORIC' REPORTS OF THE ECOFIN COUNCIL AND THE EMI THAT DEFINE THE STABILITY PACT, THE NEW EXCHANGE RATE MECHANISM (ERM 2) AND THE LEGAL STATUS OF THE EURO

Meeting in Dublin on Friday 13 December at the same time as the Summit, the Ecofin Council put the finishing touches to a document that no doubt has historic value: its report that ends negotiations between the Fifteen on transfer to the euro and on the contents of the final phase of Economic and Monetary Union. The last compromises reached concerned certain aspects of the Stability Pact, setting obligations in matters of public finances that Member States participating in the euro undertake to respect.

The Dublin Summit was not called on to discuss these issues in substance, limiting itself to approving the results of negotiations and requesting that the regulatory texts be submitted to it in June.

As follow-ups to the Ecofin Council report, may be added: a) the decision noting that the single currency cannot come into effect on the first of the two dates mentioned in the Maastricht

Treaty (1 January 1997); b) the report by the European Monetary Institute on the new exchange rate mechanism to be applied between the euro and currencies not yet part of it. These texts only exist in English and French for the moment, and it is in one of these two languages that we are sending them to all our subscribers.

REPORT BY THE ECOFIN COUNCIL TO THE EUROPEAN COUNCIL

THE PREPARATIONS FOR STAGE 3 OF EMU

Introduction

1. The European Council in Madrid a year ago confirmed that 1 January 1999 will be the starting date for Stage 3 of Economic and Monetary Union (EMU) in accordance with the convergence criteria, timetable, protocols and procedures laid out in the Treaty. Accordingly, the European Council requested the Council:

    –   to study, together with, in their respective fields of competence, the Commission and the European Monetary Institute (EMI), the range of issues raised by the fact that some countries may not initially participate in the euro area; in particular, the study should cover those issues related to monetary instability;

    –   to work on ways to ensure that, after moving to Stage 3, public finances are kept on a sound track in line with Treaty obligations. The European Council stated that budgetary discipline is of crucial significance both for the success of Economic and Monetary Union and for the acceptance of the single currency by the public; it noted the Commission's intention to present in 1996 its conclusions on ways to ensure budgetary discipline.

    It requested the Council to report on these issues as soon as possible.

    Furthermore, the Madrid European Council requested the Council to complete, at the latest by the end of 1996, the technical preparation of a Council Regulation on the legal framework for the use of the euro.

2. The Council has worked accordingly on all three issues and expects to be ready to decide on them at the same time. It has received substantial assistance from the Commission and the EMI in their respective fields of competence. The Council submitted a progress report to the European Council in Florence which urged the Council to pursue its work with a view to presenting conclusions showing further substantive progress to the European Council in Dublin. The informal meeting of Ministers and Governors in Dublin in September made further progress on these issues. On 16 October, the Commission adopted proposals for legislation on the legal framework for the euro and on budgetary discipline in Stage 3. The European Monetary Institute has prepared a report on monetary and exchange rate relationships in Stage 3 which the Council commends and attaches to this report.

3. An exchange rate mechanism would provide Member States having a derogation with a reference for their conduct of sound economic policies in general and monetary policy in particular. The Council therefore presents **proposals for a new exchange rate mechanism** (ERM 2) in Stage 3 of EMU. The details are described in **Chapter I** of this report and in the EMI report.

4. The Council sees a strong link between the exchange rate issues and budgetary discipline and therefore considered both issues in parallel. Monetary policy cannot, without adequate support from fiscal and other policies, achieve its objective of price stability and secure that lasting convergence which fosters stable exchange rates. It needs adequate and sustained support from fiscal and other policies. A Stability and Growth Pact to ensure strict budgetary discipline on an enduring basis is therefore essential.

    The Council, in its progress report to the European Council in Florence, has already submitted the outline of such a pact. Since that meeting, the Council has continued to work on this issue, and is now in a position to submit its suggestions for the **main elements of a Stability and Growth Pact**, including a possible European Council Resolution, in accordance with the procedures and principles of the Treaty. They are contained in **Chapter II** of this report.

5. In its work on the **legal framework of the euro,** the Council
    has been particularly reliant on assistance from the EMI and
    the Commission. The technical preparation for legislation
    was significantly advanced at the informal meeting of the
    Council in September. **Chapter III** reports on the state of
    preparation for legislation.

I. Relationships between Member States in the euro and those outside in Stage 3

6. In its work on the relationship between the Member States
    forming part of and those not forming part of the euro area,
    the Council was guided by principles laid out in its progress
    report which was adopted by the Florence European
    Council. There it was agreed:
    –   that all Member States, whether adopting the euro or
        not, have a strong common interest in the good
        functioning of economic and monetary union and of
        the exchange rate mechanism. As a consequence, all
        Member States will be involved in the dialogue on the
        issues raised by the move to Stage 3 of EMU, including
        monetary and exchange rate matters as well as institu-
        tional and budgetary issues;
    –   that a stable economic environment is necessary for the
        good functioning of the single market and for higher
        investment, growth and employment and is therefore in
        the interest of all Member States.
7. Over recent months, the Council has continued to work on
    these aspects of relationships between Member States
    forming part and those not forming part of the euro area.
    In so doing, it has sought to build on and to strengthen the
    unity which the Community has achieved and in particular
    to ensure that the relevant Community bodies continue to
    work effectively and harmoniously.
8. In the Council's progress report to the European Council in
    Florence, it was stated that the proper functioning of the
    single market must not be endangered by real exchange rate
    misalignments, or by excessive nominal exchange rate
    fluctuations, between the euro and the other EU currencies,

which would disrupt trade flows between Member States. Lasting convergence of economic fundamentals is a prerequisite for sustainable exchange rate stability. To this end, there is agreement that in Stage 3 of EMU all Member States must pursue disciplined and responsible monetary policies directed towards price stability. The coordination of monetary policies in the framework of the ECB General Council will therefore play a central role. Sound fiscal and structural policies in all Member States are, at least, equally essential for sustainable exchange rate stability.

9. The report adopted in Florence also made it clear that an exchange-rate mechanism can help to ensure that Member States orient their policies to stability, foster convergence among the Member States not participating in the single currency, and thereby help them in their efforts to adopt the single currency. At the same time, it could also protect them and participating Member States from unwarranted pressures in the foreign-exchange markets. In such cases, it may assist non-participating Member States, when their currencies come under pressure, to combine appropriate policy responses, including interest rate measures, with coordinated intervention. And it would help to ensure that Member States seeking to adopt the euro after 1 January 1999 receive a treatment equal to that of those initially participating with respect to the fulfilment of the convergence criteria.

10. In view of these considerations, the European Council accepted that it is indeed appropriate that a new exchange rate mechanism should replace the present ERM as from 1 January 1999. It would reflect lessons and experience gained with the present system and provide continuity. Sufficient flexibility would need to be allowed, in particular to accommodate the varying degrees, paces and strategies of economic convergence of the non-euro area Member States joining the mechanism ('the other participants'). Membership would continue to be voluntary. Nevertheless, Member States with a derogation can be expected to join the mechanism.

The new exchange-rate mechanism (ERM 2)

11. ERM 2 will be based on central rates, defined vis-à-vis the euro which will be at the centre of the system. The standard fluctuation band will be relatively wide, like the present one. Through the implementation of stability-oriented economic and monetary policies, the central rates will remain the focus for the participating Member States. Central rates and the standard fluctuation band will be set by mutual agreement between the Ministers of the euro-area Member States, the ECB and the Ministers and Governors of the central banks of the non-euro area Member States participating in the new mechanism, following a common procedure involving the European Commission, and after consultation of the Economic and Financial Committee. The Ministers and Governors of the central banks of the Member States not participating in the exchange rate mechanism would not have the right to vote in the procedure.

12. Intervention at the margins will in principle be automatic and unlimited, with very short-term financing available. However, the ECB and the central banks of the other participants could suspend intervention if this were to conflict with the primary objective of maintaining price stability. It should be ensured that any adjustment of central rates is conducted in a timely fashion so as to avoid significant misalignments. All parties to the agreement, including the ECB, would have the right to initiate a confidential procedure aimed at reconsidering central rates.

13. The exchange rate policy co-operation between the ECB and the central banks of the other participants could be further strengthened, for example by allowing closer exchange rate links between the euro and the other currencies in ERM 2, where, and to the extent that, these are appropriate in the light of progress towards convergence. The procedure to be followed would depend on the form of the closer link. The initiative to agreeing to such links would lie with the non-euro area Member State concerned. The existence of such closer links, in particular if it implied narrower fluctuation bands, would be without prejudice to the interpretation of the exchange rate criterion pursuant to Treaty Article (EC) 109j.

14. ERM 2, just as ERM 1, will require coordination of economic and monetary policies. The Treaty provides a good basis for the dialogue on assuring stability.

    – As regards Member States' economic policies, Treaty Article (EC) 103 defines the framework for coordination at Community level. It provides for the discussion and adoption by the Council of broad guidelines of economic policies, and it sets out arrangements for multilateral surveillance of economic developments and policies in order to ensure closer coordination of economic policies and sustained convergence of economic performance. Moreover, if and as long as there are Member States outside the euro area, the Economic and Financial Committee will have the task of assisting the ministers in their monitoring of the operation of ERM 2 as well as keeping under review the monetary and financial situation of these Member States and reporting regularly thereon to the Council and the Commission.

    – At the level of the central banks, the ECB General Council will monitor the functioning of the exchange rate mechanism and will serve as a forum for monetary and exchange rate policy coordination as well as for the administration of the intervention and financing mechanism.

    – While close cooperation between the Community bodies in the conduct of these various exercises will be necessary and useful, the division of responsibilities will need to respect the independence of the ECB and the non-euro area NCBs.

15. The main operational features of the new exchange rate mechanism are described in the EMI paper annexed to this report.

A framework for stability

16. All Member States have mutual interests and obligations in the monetary field. Indeed, the Treaty states that each Member State shall treat its exchange rate policy as a matter of common interest. As was reconfirmed in the Council's

report to the European Council in Florence cited above, lasting convergence of economic fundamentals is a pre-requisite for sustainable exchange rate stability.

17. For all Member States, the surveillance procedures as described in paragraph 14 will seek to ensure that their domestic policies are geared to price stability and sound public finances, thus creating the conditions for keeping exchange rates stable. While membership of ERM 2 remains voluntary Member States with a derogation can be expected to join the mechanism and thus to have a central rate vis-à-vis the euro, thereby providing a reference point which assists in judging the adequacy of their policies. Member States outside ERM 2 and thus not having a central rate will present policies, so as to enable appropriate surveillance in the Council, which can make, when necessary, non binding recommendations under Article 103, and in the General Council of the ECB. This surveillance will seek to ensure that their policies are oriented to stability and thus to avoid real exchange rate misalignments and excessive nominal exchange rate fluctuations. In this way, the provision of Treaty Article (EC) 109m, whereby each Member State shall treat its exchange rate policy as a matter of common interest, can be given effect. The policies will be presented in the convergence programmes.

The Council and the Commission are considering further the methods for the effective surveillance of exchange rate developments.

II. Ensuring budgetary discipline in Stage 3 of EMU (Stability and Growth Pact)

18. The Treaty imposes on Member States in Stage 3 of EMU an obligation to avoid excessive deficit.[1] Sound government finances are crucial to preserving stable economic conditions in the Member States and in the Community. They lessen the

---

1   Under Article 5 of Protocol 11, this obligation does not apply to the United Kingdom unless if notifies the Council that it intends to move to the third stage.

burden on monetary policy and contribute to low and stable inflationary expectations such that interest rates can be expected to be low. They are an essential condition for sustainable and non-inflationary growth and a high level of employment.

19. To that end, the Council proposes to adopt regulations on the strengthening of surveillance and budgetary discipline and on speeding up and clarifying the excessive-deficit procedure. These regulations, combined with a European Council Resolution, will constitute a Stability and Growth Pact. The Resolution would enshrine the solemn political commitment of the Commission, the Council and the Member States to the strict and timely application of the pact. The surveillance procedure and the excessive-deficit procedure (except, in particular, sanctions) will be common to all Member States. Euro-area Member States will be obliged to submit stability programmes and will be subject to agreed sanctions for failure to act effectively on excessive deficits. In the surveillance procedure, the other Member States will be obliged to submit convergence programmes only. In the excessive-deficit procedure, sanctions cannot be applied to them.

20. In this chapter of the report, the Council submits the main elements of the Stability and Growth Pact. A credible and effective pact will ensure budgetary discipline in Stage 3 of EMU in accordance with the principles and procedures of the Treaty, while in no way changing the requirements for the adoption of the euro, either in the first group or at a later date.

Reinforced surveillance of budgetary positions

21. Each Member State will commit itself to aim for a medium-term budgetary position of **close to balance or in surplus**. This will allow the automatic stabilizers to work, where appropriate, over the whole business cycle without breaching the 3 per cent reference value for the deficit. This was agreed by the European Council in Florence.

22. Member States adopting the euro will be required by

secondary legislation to present **stability programmes**, which will specify their medium-term budgetary objectives, together with an adjustment path for the government surplus or deficit ratio and the expected path for the government debt ratio. Furthermore, the programmes will contain the main assumptions about economic developments as well as a sensitivity analysis of the deficit and debt position and explain what is being done to achieve the objective.

23. A separate legislative proposal will be forthcoming from the Commission which will provide for the submission of **convergence programmes** by the non-euro area Member States. The information they will contain, as far as budgetary policy is concerned, will be similar to that of the stability programmes.

24. Member States will commit themselves to take the action they think necessary to achieve the objectives of their programmes. Stability and convergence programmes will be multiannual and will be updated annually to take account of the latest available information. Member States will make their stability and convergence programmes public.

Early warning system: monitoring and surveillance

25. The Commission and the Council will study these stability and convergence programmes and monitor Member States' budgetary performances with reference to their medium-term objectives and adjustment paths with a view to giving **early warning** of any significant deterioration which might lead to an excessive deficit. In such cases, the Council will address recommendations to the Member State concerned.

Excessive deficit procedure

26. Adherence to the objective of sound budgetary positions close to balance or in surplus will allow a Member State to deal with normal cyclical fluctuations while keeping its government deficit within the 3 per cent reference value. Nevertheless, to deter excessive deficits and to ensure that,

should they occur, they are promptly eliminated, there is a need for detailed provisions for the implementation of the excessive-deficit procedure. A Council Regulation will provide for expediting and clarifying the procedure, in particular by establishing clear definitions and setting deadlines for the various steps. Once it has decided that an excessive deficit persists, and as long as a Member State has failed to comply with a decision under Treaty Article (EC) 104c(9), the Council will, in accordance with paragraph 11 of that Article, impose sanctions on a prescribed scale. The European Council Resolution described in paragraph 37 will provide political guidance on how this procedure can be operated efficiently and speedily.

27. An excess of a government deficit over the 3 per cent reference value shall be considered exceptional when resulting from an unusual event outside the control of the relevant Member State and which has a major impact on the financial position of general government, or when resulting from a severe economic downturn.

28. The Commission will be invited to commit itself in the European Council Resolution (see paragraph 37) to prepare a report whenever the actual or planned government deficit exceeds the 3 per cent reference value, thereby triggering the procedure under Article 104c(3). The Commission, when preparing such a report, will consider, as a rule, an excess over the reference value resulting from an economic downturn to be exceptional only if there is an annual fall of real GDP of at least 2 per cent.

29. The Economic and Financial Committee will formulate an opinion on the Commission report within two weeks. The Commission, taking fully into account this opinion and if it considers that an excessive deficit exists, will address an opinion and a recommendation to the Council for a decision. In the event that the Commission considers that a deficit is not excessive, the Commission will be invited to commit itself in the European Council Resolution to present in writing to the Council the reasons for its position.

This would give the Council the opportunity to discuss the issue taking account of both the Commission's position and the opinion of the Economic and Financial Committee. The

Council could decide, by simple majority, to request the Commission under Article 109d to make a recommendation. The Commission will be invited to commit itself in the European Council Resolution to issue, as a rule, such a recommendation, in response to the Council request.

30. The Council when deciding, according to Article 104c (6) on a Commission recommendation, whether an excessive deficit exists, will in its overall assessment take into account any observations made by the Member State showing that an annual fall of real GDP of less than 2 per cent is nevertheless exceptional in the light of further supporting evidence, in particular on the abruptness of the downturn or on the accumulated loss of output relative to past trends.

31. Where it decides that an excessive deficit exists, the Council will, at the same time, make recommendations to the Member State concerned *'with a view to bringing that situation to an end within a given period'* (Article 104c (7)). These recommendations will accordingly set clear deadlines for i) the taking of effective action (within four months), and ii) the correction of the excessive deficit, which should be completed in the year following its identification unless special circumstances are given. The Council's initial judgement on whether effective action has been taken will be based on publicly-announced decisions of the Government.

32. If a Member State fails to act in compliance with the successive decisions of the Council under paragraphs 7 to 9 of Article 104c, the Council will, in accordance with paragraph 11 of that Article, impose sanctions including a non-interest bearing deposit. These sanctions would be imposed within ten months of the reporting of the figures notifying the existence of an excessive deficit. An expedited procedure will be used in the case of a deliberately planned deficit which the Council decides is excessive.

33. The excessive deficit procedure will be held in abeyance if a Member State does in fact adopt, through formal government decision, appropriate action in response to a recommendation under Article 104c (7) or a notice issued under Article 104c (9). The Commission and Council will monitor the progress of the Member State continuously until the Council decides under Article 104c (12) that the excessive

deficit has been corrected. If the action is not being implemented, or is proving to be inadequate, the procedure will resume immediately. This would lead to sanctions being imposed in accordance with Article 104c (11) within three months of the procedure's resumption.

34. If actual data demonstrate that an excessive deficit has not been corrected within the time limit specified either in the Recommendation under Article 104c (7) or the notice issued under Article 104c (9), the Council will immediately resume the excessive deficit procedure.

Structure and scale of sanctions

35. Whenever sanctions are first imposed, a non-interest bearing deposit should be included. This should be converted into a fine after two years if the deficit of the government concerned continues to be excessive. When the excessive deficit results from non-compliance with the government deficit reference value, the amount of the deposit or fine will be made up of a fixed component equal to 0.2 per cent of GDP and a variable component equal to one tenth of the excess of the deficit over the reference value of 3 per cent of GDP. There will be an upper limit of 0.5 per cent of GDP for the annual amount of deposits. The amount of the sanction will be based on outcomes for the year in which the excessive deficit occurred.

36. Further consideration is being given to the disposition of the interest on deposits and the proceeds of fines on the proviso that there would be no increase in Community spending.

European Council Resolution on the Stability and Growth Pact

37. When using the leeway which secondary legislation neces- sarily must leave to them, the Council and the Commission may receive guidance from the European Council, through, for example, a European Council Resolution. Such a Resolution would give strong political guidance to the Commission, the Council and the Member States on the implementation of the procedures. The Resolution would

invite all parties to implement the Treaty and the Stability and Growth Pact regulations strictly.

The Commission should express a clear commitment to that effect, which would include an undertaking to prepare a report on the budgetary situation in a country whenever there is the risk of an excessive deficit or the planned or actual government deficit exceeds the reference value.

The Council would be invited to take the decisions necessary for carrying the procedure forward as quickly as practicable. If the Council did not act on a Commission recommendation at any stage in the procedure, the Resolution would invite the Council always to state in writing the reasons which justify its decision not to act and to make public the votes cast by each Member State. The Resolution would also cover political agreements on the implementation of the Stability and Growth Pact. In particular, the Resolution would invite the Council always to decide to impose sanctions if a participating Member State fails to take the necessary steps to bring the excessive deficit situation to an end as recommended by the Council.

The Resolution will contain an undertaking by the Member State not to invoke the benefit of the provision in paragraph 30 unless they are in severe recession. In evaluating whether the economic downturn is severe, the Member States will as a rule take as a reference point an annual fall in real GDP of at least 0.75 per cent.

The recitals of the Council Regulation would make an explicit reference to the Resolution.

III. Legislation Establishing the Legal Framework for the Use of the Euro

38. The legal framework for the use of the euro is of the greatest importance, encompassing as it does the *lex monetae* of the monetary union and the legal provisions by which the single currency replaces the participating national currencies and the European Currency Unit (ECU).

    It was agreed at the informal meeting in Dublin that it was imperative in the interests of the smooth functioning of the financial markets that certain matters be clarified on a firm legal basis as soon as possible.

39. It was accordingly decided to separate the provisions which must be enacted soon and to envisage their early adoption in a Council Regulation under Treaty Article (EC) 235. This Regulation will cover, principally, the replacement of the ECU by the euro at a rate of one to one at the start of the third stage, the continuity of contracts when the euro is introduced and technical rules for the conversion rates, including rounding. All other provisions will be included in a Council Regulation to be adopted under Treaty Article (EC) 109l (4). Although this Regulation cannot be adopted by the Council until early 1998, earlier stages in the legislative process are being completed.

   This Regulation will provide, in particular, that the currency of the participating Member States shall be the euro from the first day of the third stage and that during a transitional period the euro shall be divided into national currency units; it will also regulate the introduction of euro notes and coins. Following the principle of 'no prohibition, no compulsion', this legislation will at the same time regulate the use of the euro and the national currency units during the transitional period and will ensure that the monetary law of participating Member States will continue to apply, subject to the provisions of the Regulation, during that period, while national notes and coins will continue to be the sole legal tender.

40. On 16 October 1996, the Commission adopted proposals for these two Regulations. Since then these proposals have been examined intensively in a Council Working Group. There is now a text for the Regulation under Article 235 as agreed within the Council Working Group. The Group also agreed the text of the other Regulation. The provisions in articles 10 and 11 of the Regulation based on Treaty Article 109 l (4), on the circulation of euro notes and coins, provide for a date to be decided, in accordance with the Madrid scenario when the regulation is adopted: for technical reasons, it is not possible to decide this date now. Further work also remains to be done on Article 8(4).

The Council, having taken into account the opinions of the European Parliament and the EMI, endorsed the text of both Regulations on 12 December 1996.

IV. Conclusion

41. The European Council is invited to approve this report. Subject to that approval, the Council proposes the following actions:

    a. The new exchange rate mechanism

    The Council will present a draft Resolution for adoption by the European Council in June of next year, setting out the fundamental elements of ERM2. In this Resolution, the European Council would be following the precedent set in 1978 in relation to the present mechanism. In parallel, the EMI would prepare a draft for an inter-central bank agreement, for submission to the European Central Bank (ECB) and the central banks of the Member States not forming part of the euro area when the ECB comes into existence.

    b. The Stability and Growth Pact

    After the Dublin European Council meeting, the Council will establish a working group which will examine intensively the Commission proposals with a view to adoption of these Regulations immediately after the European Council, in June of next year, has adopted a Resolution on the Stability and Growth Pact, a draft of which will be presented by the Council.

    c. The legal framework for the use of the euro

    The urgent Regulation under Article 235 will be adopted by the Council at an early date. Formal adoption of the Regulation based on Article 109 L (4) is not possible until 1998. Together, the two regulations establish the legal framework for the use of the euro.

Annex 1

Decisions to be taken under Treaty Article (EC) 109j (3) by the Council Meeting in the Composition of Heads of State or Government

As part of the preparations for Stage 3 of EMU and according to Article 109j (2), the Council has to assess at the end of 1996 *for each Member State, whether it fulfils the necessary conditions for the adoption of a single currency, and whether a majority of the Member States fulfil the necessary conditions*, and to recommend its findings to the Council, meeting in the composition of the Heads of State or Government. It was already clear to the European Council in Madrid a year ago, and confirmed in Florence, that at the end of 1996 there would be no majority of Member States fulfilling the conditions for the adoption of a single currency and that, therefore, 1 January 1999 (the latest date envisaged in the Treaty) would be the start date of Stage 3 of EMU.

As the basis for its Recommendation, the Council has received reports in accordance with paragraph 1 of Article 109j from the Commission and the EMI. These reports examine, as the Treaty requests, *the compatibility of each Member State's national legislation, including the statutes of its national central bank, with Articles 107 and 108 of the Treaty and the Statute of the European System of Central Banks (ESCB). The reports also examine the achievement of a high degree of sustainable convergence by reference to the fulfilment by each Member State of four criteria*. These criteria relate to price stability, the sustainability of the government financial position, the observance of the normal fluctuation margins provided for by the exchange rate mechanism of the European Monetary System and long-term interest rate levels.

The Council takes this opportunity to stress that the four criteria of sustainable convergence and the requirement of central bank independence must be strictly applied. This is essential if the coming completion of monetary union is to have the essential quality of stability and the euro is to be assured of its status as a strong currency. It is equally important that, when the criteria are applied in early 1998, they are applied with a view to ensuring that government financial positions in particular are sustainable and not affected by measures of temporary effect.

The reports under Article 109j (1) indicate that many steps have been taken towards ensuring the independence of the national central banks but that in some Member States the process is not yet complete. Similarly, with regard to convergence, progress has been achieved but much remains to be done. In particular, government financial positions remain unsatisfactory in many countries: some improvements have been achieved in recent years but substantial efforts still have to be undertaken to reduce government deficits and debt.

The (Ecofin) Council has therefore made an assessment under paragraph 2 of that Article, on a recommendation from the Commission, that at present there is not a majority of the Member States fulfilling the necessary conditions for the adoption of a single currency and presents to the Council meeting in the composition of the Heads of State or Government a Recommendation for a decision to that effect and a decision that the Community will therefore not enter the third stage of EMU in 1997 and that thus the procedure laid down in Article 109j (4) will be applied as early as possible in 1998.

The Council, meeting in the composition of the Heads of State or Government will also wish to take into account the Opinion of the European Parliament.

Annex 2

EUROPEAN MONETARY INSTITUTE

MONETARY AND EXCHANGE RATE POLICY COOPERATION BETWEEN THE EURO AREA AND OTHER EU COUNTRIES

Report to the European Council session in Dublin on 13–14 December 1996

INTRODUCTION

In accordance with the mandate given by the European Council meeting in Madrid and building on the agreement reached at the

European Council session in Florence[1] as well as on the broad support expressed at the Informal ECOFIN Council session in Dublin,[2] the EMI has finalized the first stage of its preparatory work on the future monetary and exchange rate relationships between the euro area and other EU countries. The report reflects the high level of consensus reached in the EMI Council on the objectives, principles and main operational features of the new exchange rate mechanism.

I. OBJECTIVES, PRINCIPLES AND OVERALL STRUCTURE

1. The Need for Monetary and Exchange Rate Policy Cooperation

Close policy coordination between the euro area and the other Member States from the very start of Stage Three of EMU is a matter of common interest and forms an integral part of the completion of the EMU process. In order to ensure the efficient functioning and development of the Single Market, it is especially important that real exchange rate misalignments between the euro and the other EU currencies be avoided, as well as excessive nominal exchange rate fluctuations, which would disrupt trade flows between Member States; hence the obligation under Article 109m to treat exchange rate policy as a matter of common interest.

The lasting convergence of economic fundamentals, in particular price stability, is a prerequisite for sustainable exchange rate stability. To this end, in Stage Three of EMU, all Member States will need to pursue disciplined and responsible monetary policies directed towards price stability. The coordination of monetary policies within the framework of the ECB

---

1 See 'Conclusions of the Presidency on the European Council in Florence of 21 and 22 June 1996' (SN 300/96), including the attached 'Progress report by the Ecofin Council to the European Council on preparation for Stage Three of EMU' (7940/96), dated 4 June 1996.
2 'Monetary and exchange rate policy cooperation between the euro area and other EU countries'. Report to the Informal Ecofin Council session in Dublin on 20–22 September 1996, dated 3 September 1996.

General Council will, therefore, play a central role. Sound fiscal and structural policies in all Member States are, at least, equally essential for sustainable exchange rate stability. In the absence of a convergence of fundamentals, any attempt to coordinate exchange rate policies is bound to be unsuccessful. Exchange rate policy cooperation cannot be a substitute for stability-oriented domestic policies.

The final objective of economic, monetary and exchange rate policy cooperation is convergence towards macroeconomic stability, which would lead to exchange rate stability against the euro. A nominal exchange rate mechanism may provide a reference for the conduct of sound economic policies in Member States on their way towards full economic convergence. It may help to enhance the credibility of such policies by establishing a focal point for agents' expectations. Moreover, it may provide a framework for counteracting market pressures unwarranted in the light of underlying fundamentals. In particular, it may assist any Member State, the currency of which comes under pressure, to combine appropriate policy responses, including interest rate measures in the country the currency of which is under pressure, with coordinated intervention.

Monetary and exchange rate policy cooperation should be flexible enough to accommodate different degrees and strategies of economic convergence. As noted in the Conclusions of the European Council meeting in Florence, 'Membership would continue to be voluntary; nevertheless, Member States with a derogation can be expected to join the mechanism', once they have achieved a satisfactory degree of economic convergence. In addition, the various Community mechanisms for the coordination of economic and monetary policies (see also Chapter II, Section 2) should ensure that exchange rate developments in all other Member States, irrespective of their participation in the exchange rate mechanism, are closely monitored and assessed with a view to the requirements of Article 109m of the Treaty and the smooth operation of the Single Market.

While the remainder of this report focuses on the exchange rate mechanism, the necessary broader scope of the overall policy coordination framework should be borne in mind.

2. Principles for an Exchange Rate Mechanism in Stage Three

In designing an exchange rate mechanism for Stage Three, the new economic and institutional environment which is expected to prevail by that time will have to be taken carefully into account. In particular, five elements must be underlined.

First, the statutory requirement for the ECB to maintain price stability would need to be safeguarded. It would be detrimental to the credibility of EMU if obstacles were to emerge as a consequence of exchange rate oriented measures which would hinder the newly-created ECB in the pursuit of its primary objective. These considerations would also apply to the non-euro area[3] NCBs, which should also pursue the primary objective of price stability. Second, the euro is expected to play the anchor role in monetary and exchange rate policy cooperation in the EU. This will be the natural consequence, first and foremost, of the stability of the euro and the fact that member countries with a derogation are expected to put in place the conditions to enable them to participate in the euro area at a later stage.

Third, sufficient flexibility would need to be allowed, in particular to accommodate the varying degrees, paces and strategies of economic convergence of the non-euro area Member States.

Fourth, it should be ensured that any adjustment of central rates is conducted in a timely fashion so as to avoid significant misalignments.

Finally, as a matter of principle, continuity and equal treatment among all Member States with respect to the fulfilment of the convergence criteria, including the exchange rate criterion, need to be ensured.

3. Overall structure of the mechanism

Given the respective competences and responsibilities, it would be appropriate to retain the two-pillar structure of the present

---

3   For the sake of simplicity, EU currencies and EU countries outside the euro area which participate in the new exchange rate mechanism are hereafter referred to as 'non-euro area currencies' and 'non-euro area Member States', respectively; the respective NCBs are referred to as 'non-euro area NCBs'.

ERM, which is based on two parallel agreements among governments, on the one hand, and among central banks, on the other: while a European Council Resolution would form the foundation of the new mechanism, the operating procedures would be laid down in an agreement between the ECB and the non-euro area NCBs.

II. MAIN OPERATIONAL FEATURES OF AN EXCHANGE RATE MECHANISM

In the light of the abovementioned principles, the new mechanism could be designed along the following lines.

1. Central Rates and Fluctuation Bands

The new exchange rate mechanism would be based on central rates, defined vis-à-vis the euro for the non-euro area currencies. A standard fluctuation band would be established for these currencies around their central rates. Although the exact size of the standard fluctuation band has yet to be decided, it is expected to be relatively wide.

If appropriate, non-euro area Member States could establish, on a bilateral basis, fluctuation bands between their currencies and intervention arrangements, with the aim of limiting excessive bilateral exchange rate oscillations. Prior to concluding such arrangements, the non-euro area Member States concerned would consult, on a strictly confidential basis, all the other parties to the new exchange rate mechanism.

Central rates and the standard wide band would be set by mutual agreement between the ECB, the Ministers of the euro area Member States, and the Ministers and Governors of the central banks of the non-euro area Member States, following a common procedure involving the European Commission and after consultation of the Economic and Financial Committee. The Ministers and Governors of the central banks of the other Member States not participating in the exchange rate mechanism will not have the right to vote in the procedure.

The sustainability of exchange rate relations will need to be closely monitored on a permanent basis. All parties to the agreement, including the ECB, would have the right to initiate a confidential procedure aimed at reconsidering central rates.

2. Monitoring the Functioning of the System

Intra-EU monetary and exchange rate policy coordination between the euro area and the non-euro area Member States will, pursuant to the Treaty, be conceived as a continuation of the present mechanism. The Economic and Financial Committee will, together with the European Commission, be involved in economic policy coordination. Furthermore, if and as long as there are Member States with a derogation, the Economic and Financial Committee will keep under review the monetary and financial situation of these Member States.[4] At the level of the central banks, the ECB General Council will monitor the functioning of the exchange rate mechanism and will serve as a forum for monetary and exchange rate policy coordination as well as for the administration of the intervention and financing mechanism.[5] While close cooperation between the Community bodies in the conduct of these various exercises will be necessary and useful, the division of responsibilities will need to respect the independence of the ECB and the non-euro area NCBs.

3. Intervention and Financing Facilities

Foreign exchange intervention and – after appropriate use of foreign reserve holdings – financing at the standard wide margins will, in principle, be automatic and unlimited. Intervention should be used as a supportive instrument in conjunction with other policy measures, including appropriate fiscal and monetary policies conducive to economic convergence.

The ECB and the non-euro area NCBs would have the possibility of suspending intervention and financing if these were to impinge on their primary objective. In deciding whether or not to resort to this safeguard clause, the ECB or a non-euro area NCB would take due account of all relevant factors, in particular the need to maintain price stability and the credible functioning of the new exchange rate mechanism. Without prejudice to its independent assessment, in line with Articles 105

---

4   Cf. Article 109c(4).
5   Cf. Article 44 of the Statute bf the ESCB/ECB in combination with Article 4.1 of the Statute of the EMI.

and 107 of the Treaty, as to whether there is a risk to its primary objective, the ECB would base its decision on factual evidence and, in this context, also give consideration to any conclusion which may have been reached by other competent bodies. It would appear neither advisable nor possible to define formally and ex ante the circumstances under which the possibility of suspending intervention might be used. The final decision would rest with the ECB or the non-euro area NCB concerned, but it would be understood that, time permitting, the ECB or the NCB concerned would signal as far ahead of time as possible its intention of suspending intervention and financing.

The possibility of coordinated intramarginal intervention decided by mutual agreement between the ECB, as the central bank issuing the intervention currency, and the respective NCB, in parallel with other appropriate policy responses by the latter, would be retained. As in the present ERM, unilateral intramarginal intervention would continue to be subject to prior approval by the central bank issuing the intervention currency concerned, should it exceed certain thresholds.

The present Very Short-Term Financing facility (VSTF) would be continued, following some appropriate adjustments. The initial duration (2½ to 3½ months), as well as the rules for extending maturities of VSTF financing operations (renewable twice for three months subject to certain ceilings and/or the agreement of the creditor central bank) would be retained. Outstanding balances would, as in the present ERM, be remunerated at a representative market interest rate corresponding to the duration and currency denomination of the credit. Financing balances would be denominated in the creditor's currency. VSTF balances would be settled in the creditor's currency, unless otherwise agreed between the creditor and debtor central banks.

The present ERM rules governing access to the VSTF facility for intramarginal intervention would be broadly continued, including the understanding that appropriate use of foreign reserve holdings would be made prior to resorting to the VSTF facility. The size of the ceilings for such access could, initially, be retained and adjusted in the light of experience of the practical operation of the mechanism. The Short-Term Monetary Support Mechanism (STMS) should be discontinued, given its very limited practical relevance in the past. To the extent that the STMS quotas are relevant for the definition of VSTF ceilings, the latter may have to be redefined.

4. Closer Exchange Rate Cooperation

The exchange rate policy cooperation between non-euro area NCBs and the ECB could be further strengthened. This might take various forms: inter alia, closer links may entail narrower fluctuation bands, which would be made public, with automatic intervention and financing at the narrow limits; alternatively, they may rely on informal narrower target ranges, which might be kept confidential, supported through an enhanced role for coordinated intramarginal intervention. However, a proliferation of ad hoc links should be avoided. To this effect, a standard arrangement could be used as a reference for closer links with NCBs of non-euro area Member States which have achieved a sufficiently high degree of convergence. The existence of such closer cooperation, in particular if it implied narrower fluctuation bands, would be without prejudice to the interpretation of the exchange rate criterion pursuant to Article 109j of the Treaty.

Closer exchange rate links would be agreed upon on a case-by-case basis at the initiative of the interested non-euro area Member State. The procedure to be followed would depend on the form of the closer link. Arrangements implying publicly announced narrower fluctuation bands would be agreed upon by the ECB, the Ministers of the euro area Member States and the Minister and Governor of the central bank of the non-euro area Member State concerned, after consultation of the Ministers of the other non-euro area Member States and the ECB General Council. All other closer arrangements of a more informal nature would be agreed upon by the ECB and the central bank of the non-euro area Member State concerned, after consultation of the Ministers of all Member States and the ECB General Council.

Closer exchange rate links would be subject to progress in economic convergence, although they should not be seen as the only possible strategy to be followed by non-euro area Member States on their way towards full economic convergence. They would require a continuous monitoring of the sustainability of the closer exchange rate link and an active use of accompanying policy measures by the non-euro area Member State. All parties having agreed upon a closer exchange rate arrangement, including the ECB, would have the right to trigger a confidential re-examination of the adequacy of such a closer exchange rate link and, if applicable, to suspend intervention and financing in the event of conflict with the primary objective of price stability.

CONCLUDING REMARKS

The basic features of a mechanism to succeed the present ERM should be announced well ahead of the decision on the first wave of participants in the euro area. Thus, markets would be reassured about the continuity of monetary and exchange rate policy cooperation in the EU, preserving the role of the present ERM for non-euro area currencies during the interim period. This could help to allay any incipient market fears about the management of the exchange rates of non-euro area currencies after the start of Stage Three. Full specification of the operational details would have to await the establishment of the ECB.

understood that he would not remain in office until the end of his term and that Mr Duisenberg's successor would be the Governor of the Bank of France, Jean-Claude Trichet. Lastly, they agreed on the five other members of the Bank's Board of Directors. Final decisions on the appointments will be adopted following delivery of the European Parliament's opinion.

It was not until 1.00 a.m. that Council President Tony Blair announced these results to the press. The meeting, which should have started at around 3 p.m., after a lunch for the Heads of State and Government (while, in parallel, the Finance and Foreign Ministers had a lunch separately, with Commissioners Yves-Thibault de Silguy and Hans van den Broek), did not get under way until around midnight, after long and laborious informal discussions, in a sometimes tense climate, over the appointment of the President of the future European Central Bank. The Heads of State and Government met in different configurations, including in small groups of three or four, and also in the so-called 'confessional' form, with the President-in-Office meeting privately with his colleagues (and Wim Duisenberg). In conducting the exercise, Tony Blair was accompanied by Luxembourg's Prime Minister (and Finance Minister) Jean-Claude Juncker. At around 5 p.m., these consultations seemed to have resulted in the compromise on the appointment of Wim Duisenberg for an eight-year term, as established by the Treaty, and on his resignation before the end of his term to cede his place to the French candidate, Governor of the Bank of France Jean-Claude Trichet. But it took hours to finalize this agreement in a form capable of being approved by all participants and ensuring in particular that it respects Treaty provisions. Germany was particularly opposed to any official sharing of the term of office of the Presidency of the Bank and any precise statement on the date of the early departure of Mr Duisenberg and insisted on the *voluntary nature* of this departure. The long discussions covered in particular the question of whether a written commitment was needed and whether the time at which Mr Duisenberg was to voluntarily leave his post had to be stated. France would have liked this date to be 1 January 2002, whereas one of the solutions proposed mentioned this occurring before 1 July 2002. In the end, the former Governor of the Netherlands Central Bank rejected, with the backing of his country and of Germany, any reference to either date (although the wording of his statement reveals that he will leave between 1 January 2002 and 1 July 2002, i.e. around four years after he takes office).

In conclusion, Mr Duisenberg read the following statement to the Heads of State and Government, who took note of it: '*I want to thank you for the honour of nominating me for the function of President of the ECB on this historic occasion. I explained to the President of the European Council that I will, in view of my age, not want to serve the full term. On the other hand, it is my intention to stay at least to see through the transitional arrangements for the introduction of the euro notes and coins and the withdrawal of the national notes and coins, in accordance with the arrangements agreed at Madrid. I wish to emphasize that this is my decision and my decision alone and it is entirely of my own free will and mine alone and not under pressure from anyone that I have decided not to serve the full term. Also in the future the decision to resign will be my decision alone. This must be clearly understood.*'

'We agreed to appoint Wim Duisenberg as President of the Central Bank for an eight-year term of office, in accordance with the Treaty,' Tony Blair told the press, adding that the summit had also agreed that the person appointed as his successor would be a Frenchman and had taken note of the fact that the President of the French Republic intended to appoint Jean-Claude Trichet. As to Wim Duisenberg's decision to leave his post before the end of his term, it will be 'his and his alone', the British Prime Minister repeated on several occasions. And, responding to criticisms by journalists who wondered why it had taken so long to reach this conclusion, Tony Blair replied that 'the time was worth taking' in order to ensure that 'the Treaty is fully upheld'. Why appoint for an eight-year term a person who does not plan to serve it out to the end? Because 'we believed Mr Duisenberg was the best candidate' even if he himself insisted on resigning before the end, replied Tony Blair, adding that Mr Duisenberg's position had been clear 'from the beginning'. President *Santer* voiced his satisfaction over the 'great moment' represented by the launch of the euro, a moment whose importance must not be dimmed by questions that 'may appear futile in the future'. The achievement of EMU is a 'collective success' of the governments and peoples of Europe, said Jacques Santer, who paid tribute to his two predecessors:

Pierre Werner, Luxembourg Prime Minister and author of the 1970 Werner Plan on Monetary Union, and Jacques Delors, President of the European Commission and of the Delors Committee which prepared the Treaty on EMU in 1988.

Members of Executive Board and the length of their term of office

Tony Blair also made a point of stressing the importance of the start-up of the euro (which 'will have to be strong', he said) with eleven countries and of the decisions taken on 2 May by the Heads of State and Government concerning the future European Central Bank. 'We agreed not only on the Presidency, but also on the other members of the *Executive Board* and the duration of their term of office,' he announced, listing their names: *Christian Noyer* (France), Vice-President (4 years); *Sirrka Hämïnen* (Finland, Governor of the Central Bank, 5 years); *Eugenio Domingo Solans* (Spain, member of the Council of the Bank of Spain, 6 years); *Tommaso Padoa Schioppa* (Italy, President of the Consob, 7 years); *Otmar Issing* (Germany, Chief Economist at the Bundesbank, 8 years). It was also decided that there would be some rotation in successive appointments to the ECB, said Tony Blair. And the Council adopted the following declaration on this subject: 'While reaffirming the Treaty requirement to make appointments from persons of recognized standing and professional experience in monetary or banking matters, and the roles of the European Parliament and the Governing Council of the European Central Bank, the Heads of State or Government will give appropriate weight and appropriate consideration, according to a balanced principle of rotation, in their future decisions under Article 109a(2), to the recommendations for nationals of Member States which do not provide members of the Executive Board appointed in accordance with Article 50 of the ECB Statute.'

Chancellor Kohl admits that these hours were very difficult for him

Speaking to the press after conclusion of the work, Helmut Kohl admitted that questions of 'prestige' had 'not facilitated' the summit discussions: There was a 'rather harsh exchange' and these hours were 'among the most difficult for me' (in the European context), he said. Wim Duisenberg's statement that his decision was taken of his own free will was a condition for 'our agreement', asserted the German Chancellor, who added that, had the President of the EMI dropped his candidacy, there would not have been a decision on 2 May in Brussels on the Presidency of the European Central Bank. 'We wanted Duisenberg, even though we were aware of the possible problems,' said Helmut Kohl. He qualified as 'pure invention' the report that he had promised François Mitterrand the post of the first Presidency of the European Central Bank in exchange for the Bank's location in Frankfurt. Finance Minister *Theo Waigel* admitted that there had been 'conflicts of interest' in this matter and called for the European Central Bank to be operational, if possible, even *before* 1 July. Bundesbank President *Mr Tietmeyer* simply replied 'bad', when asked how he found the compromise reached on Saturday in Brussels.

This said however, Chancellor Kohl also made a point of emphasizing the historic importance of the launch of the euro, saying it would 'give wings to pursuit of Political Union'. And, more generally, he announced that, with the backing of Tony Blair, he wished to make subsidiarity one of the main subjects of the Cardiff European Council in June.

According to the European Parliament President, Mr Duisenberg's appointment was not in compliance with the spirit of the Treaty

European Parliament President *José Maria Gil-Robles*, who was to have spoken before the Heads of State and Government around 3 p.m. before the beginning of work by the Special Council on the euro, was in the end not able to give his address until around midnight. In the shortened and amended version of his speech, he said in particular: 'You have taken a decision concerning the candidates for nomination to the Executive Board of the European Central Bank. Parliament has already expressed very clearly the need for the Treaties to be adhered to scrupulously, in both letter and spirit. It will undoubtedly consider most carefully the proposals put to it.' He went on to say: 'Today has clearly shown that it is no longer possible to reach unanimity on such important nominations and without Parliament giving its approval. I am convinced that if these two conditions had been adhered to, it would not have taken all afternoon to reach this conclusion.'

Furthermore, Mr Gil-Robles stressed that the euro must help to create jobs, that the Cardiff summit must 'demonstrate that steps are being taken in that direction' and that the decisions to be taken by the Ecofin Council and which 'will determine the Member States' entire economic policy' must not be taken 'behind the scenes' but should be discussed by the Parliament which is the only body qualified to express a European view on European economic policy guidelines. Finally, in the belief that all Member States should adopt the euro as soon as possible, Mr Gil-Robles said it 'would be regrettable if the first round of enlargements were to occur without this having taken place.' From today on, 'most of the EU Member States will form an economic and monetary federation,' he said, adding: 'The others must be brought in too and the federation must be made more transparent and democratic.'

In response to questions put by the press on how Wim Duisenberg was appointed as president of the Central Bank, Mr Gil-Robles regretted that national prestige has been put before the European interest and, to the question of knowing whether there was breach of the letter and spirit of the Treaty, he replied: 'Of course, I don't have any doubts.' 'This is a *bad start*,' he said, going on to add: 'Let's hope that the baby born in such bad conditions recovers quickly.'

Jean-Claude Juncker: response to Parliament President, criticism of insufficient preparation of debates by the Presidency

Luxembourg Prime Minister *Jean-Claude Juncker* believes there was no 'arrangement' and that the solution for the ECB Presidency is 'conform to the Treaty': 'Mr Duisenberg informed us of his intention, in view of his age, to retire early.' At any rate, 'he will remain in office until the end of the transition period, when euro notes and coins are introduced and national notes and coins withdrawn', and 'his decision will be personal' in that he 'will himself fix the date for his departure'. Mr Juncker confirmed that the length of the debates could be explained by the fact that the question was raised of knowing whether 'a set date for the end of the term of office should be included in the minutes.' Some Heads of State and Government had had difficulty in finding their marks, which he explained by the fact that they had not been 'sufficiently consulted by the Presidency *before* this meeting' and that 'many explanatory element had had to be introduced during talk.' He considered that the decision was no threat to the independence of the ECB and recalled that 'other national central banks had served as models for appointments of this kind' (he cited the Bundesbank with Mr Poehl and Mr Schlesinger). In answer to questions on the remarks by the EP president who said there was breach of the spirit of the Treaty, Mr Juncker explained that Mr Gil-Robles had made this comment before he had become aware of Mr Duisenberg's declaration to the Heads of State and Government and that, at any rate, he was 'no more qualified than others to judge the compliance or non-compliance of the decision'. According to Mr Juncker, history will not be long in casting judgement on the side issues of this historic decision.

Antonio Guterres: 'deep concern' about the way in which the appointment was made

Portuguese Prime Minister *Antonio Guterres* told the press of his satisfaction tinged with 'deep concern' about the way in which the president of the Central Bank had been appointed, which 'can in no way be acceptable'. 'A discussion that was far too long was held on the subject regarding details that reveal *national ego which, we believe, is not compatible with the European spirit,*' he declared. According to Mr Guterres, 'this form of appointment is far from what we expected from this summit, not because of the person, but because of the method (...). This meeting shows a lack of leadership and European project in most Member State.' He concluded by saying he hoped the euro would cement the Member States together and give fresh impetus to political Union.

José Maria Aznar and Romano Prodi: pleased about there being Spanish and Italian members on the Executive Board

Italian Prime Minister *Romano Prodi* and Spanish Prime Minister *José Maria Aznar* stressed at the close of work that this summit was very positive for their countries which are not only to take part in single currency but are also represented on the ECB

Executive Board. 'We trust that being represented in this way
will make it possible to play a major role in future decisions to be
taken by the Central Bank,' noted Romano Prodi. 'We put
forward someone of merit in the person of Eugenio Domingo',
stressed José Maria Aznar. Declaring that this was the 'most
important decision for Europe of the 21st century', the Spanish
Prime Minister expressed the hope that 'admission to the euro
will guarantee sustainable growth for Spain over coming years.'

Mr Prodi and Mr Aznar also presented Mr Duisenberg's
declaration as 'a personal choice'. 'At the age of 65, one can quite
understand him,' said Mr Prodi with the hint of a smile.
According to the Italian prime minister, the 'imbroglio' preceding Mr Duisenberg's appointment is in no way a negative sign:
'We have kept up the economic effort for a long while, and the
simple question of the duration of Mr Duisenberg's term of office
is not enough to give the market a negative signal,' he felt,
concluding that the results of this summit were optimistic rather
than pessimistic: 'Each State has up till now worked to reach this
decisive stage. One must understand that some States have
internal problems – the Dutch have elections in four days, the
Germans in September ... This decision was not a split mandate,'
concluded the head of the Italian Government.

*Mr Ahern (Ireland) believes the integrity of the future Central Bank is
guaranteed*

Irish Prime Minister Bertie Ahern stressed that, despite the
difficult decision concerning the presidency of the European
Central Bank, assurance has been given about the integrity of the
bank. 'It will have a powerful executive, a very strong president
and vice-president whose independence rules out any other
consideration.' The fact that Mr Duisenberg foresees remaining
in his post until the end of the period for transition to the euro
was a source of satisfaction for Ireland. 'He will see the job fully
and completely done and will ensure there is consistency and
authority.' 'It is regrettable that it took so long, but it didn't
hijack the historic decision,' he continued.

Welcoming the completion of preparations for launching
single currency, the Irish prime minister stressed the importance
for the governments to support convergence efforts and to

implement the economic policy instruments effectively, in order to make the most of the advantages of single currency. Mr Ahern noted the need for the European Union to work towards strengthening the competitiveness of its economy *while having an adequate budget*, in order to raise future challenges such as enlargement and negotiations on Agenda 2000.

Regarding Ireland, Mr Ahern confirmed his government's commitment to stability, through economic and budgetary policies that ensure strict control of spending and the maintaining of a low rate of inflation, with a view to guaranteeing the medium-term sustainability of the country's economic growth. In this context, he felt that the challenge of the economic and monetary union would require deepening of the flexible and pragmatic approach adopted by the government and social partners.

Jean-Luc Dehaene: 'The most important step since the Treaty of Rome'

Following the 'Shortest European Council with the longest lunch' in which he had ever taken part ('it could be included in the Guinness Book of Record', he commented), Belgian Prime Minister *Jean-Luc Dehaene* pointed out that, even if the 'show' was 'not brilliant seen from the outside', history would remember that 'the president of the ECB was appointed and that eleven countries are qualified', the creation of single currency being 'the most important step since the Treaty of Rome'. For Mr Dehaene, 'single currency is Europe's response to the end of the Cold War' and Belgium, by making the necessary effort for being in the first wave, 'has done itself a service by ensuring it has a future'. Finance Minister *Philippe Maystadt* confirmed he had declined the post of EBRD president, explaining that he still had 'a great deal to do in Belgium'.

Mr Chirac explains and defends the French attitude, saying he is pleased

French President Jacques Chirac welcomed the launch of the euro, the 'capital element for stability' which, without waiting its official introduction, 'has shown proof of its capacity and effectiveness', in particular in the context of the Asian financial crisis during which markets showed that they 'anticipated' and 'integrated' European single currency. The challenge which, for eleven countries, consisted in taking on this major reform 'has been raised and raised well', he said.

'What made us lose a little time,' explained Mr Chirac, 'was not at all a question of substance but a question of procedure': Mr Duisenberg has made it known that, for personal reasons – do not laugh (Ed. in response to laughter) – he did not plan to remain in office until the end of his term' and that 'nothing could be done that might run counter to the Treaty and cause a stir in capitals like Bonn', which are sensitive to market reactions. This was followed by an 'extremely sensitive and difficult debate' in which Mr Chirac's 'will was that there be a French President as soon as possible and, meanwhile, that there be a French Vice-President. This objective was attained and I am satisfied.' And he added that, even within a Community institution, such a 'combat' was not out of place: 'This may seem sad to you. But I do not find it sad at all and, to keep nothing from you, I am even very satisfied (. . .). We are in a system of Europe of nations. That does not exclude solidarity from continually growing stronger but does not prevent each country from defending its interests', he said, recalling that his proposal for a reduction in the number of Commissioners, with the introduction of a rotation system, was 'contradicted by everyone because each country wanted its own Commissioner'. Given the 'economic, monetary and financial interests,' Mr Chirac assured his listeners that he had acted 'not out of nationalism, but simply out of rationalism', going on to add, at the express invitation of Economy/Finance Minister Mr Strauss-Kahn (who, seated beside him, had passed him a note): 'The Frenchman will not be there to defend French interests in the ECB, but to manage the single currency.'

Replying to journalists, Mr Chirac also made the following statements on:

1. *the spontaneity of Mr Duisenberg's decision.* 'It is his respon-sibility, his decision' and, when speaking to him in private, the Dutch candidate mainly spoke of 'his age and desire to be able to retire', without 'ever talking of his health'. The French President then 'proposed a hearing with Mr Duisen-

berg at the plenary Council, so there is not a shadow of doubt about the way he feels'.

2. *the soundness of this declaration of intent.* This act is formal, since Mr Duisenberg explained 'collectively before the plenary Council' and 'knowing him, it would surprise me if he spoke lightly. I do not for one moment doubt his good faith.' Any written trace, he said finally, is 'in my view quite superfluous'.

3. *the reaction of the European Parliament.* 'There has been no split mandate and the EP will not, I think, have any difficulty in understanding this.'

4. *tension between Paris and Bonn on the ECB Presidency?* A 'very curious' illusion that Mr Chirac wanted to 'correct' as 'in this matter, there has been no Franco-German problem: there has been a Franco-Dutch problem.' A little later, speaking of the forthcoming elections beyond the Rhine, he expressed considerable praise of Mr Kohl, who 'had a far-sighted vision of Europe', in that 'the refused to make a monetary Yalta in Europe and this was a great opportunity for Europeans in general and for the Germans in particular'.

Invited to comment on Jacques Chirac's speech after the press conference, Mr *Strauss-Kahn* dispersed the rumours of misunderstanding between the Head of State and the Government on this question of ECB presidency appointment. Speaking to a journalist who asked him if the president had been 'good', the Ecofin minister said: 'Of course. (...) *France spoke with a single voice* and was in phase from the outset on this question of appointment of the ECB president.'

See the following pages for results of work by the Ecofin Council and for debates at the European Parliament

(EU) EU/ECOFIN COUNCIL: MINISTERS PREPARED DECISIONS ON FRIDAY AND ADOPTED THE 'WAIGEL DECLARATION', WHICH ANTICIPATES THE STABILITY PACT WITHOUT ADDING NEW CONSTRAINTS – THE UNITED KINGDOM IS CLEARLY MAKING A COMMITMENT IN THE DIRECTION OF THE EURO

Brussels, 03/05/1998 (Agence Europe) – 'This evening, the Ecofin Council took a capital decision for the long term future of Europe', said Chancellor of the Exchequer *Gordon Brown*, announcing on Friday evening that the Fifteen Finance Ministers had unanimously adopted the Recommendation (addressed to the Council meeting at Head of State and Government level on Saturday afternoon, see preceding pages) on Member States meeting the criteria for participation in the single currency, namely Austria, Belgium, Finland, France, Germany, Ireland, Italy, Luxembourg, Netherlands, Portugal and Spain. At the press conference during which Commissioner *Yves-Thibault de Silguy* was at his side, the President-in-Office of the Council stated that this decision was not 'simply the culmination of the process', but also and most importantly the 'coming of a new era' as seen in the Fifteen's simultaneous adoption, 'to make EMU a platform of stability', of a 'new Declaration on budgetary discipline' stating what will be done in the coming months to respect the undertakings made in the Stability Pact. Mr Brown said this Declaration – also adopted unanimous – went *beyond the Stability Pact* in that it 'emphasizes the necessity of economic reforms', the principal challenge to be met to enable growth to be reflected in the creation of jobs.

Answering questions, Mr Brown and Mr de Silguy added the following details.

– *'Waigel Declaration'*. Commissioner de Silguy spoke of a 'text of great importance that complements the decisions taken' in the framework of the Stability Pact through undertakings: i) to respect budget objectives in 1998; ii) to boost efforts to reduce debt, 'the primary surplus being important' in this regard; iii) 'to anticipate the stability programme to make possible a debate on 1999 budgets', which will reflect a 'reinforcement of the coordination of economic policies'; iv) to intensify structural reform efforts. For Mr de Silguy, there are no new commitments, but simply a decision to 'implement' those taken, with the realization that 'there is still work to do'. See the full text of this declaration below.

–   *Euro-11 (or Euro Council) meeting.* In accordance with the decisions taken at the Luxemburg Summit, 'the United Kingdom will participate in part of the first meeting' of this body, which will be held before the start of the Ecofin Council sitting on 5 June. And Gordon Brown added that: a) the agenda of each meeting of the Euro-11 would be 'prepared by the fifteen Member States'; b) the Euro-11's deliberations would 'always be the subject of a report to the Monetary Committee'; c) the 'prime importance of the Ecofin Council will be fully respected'.

–   *United Kingdom's participation.* Gordon Brown reported that the Blair government had, the day before, 'for the first time', informed the Commons of its 'decision to support the principle of monetary union'. And he added: 'We are going to take all necessary measures' to this effect, in concrete terms, 'drafting a programme for switchover [to the euro] next year.' 'We are preparing for the euro,' stated Gordon Brown. Asked to say whether he regretted the United Kingdom's absence from the 'first wave', the Chancellor of the Exchequer exclaimed: 'I regret that over the last five years, the other Member States have been actively preparing, which was not the case in the United Kingdom. This is why we have had to take the decision we have taken' (although he observed that 'the City has been actively preparing').

–   *The euro, a factor of division in Europe?* Asked to comment on this assessment made in his day by former Conservative Prime Minister *John Major*, Mr Brown began by observing that 'spectacular progress' had been made since that time (public deficit, inflation, etc.), with 'scepticism consequently becoming pointless'. He also pointed out that the euro would represent '20 per cent of the world economy', all of which are reasons why he 'does not share the fears of certain pessimists' and why, on the contrary, he is convinced that the euro will be a strong and very important currency. These remarks led Yves-Thibault de Silguy to tell him that he defended 'the single currency better than a Europhile Commissioner'.

For his part, German Finance Minister *Theo Waigel* told the press that the Declaration adopted on Friday contained 'what I had requested in York' (at the informal meeting of Finance Ministers). He also stated that monetary union would not be 'a Union of monetary transfers'. Belgian Finance Minister *Philippe Mavstadt* (who explained that he had 'Jacques Delors specially in mind') explained that Friday's decision was a 'point of culmination' because the euro will be a 'powerful force for integration ... Those convinced that peace on our continent is assured by integration can be happy this evening.' Regarding budgetary discipline, Philippe Maystadt stated that there would be 'no additional undertakings to make' and that the Declaration would not set any new constraints. The allusions to debt reduction are aimed primarily, in his view, at the countries (clearly, Italy) where there are 'still many privatizations to be carried out', with Belgium, for its part, envisaging the sale of gold reserves (not in the immediate future) and the sale of 'some shares' remaining to it.

(EU) EU/ECOFIN COUNCIL: DURING SUNDAY NIGHT MINISTERS APPROVE DEFINITIVE PARITIES BETWEEN CURRENCIES OF THE EURO ZONE AND ADOPT OTHER LEGAL TEXTS

Brussels, 03/05/1998 (Agence Europe) – In the wake of the Council which met at the level of Heads of State and Government and the different press conferences which punctuated it, the Ecofin Council briefly met on Sunday night under the chairmanship of the Chancellor of the Exchequer to formally adopt the following texts:

1. *Recommendation relating to the appointment of members of the Executive Board of the European Central Bank.* Finance ministers formally adopted the Recommendation finalized by the Heads of State and Government (see previous pages).
2. *Terms and conditions of employment of members of the Executive Board.* The Council appointed Luxembourg Prime Minister *Jean-Claude Juncker*, Italian Minister of the Treasury *Carlo Azeglio*, and Portuguese Finance Minister *Antonio de Sousa Franco* as members of the Committee that will propose to the

ECB Governing Council the terms and conditions of employment of the members of the Executive Board. The three other members of this Committee will be appointed by the ECB Governing Council.

3. *Practical aspects of introduction of the euro.* The Council adopted the following conclusions concerning the Commission Recommendations:

   '*The Council welcomes the attention paid to the practical aspects of the introduction of the euro. The three Commission Recommendations of 23 April 1998 form a useful complement to the preparations under way at national level in the countries concerned, insofar as they support a voluntary approach to the questions of banking charges for conversion to the euro and of the dual display of prices and other monetary amounts, while respecting the freedom of Member States to take whatever measures they consider necessary. The recommended standards of good practice as an appropriate basis for such an approach can help facilitate the transition to the euro in these areas, in particular in the light of ongoing consumer concerns. Furthermore, the Council recognizes the need for constructive dialogue among professional and consumer organizations on the various aspects of the transition to the euro, and takes note of the recommendations made regarding the monitoring of preparations and information provision.*'

4. *Regulation on the technical harmonization of euro coins.* Having decided which Member States are admitted to single currency, the Council formally adopted the Regulation relating to the denominations and technical specifications of the coins. EUROPE recalls that the Council had adopted its 'common position' on this on 20 November last and that the EP had proposed amendments on 17 December 1997.

5. *Regulation on introduction of the euro.* The Council formally adopted the Regulation which, with that adopted on 17 June 1997 for the most urgent aspects (especially continuity of contracts), will constitute the legal framework for using single currency. This Regulation will take effect on 1 January 1999.

6. *Greek convergence.* The Council noted 'substantial progress' made by Greece with a view to respecting convergence criteria. 'The Greek Government's determination to pursue

its policies of fiscal consolidation and structural adjustment with a view to joining Stage 3 of EMU by 1 January 2001 is welcomed,' states the Council which, in its Conclusions, specifies that the progress made by Greece will then be judged in the same way as that of the Member States which will join EMU on 1 January 1999.

In addition, the ministers as representatives of their respective governments set 'irrevocable' conversion rates between the currencies of the euro zone (see full text below, among 'Texts').

EUROPEAN PARLIAMENT PLENARY SESSION

(EU) EMU/EP: PARLIAMENT APPROVES BY VERY LARGE MAJORITY THE RECOMMENDATION ON COUNTRIES THAT WILL ENTER SINGLE CURRENCY IN 1999

Brussels, 03/05/1998 (Agence Europe) – During the morning of Saturday, 2 May, the European Parliament, which met in extraordinary session, had approved by *467 in favour, 65 against and 24 abstentions* the recommendation adopted on Friday by the Ecofin Council on the subject of the EU Member States that will be taking part in single currency from 1 January 1999. The Parliament, approving its rapporteur, the president of the Committee on Economic and Monetary Affairs, *Karl von Wogau,* thus, as set out in the Treaty, forwarded its opinion to the Council, which met during the afternoon of 2 May at the level of Heads of State and Government. The economic and monetary committee had first of all met *in camera* with *Gordon Brown,* President of the Ecofin Council, and the political groups then finalized their positions for the plenary. Mr von Wogau therefore presented to the plenary an oral proposal (*Hervé Fabre-Aubrespy,* on behalf of the Europe of Nations group, tried in vain at the start of the session to challenge the validity of this procedure).

Parliament's debate opened with a *very political and pro-European speech by Council President Gordon Brown,* who welcomed the Founding Fathers 'wisdom' in laying down the bases of a 'unique experiment in human history', thus recognizing that 'enduring peace in our countries could only rest in the prosperity of the peoples', and therefore, 'right from the beginning,' setting out the path 'which has led us to the historic decisions on monetary union' taken today. The resolution passed at the Messina Conference, almost 43 years ago, called for the coordination of monetary policies. Today, after half a century, Europe is entering a new era, observed Mr Brown. 'Fellow Parliamentarians, economic and monetary union is born out of our shared objectives for growth and employment,' exclaimed the Chancellor of the Exchequer, adding: 'The test of our success will not be in declarations or in documents, or even in new institutions or procedures, but in jobs for people, growth for people and prosperity for people.' Applauded on several occasions by Members, Mr Brown announced the Ecofin Council's unanimous decision, the day before, on the eleven Member States that will participate in the single currency from the outset, emphasizing that it is important for the progress made by these countries to constitute a 'continuing commitment to stability and discipline.' Hence, the importance of the 'new declaration' on 'fiscal discipline and economic reform' adopted on Friday evening by the Ecofin Council. Mr Brown stated that, 'it is by locking in our commitment to fiscal discipline that monetary union can become the platform of long term stability on which growth and employment can be built.' And he insisted on the aspect of 'economic reform' in the Ecofin Council's Waigel Declaration. (Theo Waigel proposed the part on budgetary discipline and 'I myself proposed the part on economic reform,' he said at the press conference at the Council's conclusion on Friday evening). 'Indeed, economic reform is now established as the next big challenge to create employment opportunity for Europe,' he affirmed, mentioning as necessary conditions more efficient product, labour and capital markets, improved 'adaptability' of labour markets, effective national education and training systems (in particular as a means of putting an end to social exclusion), encouragement of entrepreneurship, easier access to capital markets for SMEs, increased tax efficiency and the avoidance of 'harmful tax competition'.

'The euro is today', affirmed European Commission President *Jacques Santer*, who praised the success of the 'unprecedented efforts' made by 'peoples and nations' to reach this stage, adding that this 'investment in convergence was an investment in prosperity'. The euro, he continued, will be 'not only the guarantee of the irreversibility of these efforts, but at the same time a catalyst for formidable change', allowing the 'creative spirit, the spirit of entrepreneurship and innovation of a strong Europe to mobilize.' The euro is not a goal in itself, said Mr Sante once again, insisting on the necessity of 'continuing our fight against unemployment and exclusion.' And he stated that the euro would also be the 'most tangible messenger' of integration for citizens (it therefore cannot be built 'at the expense of consumers') and that, 'thanks to the euro, in one operation, Europe will assert itself on the global financial and monetary map', and be able to contribute to the formation of a balanced and stable international monetary system. 'It is thus a strong Union that will take in its friends from Central and Eastern Europe,' concluded Mr Santer.

'If you pass my proposal,' declared *Karl von Wogau* (German Christian Democrat), speaking to fellow Members, 'you will be saying yes to a genuine European internal market, a more competitive European economy, greater stability, a stronger position for Europe in the world. Let us vote yes, aware of the fact that this is the most important decision in the history of Europe since the signature of the Treaty of Rome in 1957 at the Capitol,' he asserted. And like several fellow Members, he mentioned among the great precursors of this decision Pierre Werner, Valéry Giscard d'Estaing and Helmut Schmidt, Jacques Delors and François Mitterrand.

Large measure of agreement by Members, but with doubts on the left and virulent hostility on the right

During debate, *Pauline Green* (Labour, UK), Chair of the Socialist Group, welcomed in particular the 'positive and sensible approach' taken by Chancellor Gordon Brown with regard to the introduction of the euro in the United Kingdom: 'the careful preparation' being made by the United Kingdom means that those who support British membership in the euro, 'of whom I am one, will be able to conduct a campaign for a "yes" vote with some confidence' (in view of a British referendum on the single currency), she stated. The European Parliament has been 'deadly serious about our role in this matter, and, said Mrs Green, 'we now expect the Council to be just as serious'. She said the president of the future European Central Bank must be in office for eight years. 'This is the first test of the euro. The Council must not fail it', she said, noting that political wrangling on the subject of the Bank's president 'demonstrated the sort of political pressure to which the ECB will be subjected' ('we all know now very clearly the phonecalls that the Governor will get in the middle of the night and we all know where they will come from', she remarked). The president of the European People's Party Group, *Wilfried Martens*, said he was convinced that monetary Union 'brings the germ of a new move forward in economic and social solidarity' that will help the transition to political Union. He continued by saying that, now 'our relations with the United States, Asia and the other great world entities will change; in addition, the euro zone will now be the *pole of stability thanks to which there is no risk the European Union will pay for its enlargement at the price of its dilution.*' The co-president of the Union for Europe Group, *Claudio Azzolini*, saw the euro as a sort of 'visiting card' which in a certain way 'tells' the story of the history of the united Europe, its successes, its problems and its 'state of health'. If one considered that eleven countries may take part in the euro from the outset, this means that one is convinced even the most backward countries structurally are able to transform 'miracles' into sustainable improvements, said the Forza Italia member. On the threshold of a new century, 'Jean Monnet's model turns out still to be very much alive,' said Mr *Gijs de Vries*, Leader of the Liberal Group. He called this model the 'Sovereignty Paradox' whereby, by 'pooling sovereignty economically interdependent states can win back power'. The president of the European Central Bank must hold office for eight years and a decision to appoint two presidents, each for a four-year term, 'would be in clear breach of the Treaty', said the Dutch MEP, stating that 'a candidate who would be prepared to serve under such conditions cannot reckon with the support of the European Parliament'. He exclaimed 'Paris is not worth such a mass.' Mr de Vries also mentioned the problem of the debt and the 'unpaid bill of the greying of the population'. Most European countries finance retirement on the basis of a 'pay-as-you-go' system and this 'a form of hidden national debt', he remarked, calling on the European Commission' as a matter of urgency to submit proposals for a common policy to deal with the pension overhang'.

'Euro, yes, but not like this,' said *Alonso Puerta*, President of the Confederal Group of the European United Left-Nordic Green Left, who pointed out that, with its different sensitivities, his group was divided between concern and hope (and this will be reflected in our vote, he added). We are neither 'catastrophist nor Euro-sceptics', we are 'critical pro-European', said the Spanish MEP. With eleven members, the euro 'will not be an element of division', noted *Claudia Roth*, co-President of the Greens Group, with satisfaction. 'Monetary Union is a good thing, but it is not everything.' It must be accompanied by a social Union and a 'democratic Union'. The president of the European Radical Alliance Group, *Cathérine Lalumière*, particularly welcomed the effort made by the southern countries, by the successive governments of her own country (France) and by Germany: these efforts for self-improvement accomplished by Member States and by the populations are a 'sign of political vitality', she affirmed. Furthermore, the former French minister for European affairs said that it is only wise to have a rapid solution to the problem of the European Central Bank presidency, and it would hardly be 'judicious' to split the presidential mandate in two. The Europe of Nations group will vote against the recommendation by the Committee on Economic and Monetary Affairs, announced Dutch MEP *Johannes Blokland*, who said his group wants a 'Europe of independent States' and reproached the Council of the EU with hiding the true extent of the debt problem. *Cristiana Muscardini* (Alleanza Nazionale), on the other hand, spoke in favour of single currency, but felt that, on its own, it will not be enough to 'undo the knots' that prevent accomplishment of political Union, that she is hoping for. The leader of the National Front, *Jean-Marie Le Pen* spoke of an act of 'expropriation', saying that 'we met here, one Saturday, to bury eleven monies', and that this vote 'has no more legal value than a society conversion'.

SEE FOLLOWING PAGES FOR OFFICIAL TEXTS ON INTRODUCTION OF THE EURO, NAMELY:

I.   Council Decision (at level of Heads of State and Government) on countries admitted to the euro (with justification of positive decision for each);

II. Declaration of the Ecofin Council on continued effort concerning public debt and convergence ('Walgel Declaration');

III. Council Recommendation on president, vice-president and members of the European Central Bank Executive Board (to be made definitive after opinion from the European Parliament);

IV. 'Joint communique' from eleven euro zone countries on irrevocable bilateral rates for their currencies (corresponding to the current central rates).

TEXT ADOPTED BY THE COUNCIL AT THE LEVEL OF HEADS OF STATE AND GOVERNMENT AND BY THE ECONOMY/FINANCE COUNCIL

COUNCIL DECISION
of 2 May 1998

in accordance with Article 109j(4) of the Treaty

THE COUNCIL OF THE EUROPEAN UNION, meeting in the composition of Heads of State or Government,

Having regard to the Treaty establishing the European Community, and in particular Article 109j(4) thereof,

Having regard to the report from the Commission,

Having regard to the report from the European Monetary Institute,

Having regard to the recommendations from the Council of 1 May 1998,

Having regard to the Opinion of the European Parliament,

(1) Whereas, in accordance with Article 109j(4) of the Treaty, the third stage of economic and monetary union (EMU) shall start on 1 January 1999;

(2) Whereas, in accordance with Article 109j(2) of the Treaty, on the basis of reports presented by the Commission and the European Monetary Institute on the progress made in the fulfilment by the Member States of their obligations

regarding the achievement of EMU, the Council has assessed on 1 May 1998, for each Member State, whether it fulfils the necessary conditions for the adoption of the single currency and has recommended to the Council, meeting in the composition of the Heads of State or Government, the following findings:

BELGIUM

In Belgium, national legislation, including the statute of the national central bank, is compatible with Articles 107 and 108 of the Treaty and the Statute of the European System of Central Banks (ESCB).

Regarding the fulfilment of the convergence criteria mentioned in the four indents of Article 109j(1) of the Treaty:

- the average inflation rate in Belgium in the year ending in January 1998 stood at 1.4%, which is below the reference value,
- Belgium is not the subject of a Council Decision on the existence of an excessive government deficit,
- Belgium has been a member of the Exchange Rate Mechanism (ERM) for the last two years; in that period, the Belgian franc (BEF) has not been subject to severe tensions and Belgium has not devalued, on its own initiative, the BEF bilateral central rate against any other Member State's currency,
- in the year ending in January 1998, the long-term interest rate in Belgium was, on average, 5.7%, which is below the reference value.

Belgium has achieved a high degree of sustainable convergence by reference to all four criteria.

Consequently, Belgium fulfils the necessary conditions for the adoption of the single currency.

GERMANY

In Germany, national legislation, including the statute of the national central bank, is compatible with Articles 107 and 108 of the Treaty and the Statute of the ESCB.

Regarding the fulfilment of the convergence criteria mentioned in the four indents of Article 109j(1) of the Treaty:

- the average inflation rate in Germany in the year ending in January 1998 stood at 1.4%, which is below the reference value,
- Germany is not the subject of a Council Decision on the existence of an excessive government deficit,
- Germany has been a member of the ERM for the last two years; in that period, the German mark (DEM) has not been subject to severe tensions and Germany has not devalued, on its own initiative, the DEM bilateral central rate against any other Member State's currency.
- in the year ending in January 1998, the long-term interest rate in Germany was, on average, 5.6%, which is below the reference value.

Germany has achieved a high degree of sustainable convergence by reference to all four criteria.

Consequently, Germany fulfils the necessary conditions for the adoption of the single currency.

GREECE

In Greece, national legislation, including the statute of the national central bank, is compatible with Articles 107 and 108 of the Treaty and the Statute of the ESCB.

Regarding the fulfilment of the convergence criteria mentioned in the four indents of Article 109j(1) of the Treaty:

- the average inflation rate in Greece in the year ending in January 1998 stood at 5.2%, which is above the reference value,
- the Council decided on 26 September 1994 that an excessive government deficit exists in Greece and this Decision has not been abrogated,
- the currency of Greece did not participate in the ERM in the two years ending in February 1998; during this period, the Greek drachma (GRD) has been relatively stable against the ERM currencies but it has experienced, at times, tensions which have been counteracted by temporary increases in

domestic interest rates and by foreign exchange intervention. The GRD joined the ERM in March 1998,

–   in the year ending in January 1998, the long-term interest rate in Greece was, on average, 9.8%, which is above the reference value.

Greece does not fulfil any of the convergence criteria mentioned in the four indents of Article 109j(1).

Consequently, Greece does not fulfil the necessary conditions for the adoption of the single currency.

SPAIN

In Spain, national legislation, including the statute of the national central bank, is compatible with Article 107 and 108 of the Treaty and the Statute of the ESCB.

Regarding the fulfilment of the convergence criteria mentioned in the four indents of Article 109j(1) of the Treaty:

–   the average inflation rate in Spain in the year ending in January 1998 stood at 1.8%, which is below the reference value,

–   Spain is not the subject of a Council Decision on the existence of an excessive government deficit,

–   Spain has been a member of the ERM for the last two years; in that period, the Spanish peseta (ESP) has not been subject to severe tensions and Spain has not devalued, on its own initiative, the ESP bilateral central rate against any other Member State's currency,

–   in the year ending in January 1998, the long-term interest rate in Spain was, on average, 6.3%, which is below the reference value.

Spain has achieved a high degree of sustainable convergence by reference to all four criteria.

Consequently, Spain fulfils the necessary conditions for the adoption of the single currency.

FRANCE

France has taken all the necessary steps to make its national legislation, including the statute of the national central bank, compatible with Articles 107 and 108 of the Treaty and the Statute of the ESCB.

Regarding the fulfilment of the convergence criteria mentioned in the four indents of Article 109j(1) of the Treaty:

- the average inflation rate in France in the year ending in January 1998 stood at 1.2%, which is below the reference value,
- France is not the subject of a Council Decision on the existence of an excessive government deficit,
- France has been a member of the ERM for the last two years; in that period, the French franc (FRF) has not been subject to severe tensions and France has not devalued, on its own initiative, the FRF bilateral central rate against any other Member State's currency.
- in the year ending in January 1998, the long-term interest rate in France was, on average, 5.5%, which is below the reference value.

France has achieved a high degree of sustainable convergence by reference to all four criteria.

Consequently, France fulfils the necessary conditions for the adoption of the single currency.

IRELAND

In Ireland, national legislation, including the statute of the national central bank, is compatible with Articles 107 and 108 of the Treaty and the Statute of the ESCB.

Regarding the fulfilment of the convergence criteria mentioned in the four indents of Article 109j(1) of the Treaty:

- the average inflation rate in Ireland in the year ending in January 1998 stood at 1.2%, which is below the reference value,
- during the second stage of EMU, Ireland was not the subject of a Council Decision on the existence of an excessive government deficit,

– Ireland has been a member of the ERM for the last two years; in that period, the Irish pound (IEP) has not been subject to severe tensions and the IEP bilateral central rate has not been devalued against any other Member State's currency; on 16 March 1998, at a request of the Irish authorities, the bilateral central rates of the IEP against all other ERM currencies were revalued by 3%,

– in the year ending in January 1998, the long-term interest rate in Ireland was, on average, 6.2%, which is below the reference value.

Ireland has achieved a high degree of sustainable convergence by reference to all four criteria.

Consequently, Ireland fulfils the necessary conditions for the adoption of the single currency.

ITALY

In Italy, national legislation, including the statute of the national central bank, is compatible with Articles 107 and 108 of the Treaty and the Statute of the ESCB.

Regarding the fulfilment of the convergence criteria mentioned in the four indents of Article 109j(1) of the Treaty:

– the average inflation rate in Italy in the year ending in January 1998 stood at 1.8%, which is below the reference value,

– Italy is not the subject of a Council Decision on the existence of an excessive government deficit,

– Italy rejoined the ERM in November 1996; in the period from March 1996 to November 1996, the Italian lira (ITL) appreciated vis-à-vis the ERM currencies; since it re-entered the ERM, the ITL has not been subject to severe tensions and Italy has not devalued, on its own initiative, the ITL bilateral central rate against any other Member State's currency,

– in the year ending in January 1998, the long-term interest rate in Italy was, on average, 6.7%, which is below the reference value.

Italy fulfils the convergence criteria mentioned in the first, second and fourth indents of Article 109j(1); as regards the criterion mentioned in the third indent of Article 109j(1), the ITL, although having rejoined the ERM only in November 1996, has displayed sufficient stability in the last two years. For these reasons, Italy has achieved a high degree of sustainable convergence.

Consequently, Italy fulfils the necessary conditions for the adoption of the single currency.

LUXEMBOURG

Luxembourg has taken all the necessary steps to make its national legislation, including the statute of the national central bank, compatible with Article 107 and 108 of the Treaty and the Statute of the ESCB.

Regarding the fulfilment of the convergence criteria mentioned in the four indents of Article 109j(1) of the Treaty:

- the average inflation rate in Luxembourg in the year ending in January 1998 stood at 1.4%, which is below the reference value,
- during the second stage of EMU, Luxembourg was not the subject of a Council Decision on the existence of an excessive government deficit,
- Luxembourg has been a member of the ERM for the last two years; in that period, the Luxembourg franc (LUF) has not been subject to severe tensions and Luxembourg has not devalued, on its own initiative, the LUF bilateral central rate against any other Member State's currency,
- in the year ending in January 1998, the long-term interest rate in Luxembourg was, on average, 5.6%, which is below the reference value.

Luxembourg has achieved a high degree of sustainable convergence by reference to all four criteria.

Consequently, Luxembourg fulfils the necessary conditions for the adoption of the single currency.

THE NETHERLANDS

In the Netherlands, national legislation, including the statute of the national central bank, is compatible with Articles 107 and 108 of the Treaty and the Statute of the ESCB.

Regarding the fulfilment of the convergence criteria mentioned in the four indents of Article 109j(1) of the Treaty:

- the average inflation rate in the Netherlands in the year ending in January 1998 stood at 1.8%, which is below the reference value,
- the Netherlands is not the subject of a Council Decision on the existence of an excessive government deficit,
- the Netherlands has been a member of the ERM for the last two years; in that period, the Netherlands guilder (NLG) has not been subject to severe tensions and the Netherlands has not devalued, on its own initiative, the NLG bilateral central rate against any other Member State's currency,
- in the year ending in January 1998, the long-term interest rate in the Netherlands was, on average, 5.5%, which is below the reference value.

The Netherlands has achieved a high degree of sustainable convergence by reference to all four criteria.

Consequently, the Netherlands fulfils the necessary conditions for the adoption of the single currency.

AUSTRIA

In Austria, national legislation, including the statute of the national central bank, is compatible with Articles 107 and 108 of the Treaty and the Statute of the ESCB.

Regarding the fulfilment of the convergence criteria mentioned in the four indents of Article 109j(1) of the Treaty:

- the average inflation rate in Austria in the year ending in January 1998 stood at 1.1%, which is below the reference value,
- Austria is not the subject of a Council Decision on the existence of an excessive government deficit,
- Austria has been a member of the ERM for the last two years; in that period, the Austrian schilling (ATS) has not been subject to severe tensions and Austria has not devalued, on its own initiative, the ATS bilateral central rate against any other Member State's currency,
- in the year ending in January 1998, the long-term interest

rate in Austria was, on average, 5.6%, which is below the reference value.

Austria has achieved a high degree of sustainable convergence by reference to all four criteria.

Consequently, Austria fulfils the necessary conditions for the adoption of the single currency.

PORTUGAL

In Portugal, national legislation, including the statute of the national central bank, is compatible with Articles 107 and 108 of the Treaty and the Statute of the ESCB.

Regarding the fulfilment of the convergence criteria mentioned in the four indents of Article 109j(1) of the Treaty:

- the average inflation rate in Portugal in the year ending in January 1998 stood at 1.8%, which is below the reference value,
- Portugal is not the subject of a Council Decision on the existence of an excessive government deficit,
- Portugal has been a member of the ERM for the last two years; in that period, the Portuguese escudo (PTE) has not been subject to severe tensions and Portugal has not devalued, on its own initiative, the PTE bilateral central rate against any other Member State's currency,
- in the year ending in January 1998, the long-term interest rate in Portugal was, on average, 6.2%, which is below the reference value.

Portugal has achieved a high degree of sustainable convergence by reference to all four criteria.

Consequently, Portugal fulfils the necessary conditions for the adoption of the single currency.

FINLAND

In Finland, national legislation, including the statute of the national central bank, is compatible with Articles 107 and 108 of the Treaty and the Statute of the ESCB.

Regarding the fulfilment of the convergence criteria mentioned in the four indents of Article 109j(1) of the Treaty:

- the average inflation rate in Finland in the year ending in January 1998 stood at 1.3%, which is below the reference value,
- Finland is not the subject of a Council Decision on the existence of an excessive government deficit,
- Finland has been a member of the ERM since October 1996; in the period from March 1996 to October 1996, the Finnish markka (FIM) appreciated vis-à-vis the ERM currencies; since it entered the ERM, the FIM has not been subject to severe tensions and Finland has not devalued, on its own initiative, the FIM bilateral central rate against any other Member State's urrency,
- in the year ending in January 1998, the long-term interest rate in Finland was, on average, 5.9%, which is below the reference value.

Finland fulfils the convergence criteria mentioned in the first, second and fourth indents of Article 109j(1); as regards the convergence criterion mentioned in the third indent of Article 109j(1), the FIM, although having entered the ERM only in October 1996, has displayed sufficient stability in the last two years. For these reasons, Finland has achieved a high degree of sustainable convergence.

Consequently, Finland fulfils the necessary conditions for the adoption of the single currency.

SWEDEN

In Sweden, national legislation, including the statute of the national central bank, is not compatible with Articles 107 and 108 of the Treaty and the Statute of the ESCB.

Regarding the fulfilment of the convergence criteria mentioned in the four indents of Article 109j(1) of the Treaty:

- the average inflation rate in Sweden in the year ending in January 1998 stood at 1.9%, which is below the reference value,
- Sweden is not the subject of a Council Decision on the existence of an excessive government deficit,
- the currency of Sweden has never participated in the ERM; in the two years under review, the Swedish krona (SEK)

fluctuated against the ERM currencies reflecting among others the absence of an exchange rate target,
- in the year ending in January 1998, the long-term interest rate in Sweden was, on average, 6.5%, which is below the reference value.

Sweden fulfils the convergence criteria mentioned in the first, second and fourth indents of Article 109j(1) but does not fulfil the convergence criterion mentioned in the third indent thereof.

Consequently, Sweden does not fulfil the necessary conditions for the adoption of the single currency.

(3) Whereas the Council, meeting in the composition of Heads of State or Government, after having made an overall evaluation for each Member State, taking into account the above reports of the Commission and the European Monetary Institute, the opinion of the European Parliament and the Council's recommendations of 1 May 1998, considers that Belgium, Germany, Spain, France, Ireland, Italy, Luxembourg, the Netherlands, Austria, Portugal and Finland fulfil the necessary conditions for the adoption of the single currency;

(4) Whereas Greece and Sweden do not at this stage fulfil the necessary conditions for the adoption of the single currency; whereas Greece and Sweden will consequently have a derogation as defined in Article 109k of the Treaty;

(5) Whereas, in accordance with paragraph 1 of Protocol No 11 of the Treaty, the United Kingdom has notified the Council that it does not intend to move to the third stage of EMU on 1 January 1999; whereas, by virtue of this notification, paragraphs 4 to 9 of Protocol No 11 lay down the provisions applicable to the United Kingdom if and so long as the United Kingdom has not moved to the third stage;

(6) Whereas, in accordance with paragraph 1 of Protocol No 12 of the Treaty and the Decision taken by the Heads of State or Government in Edinburgh in December 1992, Denmark has notified the Council that it will not participate in the third stage of EMU; whereas, by virtue of this notification, all Articles and provisions of the Treaty and the Statute of the ESCB referring to a derogation shall be applicable in Denmark;

(7) Whereas, by virtue of the above notifications it was not necessary for the Council to make an assessment under Article 109j(2) concerning the United Kingdom and Denmark,

HAS ADOPTED THIS DECISION:

Article 1

Belgium, Germany, Spain, France, Ireland, Italy, Luxembourg, the Netherlands, Austria, Portugal and Finland fulfil the necessary conditions for the adoption of the single currency on 1 January 1999.

Article 2

This Decision is addressed to the Member States.

Article 3

This Decision shall be published in the Official Journal of the European Communities.

DRAFT DECLARATION BY THE COUNCIL (ECO/FIN) AND THE MINISTERS MEETING IN THAT COUNCIL

issued on 1 May 1998

1. On 1 January 1999, the euro will be a reality, marking the end of a process culminating in the fulfilment of the economic conditions necessary for its successful launch. The Council (Eco/Fin) and the ministers meeting in that Council welcome the significant progress that has been made in all Member States in achieving price stability and sounder public finances. The convergence process has contributed to a high degree of exchange rate stability and historically low interest rates, and thus to the improved economic conditions in our economies.

2. The move to the single currency enhances further the conditions for strong, sustained and non-inflationary growth conductive to more jobs and rising living standards. It

eliminates the exchange rate risk among participating Member States, reduces transaction costs, creates a broader and more efficient financial market, and increases price transparency and competition. It thus provides the decisive step for a truly single market.

3. We, the ministers, are strongly committed to the actions necessary to realize the full benefits of Economic and Monetary Union and the single market in the interest of all our citizens. These actions include closer co-ordination of economic policies. We are confident that the full implementation of the conclusions of the Dublin, Amsterdam and Luxembourg European Councils provides a sound basis for a permanently high degree of financial stability and the smooth functioning of EMU.

4. For the coming years, strong, sustained and non-inflationary growth will continue to be based in all Member States on economic convergence. Moreover, sound and sustainable public finances are prior conditions for growth and higher employment. The Stability and Growth Pact provides the means for securing this objective and for increasing the scope in national budgets to deal with future challenges.

5. In accordance with that Pact, we will start to implement the Regulation on 'the strengthening of the surveillance of budgetary positions and the surveillance and coordination of economic policies'[1] on 1 July 1998 in the following way.

   – We are committed to ensure that the national budget objectives set for 1998 are fully met, if necessary by taking timely corrective action.
   – The Council agrees to have an early consideration of Member States' budgetary intentions for 1999 in light of the framework and objectives of the Stability and Growth Pact.

   On these first two points, the ministers of the states participating in the euro area have decided to meet informally, in the course of the coming months, to start their monitoring work in accordance with the Luxembourg European Council Resolution.
   – If economic conditions develop better than expected,

---

1. Council Regulation (EC) No. 1466/97 of 7 July 1997, OJ N. L 209

Member States will use the opportunity to reinforce budgetary consolidation so as to reach the medium-term objective of government financial positions close to balance or in surplus, as embodied in the commitments of the Stability and Growth Pact.

– The higher the debt-to-GDP ratios of participating Member States, the greater must be their efforts to reduce them rapidly. To that end, in addition to maintaining appropriate levels of primary surpluses in compliance with the commitments and the objectives of the Stability and Growth Pact, other measures to reduce gross debt should be put in place. Furthermore, debt management strategies should reduce budgets' vulnerability

– Each of the ministers undertakes to submit, at the latest by the end of 1998, national stability or convergence programmes which will reflect these important elements.

6. The Council reiterates that the responsibility for budgetary consolidation lies and remains with the Member States and that, in accordance with the provisions of Article 104b (1) TEC, the Community in particular shall not be liable for or assume the commitments of Member States. Without prejudice to the objectives and provisions of the Treaty, it is agreed that Economic and Monetary Union as such cannot be invoked to justify specific financial transfers.

7. Our work on budgetary consolidation will be complemented by increased efforts for improving the efficiency of our economies so to enhance the favourable environment for growth, high employment and social cohesion. In this context, we look forward to our meeting shortly with the social partners on Economic and Monetary Union. Together with the social partners and all other concerned parties, we will take all necessary initiatives to create the conditions for combating unemployment, particularly for young people, the long-term unemployed and the low skilled. In following up the conclusions of the Luxembourg meeting of the European Council, we commit ourselves to play our part in implementing rapidly the national Employment Action Plans drawn up in the light of the employment policy

guidelines. The Council (Eco/Fin) will consider these plans in contributing to the preparation of the Cardiff European Council and subsequent European Councils.

8. We will attach particular importance to increasing the degree to which growth can be translated into additional employment. We will thus put emphasis, inter alia, on the following structural reforms:
    − making product, labour and capital markets more efficient,
    − improving the adaptability of labour markets in order to better reflect wage and productivity developments,
    − ensuring that national education and training systems are effective and relevant to employment,
    − seeking to encourage entrepreneurship, notably by attacking the administrative obstacles which it faces,
    − enabling easier access to capital markets and to venture capital funds, particularly for small and medium-sized enterprises,
    − increasing tax efficiency and avoiding harmful tax competition,
    − addressing all aspects of social security systems in view of ageing populations.

9. The Council intends to establish a light procedure, fully respecting the subsidiarity principle, for monitoring progress on economic reform. From next year, the preparation of the broad economic policy guidelines will draw on short assessments of progress and plans by Member States and the Commission on product and capital markets, as well as on the Employment Action Plans.

COUNCIL RECOMMENDATION
of 2 May 1998

on the appointments of the President, the Vice-President and the other members of the Executive Board of the European Central Bank

THE COUNCIL OF THE EUROPEAN UNION,

Having regard to the Treaty establishing the European Community, and in particular Article 109a(2) and Article 109 l(1), second indent, and to Article 50 of the Protocol on the Statute of the European System of Central Banks and of the European Central Bank,

HEREBY RECOMMENDS

1. Wim DUISENBERG as President of the European Central Bank for a term of office of eight years.
2. Christian NOYER as Vice-President of the European Central Bank for a term of office of four years.
3. Otmar ISSING as member of the Executive Board of the European Central Bank for a term of office of eight years.
4. Tommaso PADOA SCHIOPPA as member of the Executive Board of the European Central Bank for a term of office of seven years.
6. Sirkka HÄMÄLÏNEN as member of the Executive Board of the European Central Bank for a term of office of five years.

This recommendation shall be submitted for decision to the governments of the Member States at the level of Heads of State or Government adopting the single currency after consulting the European Parliament and the Council of the European Monetary Institute.

This recommendation shall be published in the Official Journal of the European Communities.

JOINT COMMUNIQUE ON THE DETERMINATION OF THE IRREVOCABLE CONVERSION RATES FOR THE EURO

In accordance with Article 109l (4) of the Treaty, the irrevocable conversion rates for the euro will be adopted by the Council, upon a proposal from the Commission and after consultation of the European Central Bank (ECB), on the first day of Stage Three, i.e. on 1 January 1999.

With a view to guiding markets in the run-up to Stage Three, the Ministers of the Member States adopting the euro as their single currency, the Governors of the Central Banks of these Member States, the European Commission and the European Monetary Institute (EMI) have agreed on the method for determining the irrevocable conversion rates for the euro at the starting date of Stage Three.

The current ERM bilateral central rates of the currencies of the Member States which, on the first day of Stage Three, will adopt the euro as their single currency, will be used in determining the irrevocable conversion rates for the euro. These rates are consistent with economic fundamentals and are compatible with sustainable convergence among the Member States which will participate in the euro area. The central banks of the Member States adopting the euro as their single currency will ensure through appropriate market techniques that on 31 December 1998 the market exchange rates, recorded according to the regular concertation procedure used for calculating the daily exchange rates of the official ECU, are equal to the ERM bilateral central rates as set forth in the attached parity grid.

The procedure agreed upon by all parties to this Joint Communique will ensure that the adoption of the irrevocable conversion rates for the euro will by itself, as required by Article 109l (4) of the Treaty, not modify the external value of the ECU, which will be replaced on a 1:1 basis by the euro. The attached annex provides detailed information on this procedure. The final official ECU exchange rates calculated accordingly and released on 31 December 1998 will be proposed by the Commission for adoption by the Council on the first day of Stage Three, i.e. on 1 January 1999, as the irrevocable conversion rates for the euro for the participating currencies.

In compliance with the legal framework for the use of the euro, once the irrevocable conversion rate for the euro for each participating currency has been adopted, it will be the only rate which will be used for conversion either way between the euro and the national currency unit and also for conversions between national currency units.

	DEM	BEF/LUF	ESP	FRF	IEP	ITL	NLG	ATS	PTE	FIM
	100=	100=	100=	100=	1=	1000=	100=	100=	100=	100=
GERMANY: DEM										
BELGIUM/ LUXEMBOURG: BEF/LUF	2062.55									
SPAIN: ESP	8507.22	412.462								
FRANCE: FRF	335.386	16.2608	3.94237							
IRELAND: IEP	40.2676	1.95232	0.473335	12.0063						
ITALY: ITL	99000.2	4799.90	1163.72	29518.3	2458.56					
NETHERLANDS: NLG	112.674	5.46285	1.32445	33.5953	2.79812	1.13812				
AUSTRIA: ATS	703.552	34.1108	8.27006	209.774	17.4719	7.10657	624.415			
PORTUGAL: PTE	10250.5	496.984	120.492	3056.34	254.560	103.541	9097.53	1456.97		
FINLAND: FIM	304.001	14.7391	3.57345	90.6420	7.54951	3.07071	269.806	43.2094	2.96571	

DETERMINATION OF THE IRREVOCABLE CONVERSION RATES FOR THE EURO

1. Why can only bilateral rates be announced?

Article 109l (4) of the Treaty provides that the rates at which the euro will be substituted for the currencies participating in the euro area will be adopted at the start of Stage Three of the Economic and Monetary Union, i.e. on 1 January 1999. The adoption of the irrevocable conversion rates for the euro shall by itself not modify the external value of the official ECU. Likewise in Article 2 of the Council Regulation of 17 June 1997 on certain provision relating to the introduction of the euro stipulates that every reference in a legal instrument to the official ECU shall be replaced by a reference to the euro at a rate of one euro to one ECU. Therefore, the irrevocable conversion rates for the euro have to be identical to the value of the official ECU expressed in units of the participating currencies on 31 December 1998.

Since the ECU is a currency basket, which includes the Danish krone, the Greek drachma and the pound sterling,[1] it is not possible to announce before the end of 1998 the irrevocable conversion rates at which the euro shall be substituted for the

---

1.   ECU basket currencies of Member States not participating in the euro area

participating currencies. However, it is possible to announce the bilateral rates of the currencies participating in the euro area which will be used on 31 December 1998 in computing the exchange rates of the official ECU and thus in computing the irrevocable euro conversion rates for these currencies.

2. Bilateral rates which will be used in determining the irrevocable conversion rates for the euro

For currencies participating in the euro area, the current ERM bilateral central rates will be used in calculating the final official ECU exchange rates which will be adopted by the Council as the irrevocable conversion rates for the euro on the first day of Stage Three, i.e. on 1 January 1999. The table attached to the Joint Communiqué contains those rates. In order to avoid minor arithmetical inconsistencies stemming from inverse calculations, it only includes one bilateral rate for each pair of currencies, which will be relevant for the procedure to be followed on 31 December 1998, as described below.

3. Calculation of the exchange rates of the official ECU on 31 December 1998

To calculate the exchange rates of the official ECU on 31 December 1998, the regular daily concertation procedure will be used. According to this procedure, the central banks of the Member States communicate the representative exchange rate of their respective currency against the US dollar.

Three steps can be identified

Step 1: Determination of the EU currencies' concertation exchange rates against the US dollar

At 11.30 a.m. (CET), the EU central banks, including those with currencies which are not components of the ECU basket, provide to each other in the context of a teleconference, the US dollar exchange rate for their respective currencies. These exchange rates are recorded as discrete values lying within the market bid-ask spreads. While, as a rule, the discrete values are equal to the mid-points of the bid-ask spreads, the EU central banks, as is allowed by the current concertation procedure, will take into account the need to ascertain exchange rates expressed with six significant digits, like for the preannounced rates. The bilateral rates between the euro area participating currencies obtained by crossing[2] the respective US dollar rates recorded by the EU central banks will be equal to the preannounced ERM bilateral central rates, up to the sixth significant digit. The EU central banks participating in the euro area stand ready to ensure this equality, if necessary, through the use of appropriate market techniques.

Step 2: Calculation of the exchange rate of the official ECU against the US dollar

The rates as recorded by the EU central banks are thereafter communicated by the National Bank of Belgium to the Commission, which uses them to calculate the exchange rates of the official ECU. The USD/ECU exchange rate (expressed as 1 ECU = $\times$ USD) is obtained by summing up the US dollar equivalents of national currency amounts that compose the ECU.

Step 3: Calculation of the exchange rates of the official ECU against the EU currencies participating in the euro area

The official ECU exchange rates against the EU currencies are calculated by multiplying the USD/ECU exchange rate by their respective US dollar exchange rates. This calculation is performed for all EU currencies, not only the ones which are components of the ECU basket.

These ECU exchange rates are rounded to the sixth significant digit. Exactly the same method of calculation, including the rounding convention, will be used in determining the irrevocable conversion rates for the euro for the euro area currencies.

For illustrative purposes, the calculation of the official ECU exchange rates vis-à-vis all EU currencies on 31 December 1997 is shown below.

---

2.   For example. FRF/DEM = FRF/USD : DEM/USD

	STEP 1		STEP 2	STEP 3
	Amount of national currency units in the ECU basket	USD exchange rate on 31 December 1997	Equivalent in dollars of national currency amount	ECU exchange rates
	(a)	(b)	(c) = (a) : (b)	(d) = $(USD/ECU)^1$ (b)
DEM	0.6242	1.7898	0.3487541	1.97632
BEF	3.301	36.92	0.0894095	40.7675
LUF	0.130	36.92	0.0035211	40.7675
NLG	0.2198	2.0172	0.1089629	2.22742
DKK	0.1976	6.8175	0.0289842	7.52797
GRD	1.440	282.59	0.0050957	312.039
ITL	151.8	1758.75	0.0863113	1942.03
ESP	6.885	151.59	0.0454186	167.388
PTE	1.393	183.06	0.0076095	202.137
FRF	1.332	5.9881	0.2224412	6.61214
GBP	0.08784	1.6561	0.1454718 (@)	0.666755
IEP	0.008552	1.4304	0.0122328 (@)	0.771961
			USD/ECU 1.1042128^2	
FIM		5.4222		5.98726
ATS		12.59		13.9020
SEK		7.9082		8.732134

[1]The dollar exchange rate for the GBP and IEP is the number of dollars per currency unit rather than the number of currency units per dollar. Column (c) is therefore calculated for each of these two currencies by multiplying the value in column (a) by that in column (b); and column (d) by dividing the dollar equivalent of the ECU (i.e. USD/ECU) by the rate in column (b).

[2]There is a difference of one unit (i.e. 1.1042128 instead of 1.1042127 in the last significant figure because the dollar equivalents of national currency amounts are shown after rounding to the 7th decimal place, whereas an unrestricted number of digits is used for computation purposes.

In compliance with the legal framework for the use of the euro once the irrevocable conversion rate for the euro for each participating currency has been adopted, it will be the only rate which will be used for conversion either way between the euro and the national currency unit and also for conversions between national currency units. Owing to rounding, the implicit bilateral rates which could be derived from the euro conversion rates may not always correspond, up to the last (sixth) significant figure, to the pre-announced ERM bilateral central rates referred to in this Joint Communiqué.

APPENDIX 5: EUROPE DOCUMENT, NO. 2099, CONTRIBUTIONS BY EU AND MEMBER STATES TO STRENGTHENING AND REORGANIZING INTERNATIONAL FINANCIAL SYSTEM AND REPRESENTATION OUTSIDE EURO ZONE, AGENCE EUROPE, BRUSSELS, 9 OCTOBER 1998

CONTRIBUTIONS BY EU AND MEMBER STATES TO STRENGTHENING AND REORGANIZING INTERNATIONAL FINANCIAL SYSTEM AND REPRESENTATION OUTSIDE EURO ZONE

Most observers considered that the meetings of the financial institutions early-October did not provide a sufficiently forceful response to the concerns raised by the crises in Asia and Russia or to market expectations. Certainly, the ideas in favour of 'steering' these markets are making headway: the liberalization of capital markets needs to be ordered and gradual, temporary restrictions could be allowed in certain circumstances, emergency mechanisms could be provided for developing countries conducting the right policies but that are threatened, the role of the IMF's Interim Committee should bear more resemblance to that of a government, the private sector has to be further involved in crisis-solving. These guidelines, expressed cautiously, do not go as far as some EU countries would like.

This is why we are publishing the *paper that France presented to the informal Euro Council* (Group of Eleven) in Vienna end-

September, which contains a twelve-point plan and an explanatory memorandum, which was, on the whole, well received by Member States. In part B, we publish the Belgium's *paper on representation outside the euro zone*, and which should provide the basis for forthcoming talks in the EcoFin Council on this delicate issue.

A. FACING INTERNATIONAL INSTABILITY: TWELVE FRENCH PROPOSALS FOR A EUROPEAN INITIATIVE

France proposes two sets of measures:

- in the short term, Europe must contribute to stabilizing the international economic and monetary situation in order to promote worldwide growth;
- Europe must also make an active contribution to laying foundations for a new international monetary and financial system, a new 'Bretton Woods arrangement' that we intend to be more legitimate and more effective.

I. EUROPE'S CONTRIBUTION TO PROMOTE WORLDWIDE GROWTH

1. Close coordination of economic policies within Europe, and within the Euro-11 framework in particular, to promote our own growth.
2. Close coordination between Europe and the United States on economic policy, and a political initiative towards Japan on structural reform to maintain growth and preserve international monetary stability.
3. A European approach to American authorities to obtain rapid ratification of the IMF's quotas increase. Europe must also be ready to provide exceptional financial resources within a multilateral framework so as to maintain the IMF's ability to act.
4. Extension of the euro area of monetary stability:
   - by having the other countries of the European Union join ERM2 as soon as they deem it possible
   - and through consultation with countries applying for accession. The euro could serve as a benchmark for the

countries that made the most progress towards convergence.
5. Encouragement for implementation of reforms identified as
necessary in Russia, via the IMF and through more effective
European assistance (TACIS targeting).

Making European assistance (TACIS) more effective through
better targeting.

II. BUILDING A NEW BRETTON WOODS ARRANGEMENT

6. Instituting genuine political governance of the IMF, including voting on strategic choices.

This will mean transforming the Interim Committee into a
Council, as called for in the IMF's Articles of Agreement so that it
becomes an authentic decision-making body that meets on a
more regular basis.
    The Ministers should also debate the social consequences of
adjustment plans. The World Bank has a key role to play in this
area.

7. More frequent consultation between industrialized countries
and emerging countries.

The IMF Council proposed above will be the appropriate forum
for such consultation, since the 24 ministers sitting on it will
represent constituencies covering all countries.

8. A sound and transparent international financial system.

This will require:

– better prudential supervision of financial institutions,
  whether or not they are banks, in all financial centres;
– enhanced gathering and disclosure of information. The
  INIF should work for the adoption of a Disclosure
  Charter for private institutions;
– enforcement of international rules in off-shore centres.

9. More progressive and orderly opening up to global financial
markets in emerging countries.

Without challenging the principle of free movement of capital, a more progressive approach is called for, which takes into account the quality of financial infrastructures in each country and the nature of capital flows.

In case of severe instability, countries that have already deregulated capital movements should be able to use a 'financial safeguard clause', in consultation with the IMF.

10. Maintaining the flow of Official Development Assistance.

The Paris Club must strengthen its co-ordination and work to tailor its action to each emerging country's individual situation.

It is absolutely necessary that the richest countries maintain high levels of Official Development Assistance to attenuate the impact of volatile private capital flows in developing countries.

11. A crisis-solving partnership in which the private sector works alongside the IMF and the Paris Club in finding negotiated solutions.

Regional consultation mechanisms need to be put in place.

12. Europe's role in international monetary co-operation.

Europe will have greater responsibilities on the international scene with the changeover to the euro. The euro will be a foundation for promoting international monetary stability through coordinated macroeconomic and foreign exchange policies.

European countries will have to organize themselves quickly to define methods for elaborating their positions and expressing them at international level. Positions concerning the euro should henceforward be discussed within the Euro-11 framework.

The French government suggests that the ideas in this paper be used as a basis for the positions Europe will express at sessions taking place during the upcoming Annual Meetings of the IMF and the World Bank.

FACING INTERNATIONAL INSTABILITY: FOR A EUROPEAN INITIATIVE

Up until now, the European Union has been mainly concerned with internal aspects of the changeover to the euro, but it must now shoulder the responsibilities that come with its weight in the world economy. The economic weight of the euro area will be comparable to that of the United States. The current economic and financial environment makes such a step all the more necessary.

As massive outflows of foreign capital indiscriminately affect financial markets in most emerging countries, the leading players in the international financial community must act together to limit the impact of irrational capital movements. The European Union must now fully participate in the resolution of the current crisis, in particular:

- by being ready to adapt its macro-economic policies in collaboration with the United States and Japan in order to maintain growth and international monetary stability;
- by acting vigorously so that the IMF obtains the resources it needs to deal with the crisis, including contributing extra resources if necessary;
- by focusing its development and transition aid, along with its technical assistance, on the structural and social weaknesses revealed by the crisis.

Europe has based its economic development on a balance between market forces and public responsibilities. Experience has taught us that rules and institutions are needed for smoothly operating markets, and especially financial markets. This experience should enable Europe to play a decisive role in elaborating a new international monetary and financial system based on:

- stronger political governance of international financial institutions, such as the IMF,
- more frequent consultation between industrialized countries and emerging countries;
- a more progressive and orderly approach to liberalizing financial markets;
- mechanisms for cooperative crisis management involving the private sector.

To meet these objectives, the European Union and the euro area will also have to decide quickly how they are to be represented on the international economic stage.

I. IN THE SHORT TERM, EUROPE MUST HELP TO REDRESS THE INTERNATIONAL ECONOMIC AND FINANCIAL SITUATION

I.1. Europe, or more specifically the euro area, has followed a policy of convergence and is now reaping the benefits, such as very low inflation and renewed growth. International organizations forecast that the euro area will enjoy the strongest growth among the industrialized economies in 1999. The deterioration of the international economic and financial environment, however, is a threat to continued non-inflationary job-creating growth in Europe and other areas.

Under these circumstances, each of the world's leading economic areas should do its part to boost world demand and therefore persistently sluggish demand in Japan is a cause for grave concern. France proposes undertaking a concerted European initiative to express to Japanese authorities how much concern the current situation is causing, stressing the urgent need for a rapid and credible implementation of the decisions that have been announced with regard to restructuring the banking sector.

I.2. The fear that the IMF will be short of resources has intensified the pressure on emerging countries, especially in Latin America. The participating European countries must now state their willingness to implement the General Agreements to Borrow, but the real priority now is to implement rapidly IMF's quotas increase and the New Agreements to Borrow. France proposes a concerted European initiative to stress to the American authorities, and especially to Congress, how critical immediate ratification of the IMF's quotas increase has become. Moreover, the Member States of the European Union should be ready to provide immediate exceptional financial resources, shared fairly in a multilateral framework, so as to ensure that the IMF is able to act.

I.3. The European Union currencies should join the new European Exchange Rate Mechanism as soon as the countries concerned deem it possible in order to extend the European area of stability beyond the euro area. Financial and economic stability is also of major importance for the countries applying to join the Union, starting with those most likely to be able to accede to the Union in coming years. The euro could be a helpful benchmark for the applicants that have made the most progress towards convergence. The French government suggests that the Finance Ministers of the Union start consultations with their colleagues from the countries concerned on these issues.

I.4. Europe must encourage Russia to carry out the economic reforms necessary for its development. We know what is required and what must be vigorously pursued: macro-economic stabilization, which means solving the fiscal problem through better tax collection, building a more effective government without overlooking its social responsibilities, restructuring the banking system and maintaining openness to the world.

The IMF must play a central role, in conjunction with the EBRD and others, in implementing urgent action. But Russia must also come up with a long-term political strategy for its recovery. It must resume constructive dialogue with the international community, which is needed to make international assistance more effective. Europe must be ready today to provide coordinated support for Russian authorities to back them in their efforts. In particular, TACIS programme funding must be targeted precisely and used effectively to enhance the rule of law, taxation and banking supervision.

The Member States of the European Union taken together are the leading shareholders in international organizations and they should continue to support these institutions, since they provide the means for organizing international solidarity in favour of developing countries. However, the European countries must also act as vigilant shareholders in International Institutions, as this is where we may have failed to play our full role in the past. Today, the Bretton Woods Institutions at the heart of the International monetary and financial system need to be given a new impetus through enhanced political legitimacy and a review of the practical procedures for intervention. This leads the French Government to propose a revamping of the existing international financial structures to create a 'new Bretton Woods arrangement' that we intend to be more legitimate and more effective.

II. REFORM OF THE INTERNATIONAL MONETARY AND FINANCIAL SYSTEM IS NOW A PRIORITY

Successive international financial crises in recent years have shown us that if the international financial system is to contribute to growth and development, we need regulations and institutions tailored to today's global economy. Massive private capital inflows helped to finance developing countries' economies, and this trend should be encouraged, especially as there is an unfortunate tendency towards smaller flows of Official Development Assistance from the richest countries. However, private capital can also have destabilizing effects and it is up to us to prevent this from happening.

II.1. We must endow international financial institutions with genuine political legitimacy.

A global economy needs strong and legitimate institutions that are able to enforce the international economic and financial ground rules and deal with emergencies. The French Government feels that the institutional framework of the world's financial system needs to be given greater political strength.

The IMF must be endorsed as the cornerstone of the international financial edifice. This will mean granting a bigger role to the Interim Committee to make it a genuine 'Council', as called for in the IMF's Articles of Agreement, so that it can become a real decision-making body. The Ministers of Finance representing the entire international community, including developing countries, should vote on matters concerning the IMF's strategic choices, including its major financial commitments. The Council should meet more frequently than the Interim Committee currently does. Of course, the operational implementation of guidelines will still be up to the Executive Board.

The World Bank should make its action for development more effective. Greater understanding of international institutions' programmes will be achieved by paying more attention to the social impact of adjustment plans. Special support measures should be aimed at the most vulnerable population categories. The coordination between the Development Committee and the IMF Council will have to be more effective so that these issues are actually discussed in the Ministers' meetings.

II.2. More thorough consultation between industrialized countries and emerging countries is needed.

Consultation between industrialized countries and emerging countries should be developed as the role of the latter in the world economy is growing and more especially as they have been affected by each recent financial crisis. If it is to develop, this consultation needs an organized forum, which will be provided by the IMF Council. The 24 Ministers sitting on the Council should represent all countries, as suggested earlier. Even though they may be useful for emergency meetings, the other initiatives put forward for organizing consultations do not seem appropriate for the longer term, since they do not ensure representation for all players concerned.

II.3. The international financial system needs to be made stronger and more transparent.

Recent crisis have often stemmed from faulty assessment of financial risk. This led to excessive capital inflows to some emerging economies, followed by equally excessive withdrawals.

Volatile capital movements are a destabilizing factor that impedes growth and the allocation of resources. New worldwide financial regulations are called for to improve the allocation of capital available from international markets and to prevent or, when necessary, to manage financial crises.

● First, an effort must be made to improve financial transparency in the public and private spheres, as well as within international financial institutions, to ensure smoother operation of markets and to deter excessive risk-taking by financial institutions. Existing economic and financial information must be improved to ensure that governments and private sector investors have continuing access to reliable information.

The private sector must be urged to use this information to develop sounder analysis of financial risk. It must also be urged to apply the principle of transparency in its own dealings by disclosing detailed information to public institutions. For this purpose, the French Government proposes that the IMF start work on a Disclosure Charter for private institutions, which the Member States could transpose into their domestic legislation.

The principles should apply not only to banks, but to other institutions in the financial sector as well, such as insurance companies, pension funds and mutual funds. Moreover, tighter supervision of the non-bank financial sector is also needed, especially as pension funds and investment funds own a growing share of the emerging countries' public and private debt.

● Secondly, international financial institutions must work to promote modern financial, legal and social infrastructures in developing countries. As a preliminary step towards stronger infrastructures, international standards for supervision and prudential regulation must be developed and implemented. The Basle Committee and the IMF have an important role to play in this matter. Their respective attributions, and the procedures for coordinating their work with that of the World Bank, must be clearly defined as soon as possible.

● Finally, the enforcement of international financial rules in off-shore centres must become a priority for international action. Every financial centre should comply with rules governing transparency, international cooperation and supervision. This means inter alia providing detailed information on banking transactions to the BIS.

II.4. A progressive and orderly approach to opening markets up to international capital is called for.

A progressive and orderly approach to opening markets up to international capital under the aegis of the IMF should be recommended. We must fight ideas that lead to financial isolation, such as debt repayment moratoria or a sudden return to currency controls. Such moves inflict heavy and lasting damage on countries that adopt them. Similarly, financial difficulties must not be used as an excuse for putting up trade barriers. In this regard, the World Trade Organization has an important role to play. On the other hand, it is important to define how liberalization can be carried out in an orderly fashion.

● The degree of openness in a country's economy should be consistent with the quality of its financial infrastructures.

Orderly opening to international capital should promote inflows of long-term capital and foreign direct investment. The IMF's prerogatives should be extended to the Financial Sector and the Capital Account so that it can filfil its surveillance role in this area. Countries should be able to use specific regulatory or tax measures in cooperation with the IMF to curb destabilizing capital flows.

● In case of severe instability stemming from destabilizing movements of short-term capital, countries that have already deregulated capital movements should be able to use special regulatory or tax measures under the financial escape clause, as provided for in the IMF Articles of Agreement. Such measures must be temporary and their implementation must comply with specific legal rules. The measures must also protect the interests of non-resident investors and be implemented in cooperation with the International Monetary Fund.

● In their capacity as creditors, the European countries are the leading members of the Paris Club. France would like the Paris Club to tailor its action to each emerging country's individual situation and to strengthen its coordinating role to deal with the new international financial environment.

● Europe is the leading provider of Official Development Assistance, accounting for 56 per cent of the worldwide total. This means it has a key role to play in preventing crises in developing countries by using its assistance as an instrument for structural and social reform. It is essential to maintain high levels of Official Development Assistance, in addition to private capital, which has shown how volatile it can be.

The World Bank and the multilateral development banks must do more to strengthen development infrastructures. They should be encouraged to cooperate closely with non-governmental organizations.

II.5. Crisis management calls for special tools.

Recent financial crises have shown that the private sector can underestimate risks in emerging countries. In consequence, it must be made to shoulder the responsibility for its actions, through informal coordination with international organizations, which will provide the appropriate signals when warranted, and through a financial contribution towards solving the crises.

France proposes that the private sector should be more directly involved in crisis management, alongside the IMF and the Paris Club, and within a framework of negotiated solutions. Regional consultative mechanisms, bringing together the IMF, the Paris Club, the national authorities of the countries in the region and their main private creditors, should be set up with the aim of preventing and managing crises.

III. BETTER INTERNATIONAL MONETARY BALANCE MUST BE SOUGHT

III.1. The euro must be used as a foundation for promoting international monetary stability, which will require intense international coordination of macro-economic and foreign exchange policies. This will provide the basis for a more satisfactory monetary balance in the world as a whole, limiting excessive swings in exchange rates and preventing major distortions with regard to economic fundamentals. Closer coordination is especially critical at a time when a new international currency is being introduced into an unstable financial environment.

Regional monetary unions should be encouraged, following the European example, which has shown how important it is to build a macro-economic framework that promotes growth.

III.2. In the run-up to the introduction of the single currency, representation of the euro area must be organized quickly, effectively and pragmatically, so that it can contribute to smooth international monetary relations and so that Europe's weight in the world economy is given concrete expression. The role of the Euro-11 should be enhanced to facilitate coordination on matters of special concern for the 11 EMU countries in their preparations for international meetings. The Euro should arrive at a coordinated position on all issues relating to the euro in advance of IMF or G7 meetings, for example. France is ready to respect the discipline that this would imply, since it would reinforce the impact of our respective actions.

The French government suggests that the ideas in this paper be used as a basis for the positions Europe will express at sessions taking place during the upcoming Annual Meetings of the IMF and the World Bank.

B. EXTERNAL REPRESENTATION OF THE EURO-ZONE PROPOSALS BY JEAN-JACQUES VISEUR, MINISTER OF FINANCE OF BELGIUM

Meeting of the enlarged Euro-11-group Vienna, Saturday 26 September 1998

I. Role of the Commission

1. A distinction has to the made between its role in the preparation of the decision-making proposals in accordance with article 109(4) and its role in the representation itself, keeping in mind that it was agreed in Luxemburg that *'the Commission will be involved in external representation to the extent required to perform the role assigned to it by the Treaty'*.

II. External representation: general principles

2. The procedure provided for in article 109(4) would apply for positions to be taken in international fora; in the other cases, one should seek pragmatic formulas in order to reach common understandings.
3. A parallelism has to be ensured between the representation of the monetary pole and the economic pole of the euro-zone. Therefore, at top level, the euro-zone should be represented by the Presidency of the ECB and the Presidency of the Euro-11-group, in association with the Commission. The precise modalities of this representation have to be specified according to the fora and circumstances (G7, IMF, missions abroad).
4. The positions shall, as a rule, be prepared within the Economic and Financial Committee on the basis of a proposal by the Commission.
5. A special procedure will have to be established to solve the problem of representation in situations of urgency.
6. It could be appropriate to reflect on the possibility to

strengthen the representation of the euro by entrusting it to a President of the Euro-11-group, who would be designated by his colleagues for a period of specified or unspecified duration. This solution would offer more continuity to the representation of the 'economic pole' at international level. It would also allow to rebalance the relationship between that pole and the monetary pole represented by the President of the ECB. The President of the Euro-11-group could also be assisted by a Vice-President. When 'small' countries hold the presidency, 'large' countries would hold the Vice-Presidency, and vice-versa. The balance in the representation between the two groups of countries would thereby be secured. An adequate cooperation would have to be found between the President of the Euro-11-group designated in this manner and the President of the Council.

III. External representation at the G7-Finance

7. Ideally, the President of the ECB and the President of Euro-11-group would represent the euro-zone at the G7-Finance, in association with the European Commissioner in charge of economic and monetary issues. This form of representation would be in line with the situation prevailing in the G7 at the level of heads of states and governments.

8. A fallback position could be articulated around point II.6. If the President of the Euro-11-group is the Minister of Finance of a G7-country, he would represent the euro-zone at the G7-Finance with a clearly-defined mandate, if the Presidency of the Euro-11-group is held by a 'small' country, the Vice-President of the Euro-11-group would attend the G7-Finance meetings on behalf of the euro-zone. If this formula is adopted, its efficiency should be examined sooner rather than later.

9. Whatever the solution chosen, representatives of the euro-zone at the G7-Finance will have to be mandated.

IV. Representation at IMF level

10. One has to distinguish between short-term requirements and possible medium-term ambitions for the representation of the euro at the IMF.

11. At the Executive board, the euro-zone could be represented by an observer from the ECB and a representative from the Presidency of the Euro-11-group, with a clear mandate.
12. The procedure for defining the mandates has to be specified. The Commission will have a role to play in this.
13. At the level of the Interim Committee, the euro-zone should be represented by the President of the Euro-11-group, the President of the ECB and the European Commissioner concerned.

V. Missions abroad

14. The circumstances that call for a representation of both poles of the euro-zone will have to be determined.
15. When only the economic pole is concerned, the general rule could be to organize missions of the Presidency of the Euro-11, in association with the Commission and with the assistance of the Chairman of the Economic and Financial Committee and, if the idea should be adopted, the Vice-President of the Euro-11-group.

APPENDIX 6: EUROPEAN COMMISSION, FINANCIAL SERVICES: IMPLEMENTING THE FRAMEWORK FOR FINANCIAL MARKETS: ACTION PLAN, BRUSSELS, MAY 1999

FINANCIAL SERVICES: IMPLEMENTING THE FRAMEWORK FOR FINANCIAL MARKETS: ACTION PLAN

FINANCIAL SERVICES ACTION PLAN

Based on the extensive consultations around the Commission's Framework for Action, the following plan confirms the work that must be set in hand to reap the full benefits of the euro and ensure continued stability and competitiveness of EU financial markets. The future Commission will need to decide conditions under which different actions will be taken forward. The optimal timeframe reflects the priorities which have emerged from discussions in the FSPG, with the European Parliament and with other interested parties.

The European Parliament and the Council are invited to endorse the content and urgency of the Financial Services Action Plan. The European Parliament and the Council are also invited to make every effort to ensure rapid agreement and implementation of the individual legislative measures. Commitments are also called for to ensure the investment of political will and concentration of the necessary resources to achieve the ambitious deadlines that are set in response to the changing demands of the market, the need to safeguard consumer interests and to enhance the competitiveness of EU industry as a whole.

Three indications of priority have been set for each measure, identified in the Action Plan:

Priority 1 actions:

There is broad consensus that these actions call for immediate attention. These measures are crucial to realization of the full benefits of the euro and to ensuring the competitiveness of the Union's financial services sector and industry whilst safeguarding consumer interests.

- Where legislative proposals are already on the table European Parliament and Council are invited to take all steps necessary to secure the maximum possible agreement before January 1, 2000.
- The Commission confirms that where an initiative is required, it will come forward with the necessary action without delay.
- Based on any necessary preparatory work by the Commission, the Council and European Parliament are invited to ensure rapid agreement within two years, or at the latest by the end of the euro-transitional period, and to expedite implementation of agreed measures without delay.

Priority 2 actions:

The Commission regards these priorities as important to the functioning of the Single Market for Financial Services – in particular, by amending existing legislation or adapting present structures to meet new challenges.

Priority 3 actions:

These actions concern important areas where a clear and general consensus exists that new work should be set in hand with a view to finalizing a coherent policy by the end of the euro-transitional period.

STRATEGIC OBJECTIVE 1
A single EU wholesale market

Speedy adoption and implementation of the following actions[12] in order to achieve this strategic objective will:

- enable corporate issuers to raise finance on competitive terms on an EU-wide basis;
- provide investors and intermediaries with access to all markets from single point-of-entry;
- allow investment service providers to offer their services on a cross-border basis without encountering unnecessary hindrances or administrative or legal barriers;
- establish a sound and well integrated prudential framework within which asset managers can put funds at their disposal to their most productive use;
- create a climate of legal certainty so that securities trades and settlement are safe from unnecessary counterparty risk.

---

12 The proposed actions are structured in accordance with the presentation in the introductory paper

Raising capital on an EU-wide basis:

Action	Priority	Objective	Actors	Optimal Timeframe
Upgrade the Directives on Prospectuses through a possible legislative amendment	1	Overcoming obstacles to the effective mutual recognition of prospectuses, so that a prospectus or offer document approved in one Member state will be accepted in all. In addition, incorporating 'shelf registration' will provide for easier access to capital markets on the basis of streamlined prospectuses, derived from annual accounts.	Commission, building upon work by FESCO[13]	For issue by mid 2000 Adoption: 2002
Update the Directive on Regular Reporting (82/121/EEC)	3	More frequent and better quality information will enhance market confidence and attract capital.	Commission, following consultation with FESCO and the market	Launch consultation by mid 2000 Proposal: 2001 Adoption: 2002

Establishing a common legal framework for integrated securities and derivatives markets:

Action	Priority	Objective	Actors	Optimal Timeframe
Issue a Commission Communication on distinction between 'sophisticated' investors and retail investors	1	Summary of common interpretation of use of investor protection rules, including conduct of business rules to determine conditions under which host country business rules apply to cross-border securities transactions.	Commission, building upon work by FESCO and after consultation with Member States	Draft for issue by end 1999
Directive to address market manipulation	2	Enhance market integrity by reducing the possibility for institutional investors and intermediaries to rig markets. Set common disciplines for trading floors to enhance investor confidence in an embryonic single securities market.	Commission: after consultation with Member States and markets	Proposal by end 2000 Adoption: 2003
Green Paper on upgrading the ISD	2	Wide-ranging review of ISD as basis for integrated and efficient market for investment services. Tackle remaining obstacles to market access for brokers/dealers, obstacles to remote membership, and restrictions on trading in T-bonds. Address new regulatory challenges such as Alternative Trading systems.	Commission	Publish Green Paper: mid-2000

13   Forum of European Securities Commissions

Towards a single set of financial statements for listed companies:

Action	Priority	Objective	Actors	Optimal Timeframe
Amend the 4th and 7th Company Law Directives to allow fair value accounting	2	Enabling European companies to account for certain financial assets at fair value, in accordance with International Accounting Standards.	Commission, Council, EP	Proposal autumn-99 Adoption: 2001
Commission Communication updating the EU accounting strategy	1	Map out strategy for enhancing comparability of financial reports issued by listed EU companies. based on combination of EU accounting Directives and financial statements issued in accordance with agreed international accounting standards. Strategy should prefigure mechanism for vetting international benchmark standards so that these can be used (with no national variations) by EU listed companies.	Commission	For issue by end-99
Modernization of the accounting provisions of the 4th and 7th Company Law Directives	2	Bringing the 4th and 7th Directives in line with the needs of the Single market and to take into account developments in international accounting standard-setting.	Commission, Council, EP	Proposal end-2000 Adoption: 2002
Commission Recommendation on EU auditing practices	2	Upgrading the quality of statutory audits in the EU by recommending specific measures in the areas of quality assurance and auditing standards.	Commission	For issue by end-99

Containing systemic risk in securities settlement:

Action	Priority	Objective	Actors	Optimal Timeframe
Implementation of the Settlement Finality Directive	1	Common and coherent application of the Directive throughout the EU is important for a smooth functioning of systems.	Member States	Commission to continue monitoring of implementation in a working Group. Commission report to Council end 2002
Directive on cross-border use of collateral	1	Legal certainty as regards validity and enforceability of collateral provided to back cross-border securities transactions.	Commission in consultation with Member States and market experts	Launch consultation autumn-99: proposal end-2000. Adoption: 2003

Towards a secure and transparent environment for cross-border restructuring:

Action	Priority	Objective	Actors	Optimal Timeframe
Political agreement of the proposed directive on Take Over Bids	1	Create EU-wide clarity and transparency in respect of legal issues to be settled in event of take-over bid. Prevent pattern of EU corporate restructuring from being distorted by arbitrary differences in governance and management cultures.	Council, EP	Mid-99 Adoption: 2000
Political agreement on the European Company Statute	1	Create optional legal structure to facilitate companies to place pan-European operations on a rationalised single legal umbrella. Within this context clarify scope for participation by employees – thereby create further common ground in respect of corporate governance practices.	Council, EP	Mid-1999 Adoption: 2000
Review of EU corporate governance practices	3	Identification of legal or administrative barriers and resulting differences in corporate governance regimes.	Commission, Member States, markets	Launch review early 2000
Amend the 10th Company Law Directive	3	Create the possibility for companies to conduct cross-border mergers.	Commission	Proposal in autumn 1999 Adoption: 2002
14th Company Law Directive	3	Allow companies to transfer their corporate seat to another Member State.	Commission	Proposal in autumn 1999 Adoption: 2002

A Single Market which works for investors:

Action	Priority	Objective	Actors	Optimal Timeframe
Commission Communication on Funded Pension Schemes	1	Consultation on prudential framework for second-pillar pension fund schemes to protect beneficiary rights through stringent prudential safeguards and rigorous supervision.	Commission	Issue by May 1999
Political agreement on the proposed directives on UCITS	1	Proposal 1 will remove barriers to cross-border marketing of units of collective investment by widening assets in which funds can invest. Proposal 2 would provide a European passport for management companies, and widen the activities which they are allowed to undertake (also be authorized to provide individual portfolio management services).	Council, EP	End-1999 Adoption: 2000
Directive on the prudential supervision of pension funds	1	Following the policy outlined in its Communication, the Commission will propose a Directive on the prudential supervision of pension funds. It will take into account the diversity of pension funds currently operating in the EU and will cover authorization, reporting, fit and proper criteria and rules on liabilities and investments.	Commission	Proposal: Mid 2000 Adoption: 2002

STRATEGIC OBJECTIVE 2
Open and secure retail markets

Concerted efforts by EU institutions and all interested parties, along the lines listed below, are needed to:

- Equip consumers with the necessary instruments (information) and safeguards (clear rights and effective dispute settlement) to permit their full and active participation in the single financial market;
- Identify and roll back unjustified insistence on non-harmonized consumer-business rules as an obstacle to cross-border provision of services;

- Promote the emergence of effective mechanisms for overcoming fault in the single retail financial market which have their origin in differences in private law;
- Create legal conditions in which new distribution channels and distance technologies can be put to work on a pan-European scale;
- Encourage the emergence of cost-effective and secure payment systems which enable citizens to effect small-value cross-border payments without incurring exorbitant charges.

Action	Priority	Objective	Actors	Optimal Timeframe
Political agreement on proposal for a Directive on the Distance Selling of Financial Services	1	Proposal aims to bring about convergence of rules on business-to-consumer marketing and sales techniques. This will limit exposure of consumers to undesirable marketing techniques (inertia and pressure-selling) through inclusion of appropriate provisions (generous right of withdrawal rights, prohibitions). Once in place, distance selling via remote technologies should be free from this category of impediment.	Council, EP	End 99 Adoption: 2000
Commission communication codifying clear and comprehensible information for purchasers	2	Establish over-arching view of basic information requirements consumers need in order to assess credential of (cross-border) service suppliers, security/performance of services offered by latter (plus redress). Examine extent to which these requirements are complied for range of retail financial services.	Commission, Member States	Review to begin end 99: Communication: mid 2000
Recommendation to support best practice in respect of information provision (mortgage credit)	1	Building on discussions in Consumer Dialogue, the Commission will publish a communication to endorse understanding in respect of information to be provided in event of cross-border provision of mortgage credit services. Commission involvement in monitoring of compliance.	Commission, bank and consumer representatives	For issue by end-99

Action	Priority	Objective	Actors	Optimal Timeframe
Commission report on substantive differences between national arrangements relating to consumer-business transactions	3	The report will catalogue obstacles to cross-border business-to-consumer transactions for relevant financial services. This will provide analysis of whether, how and why host-country consumer rules apply and determine conditions under which equivalence of national rules does/does not exist. Provide objective and empirical basis for discussion with MS and EP on how to facilitate cross-border provision of retail financial services without jeopardising consumer safeguards.	Commission, Member States	Review to begin autumn-99: status report – mid-2000: Discussions with Council, EP to begin end-2000
Interpretative Communication on the freedom to provide services and the general good in insurance	2	Greater legal certainty and clarity for Member States, insurance undertakings and citizens, contributing to the creation of the single market.	Commission	For issue by: summer-99
Proposal for amendment of Insurance Intermediaries Directive	2	Facilitation of the free provision of services by insurance intermediaries and enhanced consumer protection by updating and introducing safeguards on professionalism and competence. By creating stringent common ground-rules for intermediaries can facilitate placing on market of insurance premia by partner country underwriters.	Commission (IC[14])	Proposal mid-2000 Adoption: 2002
Commission Communication for a single market for payments	2	Will provide a road-map for public and private agencies with a role to play in ensuring that secure and cost-effective retail payments can be effected on a cross-border basis. At present, such transactions incur charges which are much higher in average than those within domestic payments systems – a situation which is untenable within a single currency zone. The Communication will focus heavily on credit transfers but will also address card payments, cheques and cash.	Commission, ESCB, market, consumers	For issue by summer 1999
Commission Action Plan to prevent fraud and counterfeiting and payment systems	2	Agree on ways to prevent fraud, e.g. in organizing the exchange of data or increasing the security of technical systems.	Commission industry users and Member States	Communication for issue by: end-1999
Commission green paper on an e-commerce policy for financial services	1	A clear and coherent policy for the whole financial sector, which takes account of existing rules, wider international developments, and technological progress.	Commission	For issue by: mid-2000

STRATEGIC OBJECTIVE 3

State-of-the-art prudential rules and supervision

Urgent headway must be made in order to:

- Eliminate any lacunae in EU prudential framework, arising from new forms of financial business or globalization, as a matter of utmost urgency.
- Set rigorous and appropriate standards so that the EU banking sector can successfully manage intensification of competitive pressures.

- Contribute to the developing of EU supervisory structures which can sustain stability and confidence in an era of changing market structures and globalisation.
- Develop a regulatory and supervisory approach which will serve as the basis for successful enlargement.
- Enable the EU to assume a key role in setting high global standards for regulation and supervision, including financial conglomerates.

Action	Priority	Objective	Actors	Optimal Timeframe
Adopt the proposed directive on the winding-up and liquidation of insurance undertakings	1	Provide a coherent legal framework for the winding-up and liquidation of insurance companies in the single market through the mutual recognition of proceedings and the principles of unity, universality, publicity and non-discrimination.	Council, EP	New first reading in EP end 1999 Political agreement as soon as possible Adoption: 2001
Adopt the proposed directive on the winding-up and liquidation of banks	1	Common rules on winding-up and liquidation will establish common principles for procedures to be followed in event of bank insolvency, identify responsible authority. As such will safeguard against continued activities by insolvent institutions which could represent source of counterpart risk.	Council, EP	Common position: end-99 Adoption: 2001
Adopt the proposal for an Electronic Money directive	1	Ensure market access and adequate regulation of e-money providers: clarify the prudential rules under which institutions other than traditional credit institutions can provide e-money services. Enable provision of this activity on cross-border basis.	Council, EP	Common position: autumn 99 Adoption: 2000
Amendment of the money laundering directive	1	Combat fraud and money laundering in the financial system to widen definition of predicate offences and to extend reporting ('suspicious transactions') requirements to relevant non-financial professions.	Commission	Proposal mid 1999 Adoption: 2000

Action	Priority	Objective	Actors	Optimal Timeframe
Commission Recommendation on disclosure of financial instruments	2	Enhanced disclosure of the activities of banks and other financial institutions to allow investors to take informed decisions, and to foster market transparency and discipline as a complement to prudential supervision.	Commission	Communication mid 1999
Amend the directives governing the capital framework for banks and investment firms	2	Work on a review of the bank capital framework to reflect market developments is running in parallel with that of the G-10 Basle Committee on Banking Supervision. This work is expected to result in a overhaul of the EU's bank and investment capital framework.	Commission (BAC, HLSS[15]) Member States, markets	Proposal for directive: spring 2000, pending developments in Basle Adoption: 2002

GENERAL OBJECTIVE
Wider conditions for an optimal single financial market

- Addressing disparities in tax treatment

- An efficient and transparent legal system for corporate governance

Action	Priority	Objective	Actors	Optimal Timeframe
Adopt a Directive on Savings Tax	1	The objective of the proposal is to remove disparities in tax treatment of private savings to complement the removal of obstacles to the free movement of capital and financial services will benefit the financial sector.	Council	Political agreement by November 1999 Adoption: 2000
Implementation of the December 1997 Code of Conduct on business taxation	1	Counter harmful tax competition which may significantly affect the location of business activity in the Union.	Commission, Member States, markets	Discussions in Tax Policy Group
Review of taxation of financial service products	3	Lower costs and remove disincentives for cross-border business	Commission, Member States, markets	Discussions in Tax Policy Group
Commission proposals for co-ordination of the tax arrangements governing supplementary pensions	2	Building on discussions in Tax Policy Group, proposal for legislative action will be prepared to address tax treatment of cross-border contributions of migrant workers to supplementary pension funds. Will serve as a contribution to labour mobility.	Commission	Proposals end-99 Adoption: 2002

15   Banking Advisory Committee, *High Level Securities*

Action	Priority	Objective	Actors	Optimal Timeframe
Review of EU corporate governance practices	3	Identification of legal or administrative barriers and resulting differences in corporate governance regimes.	Commission, Member States, markets	Launch review early 2000
Amend the solvency margin requirements in the insurance directives	3	Protection of consumers in the single market by ensuring that insurance undertakings have adequate capital requirements in relation to the nature of their risks.	Commission (IC), Member States, markets	Proposal for directive: mid-2000 Adoption: 2003
Proposal to amend the insurance directives and the ISD to permit information exchange with third countries	3	Basis for international exchange of information to underpin financial stability.	Commission	Proposal autumn 1999 Adoption: 2001
Development of prudential rules for financial conglomerates following the recommendations of the 'Joint Forum'.	1	Addressing loopholes in the present sectoral legislation and additional prudential risks to ensure sound supervisory arrangements.	Commission: BAC/IC/HLSS, Member States, supervisors and markets	Proposal: end-2000 Adoption: 2002
Creation of a Securities Committee	2	A formal regulatory committee in this field will contribute to the elaboration of EU regulation in the securities area. Requires willingness on part of EU institutions to agree an appropriate comitology procedure.	Commission, Council, EP	Proposal: end 2000 Adoption: 2002

APPENDIX 7: CO-ORDINATED PUBLIC DEBT ISSUANCE IN THE EURO AREA – REPORT OF THE GIOVANNINI GROUP, BRUSSELS, 8 NOVEMBER 2000

CO-ORDINATED PUBLIC DEBT ISSUANCE IN THE EURO AREA REPORT OF THE GIOVANNINI GROUP

Executive Summary

The introduction of the euro has created the conditions for a substantially more integrated euro-area public debt marker. A considerable harmonization of national market conventions has already been achieved but important differences remain in the issuance techniques and instruments of the national debt agencies. These differences are a source of market fragmentation, evidence of which is to be found in euro-area yield spreads, where some issuers are obliged to offer a premium greater than would seem to be justified by credit risk. Accordingly, greater coordination in debt issuance would suggest scope for efficiency gains to the extent that market fragmentation would be reduced.

The extent to which more co-ordinated debt issuance could reduce market fragmentation would depend upon the degree of coordination involved. The Group considered four hypotheses for tighter coordination in debt issuance. While not exhaustive, these hypotheses cover the spectrum of possible arrangements, ranging from a limited extension of current procedures to the most advanced form of coordination involving the establishment of a single benchmark issuer for the euro area as a whole. In assessing the four hypotheses, the Group distinguished between looser coordination arrangements which would be agreed outside the framework of the Treaty and more advanced arrangements that would be likely to require legal or institutional changes.

The views of the Group on the benefits of more coordinated debt issuance were mixed. Some pointed to liquidity premia and problems of deliverability into futures contracts, as evidence that decentralized issuance is a source of inefficiency in the functioning of the euro-area market. Others argued that the market is still young in terms of its functioning and that spreads are not sufficiently large or volatile to cause any great concern. Moreover, it was argued that any proposal requiring significant and time-consuming change would face scepticism in markets that are evolving so rapidly, and consequently priority should be given to the transparency and predictability of issuance and to improving the existing market infrastructure. Coordination involving a joint or single debt instrument was not regarded as a practical option for the euro area as a whole. However, it was agreed that such arrangements could benefit smaller Member States that have limited issuance and that are currently paying a liquidity premium on their debt.

The Group acknowledged that the pace of structural change in euro-area financial markets means that the context for assessing the merits of coordinated public debt issuance may change significantly in the coming years. Accordingly, there will be a need to keep the topic under review and, if necessary, to update the analysis presented in this report.

1. Introduction

1.1 The introduction of the euro on 1 January 1999 created the conditions for a substantially more integrated public debt market in the euro area. From the outset, the euro-area Member States agreed that all new issuance and outstanding stocks of their debt should be re-denominated into euro. The result was to create a euro-area public debt market that is comparable to the US Treasuries market both in terms of size and issuance volume.[1] Unlike the situation in the United States, however, issuance of public debt in the euro area is decentralized under the

---

1.   The euro-area government debt market was about € 3,200 billion in
      1999, equivalent to approximately 52 per cent of GDP.

responsibility of 11 (soon to be 12) separate national agencies. Differences in issuance techniques and instruments between these national agencies continue to fragment the euro-area market.

1.2 There has already been a considerable harmonization of market conventions for euro-area public debt, based on bilateral cooperation between national debt agencies and multilateral cooperation within the Brouhns Group.[2] As part of this effort, national debt agencies have also agreed to exchange information on issuance techniques and have published indicative calendars of issuance. Despite these initiatives, euro-area public debt issuance remains an essentially non-cooperative activity in which issuers compete for investors. While competition in public debt issuance is a positive force for market integration, it can give rise to price distortions and to persistently less favourable terms for the relatively illiquid instruments of smaller issuers. The liquidity premium has already become a concern for smaller euro-area issuers and is likely to grow in importance as budgetary consolidation reduces the supply of public debt across the area as a whole. In light of continued market fragmentation and the associated liquidity premia paid by smaller issuers, there have been calls – echoed in the conclusions of the special Lisbon European Council – for a more coordinated approach to euro-area public debt issuance.

1.3 Arguments in favour of more coordinated public debt issuance focus on improving the efficiency of euro-area financial markets, although some investors and financial intermediaries might see their investment options and arbitrage possibilities reduced. At this stage, smaller euro-area issuers would seem to have most to gain. A more homogenous public debt market would imply greater substitutability between various euro-denominated issues and would thereby help to ease liquidity constraints in the smaller markets. For the benchmark issuers, i.e. Germany and France, the likely gains from further market

---

2. This is the Economic and Financial Committee sub-group on EU Government Bonds and Bills Markets, which is chaired by Gregoire Brouhns of the Belgian Treasury.

integration seem more limited. It is conceivable, therefore, that measures to increase coordination in debt issuance could be confined to a subset of euro-area Member States.

1.4 This report examines four hypotheses for increased coordination in public debt issuance in the euro area, ranging from a limited extension of current procedures to the establishment of a single benchmark issuer for the euro area as a whole. As background to the analysis, Section 2 summarizes recent developments in the euro-area public debt market focusing on the evolution of sovereign yield spreads as evidence of market fragmentation. In Section 3, the rationale for more coordinated debt issuance is explored and, on this basis, Section 4 presents the four progressively advanced hypotheses for coordination. Section 5 reports the views of the Group participants on the need for and the benefits from coordination.

2. Evidence of fragmentation in the euro-area government debt market

2.1 Two main parameters can serve as indicators of the remaining fragmentation in the euro-area public debt market. These are the size and structure of the market and the spreads between sovereign issuers.

● *Size and structure:* At the beginning of 1999, government bond markets in the three main world currencies were of roughly equal size, €2,500–3,000 billion. If the euro-area market is disaggregated, however, it is clear that even the largest segment – the Italian market – is less than half the size of the US market. Excluding the three largest national segments (Italy, Germany and France), the remaining euro-area public debt market constitutes less than ten per cent of the US market (see Table 1). Current trends in issuance diverge sharply between the three markets. Net issuance has been falling in the United States, while there has been a slight increase in euro-area net issuance. Japan has experienced a massive increase in net issuance, making it the world's largest issuer of public debt at the beginning of 2000. These trends are likely to continue for at least the coming two to three years.

Table 1 Size and structure of world government bond markets

Outstanding at end of year	1999	2000	% of Total National Bond Market	Gross	Redem.	Net
Germany	768	793	30	152	127	25
Italy	928	943	78	145	130	15
France	711	758	76	90	43	47
Netherlands	174	182	57	26	18	8
Belgium	195	198	70	25	22	3
Spain	223	239	74	19	3	16
Austria	80	84	54	18	14	4
Finland	44	45	79	4	3	1
Portugal	36	38	76	9	7	2
Ireland	23	21	73	2	4	−2
United Kingdom	466	456	44	12	22	−10
Sweden	94	84	46	3	13	−10
Denmark	82	78	29	8	12	−4
Euro area	3182	3301	46	490	371	119
EU	3824	3919	44	513	418	95
US	2460	2310	15	130	280	−150
Japan	2795	3465	73	700	30	670

Note: Amounts in € bn. For Japan, end of fiscal year, March
Source: European Commission, Merrill Lynch

● *Spreads between Sovereign issuers:* A brief review of secondary market trading in the euro area supports the view that liquidity is increasingly concentrated in the very big

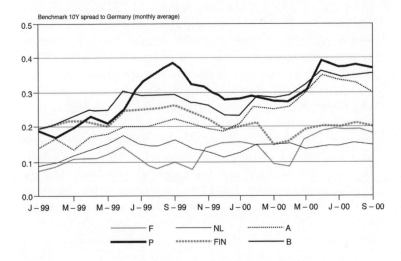

Graph 1 Sovereign yield spreads in bps, January 1999–September 2000

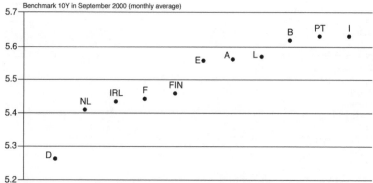

Graph 2   Sovereign yield spreads in bps, September 2000

benchmark issues. As a result, it seems that smaller euro-area Member States with limited issuing volume are obliged to offer a spread over benchmark greater than could be justified by differences in credit rating alone. On the other hand, the benchmark issuers, Germany and to some extent France, enjoy very favourable issuing terms. The impact of the perceived liquidity premium can be seen in the evolution of the spreads vis-à-vis the relevant benchmark over the last two years (see Graphs 1 and 2). As an example, Austrian and Dutch securities used to trade in a very narrow range to German government bonds (+/− 5 basis points) due mainly to the stability of the exchange rate between the three currencies. Although the introduction of the euro implies the elimination of exchange risk, the spreads between the three bonds have widened substantially (by about 20 basis points) against the two smaller issuers. In other Member States such as Finland and Ireland, the picture is more complex. These two issuers have significantly reduced the supply of securities, and the spread to the German bond has been more stable, implying that scarcity rather than liquidity has been the dominant factor.

Smaller Member States with limited financing needs have also seen increased competition from non-sovereign borrowers such as large corporate and pfandbriefe issuers. On a few occasions, corporate multi-currency bond issues have totalled €10 to €15 billion with over €3 billion raised in euro. Some Jumbo Pfandbriefe issues reach €3 to €5 billion in outstanding amount in a continuous fashion that closely resembles the borrowing practice of governments. Freddie Mac, the US Federal Mortgage Agency, has recently implemented plans to issue €5 billion of euro-denominated reference notes on a quarterly basis.

3. Rationale for more coordinated issuance of euro-area public debt

3.1 The rationale for more coordinated issuance of euro-area public debt derives from a view that the current decentralized approach is an obstacle to full market integration. The persistence of significant yield spreads between euro-area sovereign issuers with highly comparable credit standing has been cited as evidence of market fragmentation due to national differences in instruments, primary issuance techniques and liquidity. By addressing these sources of fragmentation, it has been argued that the non credit-risk components of euro-area yield spreads could be substantially reduced.

3.2 While allowing for differences in Member States' perceptions, a number of general arguments can be made in favour of more coordinated public debt issuance in the euro area. These are:

● Market fragmentation would be reduced to the extent that coordination went beyond current arrangements to include harmonization of issuing techniques, standards, procedures and regulations. Harmonization in these areas would tend to increase the homogeneity of euro-denominated public debt and thereby improve market liquidity.

● Coordination based on a common issuing calendar would avoid inefficiencies arising from competition among issuers, e.g. a tendency towards more discretionary issuance so as to avail of temporary improvements in market liquidity. A single issuing calendar would also benefit investors by ensuring steadier and more predictable supply conditions, thereby minimizing the risk of market distortions due to uncertainty and/or clashes in the timing of issuance.

● More advanced coordination based on some form of joint issuance would substantially improve market integration, while creating scope for larger volume issues. Larger issue sizes would enhance liquidity in the cash market and would widen the potential to establish area-wide benchmarks along the yield curve.

● The larger and more liquid debt issues facilitated by coordination based on joint issuance would improve the possibilities of delivery into actively traded futures contracts. By allowing more active interest risk management, successful futures contracts would further enhance liquidity in the cash market in a mutually reinforcing process.

The common theme in these arguments is that coordination offers efficiency gains by creating a more homogenous public debt market that would imply greater substitutability between various euro-denominated issues and would thereby help to ease liquidity constraints, particularly for smaller issuers.

4. Some hypotheses for coordination of euro-area government debt issuance

4.1 The extent to which more coordinated issuance of euro-area public debt can reduce market fragmentation and increase liquidity will, of course, depend upon the degree of coordination involved. In this section, a set of four hypotheses for intensified coordination is considered. The set of hypotheses is not meant to be exhaustive but spans the range of possible coordination arrangements, i.e. from relatively loose coordination on technical issues to a very advanced form of cooperation involving a single debt issuer and single debt instrument for the euro area.

Hypothesis 1: Coordination on technical aspects of debt issuance

4.2 There is already limited coordination between national debt agencies in the euro area in the form of bilateral and multilateral exchanges of information on issuance techniques, instruments and issuing calendars. It is difficult to assess the extent to which these arrangements have reduced market fragmentation. However, current euro-area yield spreads would suggest that there is scope to develop further coordination on technical aspects of debt issuance for some or all of the Member States. In more developed form, this type of coordination could be extended to include agreement on:

- a common issuance calendar to improve efficiency in market supply;
- identical coupon and maturity dates to allow greater comparability between different national issues;
- a common primary dealership system, including similar or overlapping membership, standard terms of remuneration and identical quote sizes, bid/ask spreads; and
- a common real-time clearing and settlement system that ensures a uniform processing of completed transactions thereby facilitating the management of cross-border sales and purchases.

4.3 The extent to which increased coordination on these technical matters would improve the overall liquidity of euro-area public debt is unclear. However, the smaller euro-area issuers could gain substantially in terms of liquidity, resulting in a compression of euro-area yield spreads. The compression of spreads would also depend on the evolution of other spread components such as the derivatives premium. Development of a successful multi-deliverable futures contract among the participating issuers might be possible, although the issuers would need to be broadly of the same credit quality with the basis risk in the contract being influenced by changes in their perceived credit standing. If one issuer were to have a systematically lower credit standing, the futures contract would be likely to become a single deliverable contract.

Hypothesis 2: Creation of a joint debt instrument with several country-specific tranches

4.4 A second hypothesis for coordination in public debt issuance would involve not only common issuance terms and conditions but also a joint debt instrument underpinned by the *several* guarantees of the participants. Guarantees of a several nature would mean that each participant guarantees only its portion (or tranche) of the joint instrument, turning each tranche into an individually distinguishable legal object. As with hypothesis 1, this type of arrangement would appeal mainly to smaller issuers but would probably have a greater effect in reducing yield spreads because the joint instrument would imply greater liquidity. Development of an active futures contract would be facilitated by the use of a joint instrument, so long as issuance were of sufficient volume and regularity to maintain the necessary liquidity in the underlying cash market. The absence of a joint guarantee should ensure no change in the credit risk premium faced individually by the participant issuers, although the credit component of the spread on the joint instrument would be likely to emerge as an average of the issuers' credit spreads.

4.5 A possible approach to this type of issuance would be for a group of (smaller) Member States to issue instruments under a common title but with each instrument guaranteed by the issuing Member State. To create market liquidity, the instruments issued under common title would need to have identical characteristics, e.g. coupons and maturity, and the participant issuers would need to have identical credit ratings, probably AAA. The participant issuers could then agree to re-open issues as they each required. Investors would choose either to buy the instruments in generic form, i.e. under the common title, or they could specify a particular Member State instrument. The intention would be to induce investors to value each Member State instrument more clearly and to emphasize their substitutability. A potential problem would be the small size and limited frequency of issuance under the common title due to the relatively modest borrowing requirements of the smaller Member States with AAA credit rating. However, this problem might be overcome by enriching the issue with an exchange programme or by issuing with identical characteristics to the instrument of a more liquid issuer. The main attractions of this approach would be the possibility of replication in issuance and the fact that the success of the instrument would be decided on the basis of a market assessment.

Hypothesis 3: Creation of a single euro-area debt instrument backed by joint guarantees

4.6 A third hypothesis for coordination in public debt issuance would again involve the creation of a single debt instrument, but backed by the *joint and several* guarantees of participating issuers. Unlike in hypothesis 2, guarantees of a joint and several nature mean that each participant guarantees the totality of the obligations of the joint instrument, thereby making it an indivisible legal object. This would give an investor legal recourse to all the participating issuers, in the case that not all the obligations under the terms and conditions of the single debt instrument have been fully met. The single instrument would facilitate a reduction in liquidity premia and derivatives premia to the extent that issues were sufficiently large and regular and to the extent that there would be delivery into an actively traded futures contract. In this arrangement, however, the cross-default nature of the guarantees would be likely to have an effect on credit spreads if the participant issuers were of different standings. Legal certainty on the structure and nature of the guarantees would be essential to sustain this form of coordination.

4.7 The relatively advanced form of coordination implied by a jointly backed single debt instrument would hold out the prospect of securing a substantial reduction in euro-area yield spreads. On the other hand, the implementation of such an arrangement would be complex for a variety of legal and technical reasons. For example, the cross-default element would need to be made consistent with the Treaty provisions on fiscal discipline, particularly Article 103 which prohibits Member States from being liable for or assuming the commitments of other Member States. Second, the joint guarantee would need to be carefully structured so as not to violate the covenants in existing bond prospectuses and loan agreements. Third, the institutional arrangements needed for issuance of the single instrument – for example, the creation of a body responsible for such issuance – would require special attention. Fourth, the set of participating issuers would probably need to be closed so as to ensure the comparability of different issues over time, thereby precluding any extension of participation in the arrangement over time.

Hypothesis 4: Borrowing by a Community institution for on lending to euro-area Member States

4.8 A fourth hypothesis for coordination in euro-area public debt issuance would involve borrowing by a Community institution for on-lending to Member States.[3] A precedent for such an arrangement exists in that the European Commission borrows on capital markets to fund, for example, its balance of payments facility and to finance programmes of financial assistance for third countries. These borrowings have a AAA rating on the basis of a joint and several guarantee of the 15 Member States (which in turn derives from their Treaty obligations). Clearly, however, an arrangement under which all or a part of the borrowing of euro-area Member States were to be conducted via a Community institution would be materially different from existing activities in terms of the volume of borrowing and the permanence of the borrowing programme.

4.9 The sustainability of a Community guarantee of this type would, as a minimum, necessitate strict adherence by individual participants to the limits on deficits and debts laid down in the Treaty and elaborated in the Stability and Growth Pact. Unlike in hypothesis 3, participation in this arrangement could be extended over time since the comparability of different issues would not be affected. To create benchmark issues, the Community institution responsible for issuance would need to issue at a limited set of maturities and on the basis of a pre-announced calendar to reach targets for size and liquidity as well as the desired level of transparency. For reasons of efficiency, it would seem desirable to avoid issuing debt each time a participating Member State required funding at a particular maturity. Also, a situation should be avoided where the Community institution would be required to hold money and assume substantial interest rate risk (or be highly active in swaps

---

3.   An idea of this type was proposed by former Commissioner de Silguy in a speech to the Corporation of London in July 1999.

and futures markets to manage that risk). To ensure stable and predictable issuance by the Community institution, a substantial part of the borrowing requirements of the participating Member States would have to be covered by such an arrangement.

4.10 The creation of a new Community institution for debt issuance could be time consuming and might even require a Treaty amendment. Moreover, the new institution would issue on behalf of the Community as a whole so that non-participating Member States (and even non euro-area Member States) would be required to guarantee the debt of the participating Member States. The net result could be a deterioration in the borrowing terms for non-participant Member States with relatively high credit ratings particularly if they were cross-guaranteeing the debt of participant Member States with lower credit ratings. As in hypothesis 3, the compatibility of this arrangement with the Treaty provisions on fiscal discipline would need to be addressed.

5. Assessment and views of the Group

5.1 While there was recognition within the Group that the market for euro-area public debt remains fragmented, views on the benefits of more co-ordinated debt issuance were mixed. Some members argued that imperfections in the functioning of the market, such as lack of liquidity and problems with deliverability into futures contracts, could be linked to the current structure of decentralized issuance. Among the factors seen as pointing in this direction were (i) the persistent out-performance of some sovereign issues relative to others with identical credit rating; (ii) the appearance of three distinct segments in the euro-area market in terms of spread between issuers; (iii) the persistent home bias among investors in the euro area (except Germany); and (iv), non-EU investors' perference for particular sovereign issues. In light of these factors, there was some sympathy for the argument that some issuers might benefit from more coordinated debt issuance.

5.2 Others argued that it is too early to make a definite judgement on the longer-term functioning of the euro-area public debt market. In view of the time required to rollover a bond portofolio, it could be several years before investors can act in an unconstrained manner in the market. Meanwhile, tax and accounting implications from the 'pre-EMU' period could also be a distorting factor in the market. On this basis, there was a view that existing arrangements for coordination were broadly adequate and that any changes would need to be undertaken with caution. It was noted that no major conflict in the calendars of issuers has been experienced to date and that most issuers have become more transparent and predictable in their issuance policies. While market inefficiencies clearly exist, e.g. linked to difficulties with clearing and settlement and with differences in regulatory environment, these could be solved more directly rather than by measures to centralize debt issuance. Similarly, problems in the futures market with an insufficient pool of deliverable securities could be addressed directly by restructuring the way contracts are settled in the direction of cash settlement or settlement against an index of bonds.

5.3 As the Group examined the four hypotheses for more coordinated debt issuance, it was noted that arrangements under hypotheses 1 and 2 differ qualitatively from those under hypotheses 3 and 4. Arrangements under the first two hypotheses would be on a strictly intergovernmental basis. As these would be agreed outside the framework of the Treaty, no change either in Community legislation or institutional infrastructure would be needed. While participating issuers would be required to abide by common rules on technical issues, there would be no cross-guarantees of debt issued by the participants. Consequently the credit risk of individual issuers would not be affected. On the other hand, the credibility of these looser forms of coordination would reflect their vulnerability to the eventual termination of such schemes.

5.4 The coordination arrangements under hypotheses 3 and 4 would involve a cross-guarantee of the debt issued. Although the scope for further market integration would be greater in these more advanced forms of coordination and the possibility of large, liquid and predictable issues based on one issuing calendar would facilitate the emergence of benchmark debt instruments, issuance would have to be based on a timetable established by the issuing entity in close co-operation with the Member States. The credit rating of all participating Member States would be merged both in contractual terms and in terms of financial market perception. If a Community institution were to become the single issuer, the question of non-participating Member States which would de facto cross guarantee the debt of the participating Member States would have to be addressed. This raises legal and institutional aspects that go beyond the scope of this report.

5.5 Coordinated debt issuance was seen as most attractive for the smaller issuers and there was a relatively detailed discussion of the possibilities for joint issuance by the relevant Member States. For joint issuance to be successful in boosting liquidity in the cash market and in allowing deliverability into an actively traded futures contract, single issues of between € 15 billion and € 20 billion would be required on a regular basis. It was felt that most (if not all) of the smaller Member States would need to participate in the joint issuance to ensure the necessary size and regularity in issuance. Without wide participation, it could take too long to build up liquidity in any jointly issued instrument, given differences in maturity profiles among the participants and other constraints.

5.6 In terms of narrowing of spreads, there was scepticism about the scale of benefits to be derived from increased coordination in debt issuance, even for the smaller issuers. As euro-area yield spreads have remained below 50 basis points for 10-year maturities, savings from compression of spreads would be relatively modest. These savings would be further reduced to the extent that they were achieved at the cost of an increase in the yields of larger issuers. Moreover, it was argued that yield spreads might not be susceptible to complete elimination, even between issuers of identical credit rating. To the extent that bonds are used for collateral purposes, they can become 'special' in repo transactions. Tax effects can also be important in this context.

5.7 The advantages of creating a single euro-area debt instrument that could successfully compete for funds on the global capital market in competition with US Treasuries and JGBs were acknowledged in principle. It was also agreed that the euro-area market could benefit from the establishment of a clear 'benchmark' issuer, e.g. through facilitated pricing of non-sovereign issuance and the creation of a homogeneous euro yield curve. However, there was a broad consensus that there would be difficulties associated with such far-reaching coordination that are of a nature which go beyond the remit of the Group. In this context, it was argued that any proposal requiring significant and time-consuming change would face scepticism in markets that are evolving so rapidly.

5.8 The Group also drew attention to an important caveat to these findings: financial markets are experiencing significant changes as a result of globalization, structural change, deregulation and, of course, the impact of the euro itself. Any analysis therefore risks being bypassed by events. While they go beyond the scope of this report, the Group noted several relevant developments. Concerning the role of government issues as benchmarks, for example, the development of non-public debt markets and the decline in the share of government issuance in total debt issuance have important implications. Debt issues of US institutions such as Fannie Mae and Freddie Mac, or European Pfandbriefe, to the extent that they have characteristics similar to those of government issues, may eventually act as substitutes for government debt and obtain benchmark status. The US swap market has indeed already become a benchmark for pricing corporate debt. In the secondary markets, the development of electronic trading systems has important implications for liquidity and has already led to changes in issuing strategies and techniques.

BIBLIOGRAPHY

BOOKS AND MAJOR MONOGRAPHS

Agence Internationale D'information por la Presse. 'Special edition on the European Council and European Parliament sessions, 1 and 2 May 1998: On the creation of EURO, EUROPE', Bruxelles, 3 May 1998.

Basel Committee on Banking Supervision. *A New Capital Adequacy Framework* BIS, Basel, June 1999.

Begg, D., Hagen, J.V., Wyplosz, C. and Zimmermann, K.E. *EMU: Prospects and Challenges for the Euro*, Blackwell, Oxford, 1998.

Bishol, G., Péres, J. and Tuyll, S.V. *User Guide to the Euro*, Sweet and Maxwell, Federal Trust, London, 1996.

Coffey, P. *The European Monetary System – Past, Present and Future*, 2nd edn, Kluwer Academic Publishers, Dordrecht and Boston, 1987.

ECB *Monthly Bulletin*. 'Inflation differentials in a monetary union', Frankfurt, October 1999.

ECB *Monthly Bulletin*. 'The international role of the euro', Frankfurt, August 1999.

ECU. 'The commercial use of the ECU: Invoicing and import–export practices', San Paolo Bank and IAFEI, ECU *Newsletter*, January 1990.

European Commission. 'The Treaty on European Union (Maastricht)', Brussels, 1992.

European Commission. 'Green Paper: On the practical arrangements for the introduction of the single currency', EC Office for Official Publications of the European Communities, Luxembourg, May 1995.

European Commission. 'Economic policy in EMU', Economic Policy Papers, No. 124, Brussels, 1997.

European Commission, Competitiveness Advisory Group. 'Capital markets for competitiveness', Brussels, June 1998.

European Commission. 'A review of regulatory capital requirements' Brussels, November 1999.

European Commission. 'Co-ordinated public debt issuance in the euro area – Report of the Giovanni Group', Brussels, November 2000.

EMI. *The Changeover to the Single Currency*, November 1995.

Kenen, P. *Economic and Monetary Union in Europe,* Cambridge University Press, 1995.

Krueger, T., Nasson, P. and Turtelboom, B. *European Monetary System,* IMF, Washington D.C., 1997.

Onida, F. *The Theory and Policy of Optimum Currency Areas and their Implications for the European Monetary Union,* Societe Universitaire Europeenne de Recherches Financieres (SUERF), 1972.

Smets, J., Maes, I. and Michielsen, J. 'EMU from a Historical Perspective', Belgian National Bank, Brussels, April 2000.

Vedrine, H. *Les Cartes de la France,* Fayard, Paris, 2000.

ARTICLES AND DOCUMENTS

Currencies/Finance

Bulletin Quotidien Europe. 'G/7 Finance Ministers to discuss euro/dollar exchange relationship, reform of international monetary system and external representation of euro', February 1999.

Bulletin Quotidien Europe. 'European Commission: According to the first "Quarterly Note" from the Commission, the use of the Euro is increasing in administrations and is widely used in international payments by companies, although it is still very low among private individuals', December 1999.

Bulletin Quotidien Europe. 'EP/Financial Services: Parliament hopes to strengthen legislation on undertakings for collective investments to improve consumer protection', February 2000.

Bulletin Quotidien Europe. 'EU/Single Currency: European Commision strategy for introduction of Euro', July 2000.

Financial Times. 'Fed funds rate edges upwards to 5.25%', August 1999.

Ecofin

Bulletin Quotidien Europe. 'Reform of IMF, role of EU, conditions for supporting Russia', September 1998.

Bulletin Quotidien Europe. ' "Euro Group" agrees on economic situation, whereas differences remain on presence of commission in external representation of Euro', November 1998.

Bulletin Quotidien Europe. 'Council fixes irrevocable conversion rates between Euro and Currencies of the eleven member states adopting the Single Currency', January 1999.

Bulletin Quotidien Europe. 'Council approves updated stability and convergence programmes – Content of opinions on Germany, Italy, Spain and Belgium', February 2000.

Bulletin Quotidien Europe. 'Greece's third stage on its march towards joining Euro – Improvement in productivity enables Ireland to increase wages', February 2000.

Bulletin Quotidien Europe. 'EU/Council: Council reacts favourable to Danish and UK convergence programmes – some criticism and a few suggestions', March 2000.

Bulletin Quotidien Europe. 'EU/ECOFIN Council: In Monday's "open debate"', several ministers made practical suggestions or introduction of euro and for funding innovation', July 2000.

Euro

Bulletin Quotidien Europe. 'EP/Single Currency: Duisenberg tells parliament ecosystem is well equipped to face up to uncertainties inherent in "new economy" (of which as yet there is no clear evidence in Euro Area)', July 2000.

Bulletin Quotidien Europe. 'EU/Information Society: Agreement by EU 15 at Coreper level on copyright', June 2000.

Financial Times. 'Employers, leader upbeat about Euro', July 2000.

Financial Times. 'Euro-Zone will see faster growth', July 2000.

Financial Times. 'Paris minister hints at control over ECB target', July 2000.

European Economic and Monetary Union

Bulletin Quotidien Europe. 'Eurochambres calls of Ecofin Council to review its approach concerning modalities for introducing note and coins in Euro', October 1999.

Bulletin Quotidien Europe. 'Parliament calls for period of dual circulation of National Currencies and the Euro in early 2002 to be limited to two months,' December, 1999.

Bulletin Quotidien Europe. 'Eurostat study (in cooperation with ECB) shows an evolving European Banking Sector, marked by Mergers and Internationalisation', January 2000.

Bulletin Quotidien Europe. 'EU/Economic and Monetary: Franco Modigiliani Noble Prizewinner accuses ECB of programming 10% unemployment and encourages Europe not to give up until unemployment has been brought down to 3%', April 2000.

Bulletin Quotidien Europe. 'EU/Euro: Euro Group finance ministers release a reassuring statement noting that the exchange rate of the European Currency is a "common concern"', May 2000.

Bulletin Quotidien Europe. 'Plans towards an European economic government are just as important for future of Europe and Euro as Intergovernmental Conference on Institutional Reform', June 2000.

Bulletin Quotidien Europe. 'EU/Euro: Content and aims of new measures proposed by European Commission to fight against Euro-Counterfeiters', July 2000.

Bulletin Quotidien Europe. 'EU/Euro Group: Strengthening and visibility of group decided on – broader powers? Step-up balance of budgets – confirmation of positive economic developments', July 2000.

Bulletin Quotidien Europe. 'EU/Financial Services: Committee of wise men chaired by Lamsfalussy launches questionnaire on European Commissions "Internal Market" site', September 2000.

Bulletin Quotidien Europe. 'Council clarifies practical arrangements for introduction of Euro Notes and Coins' November 2000.

Economist, The. 'Europe's immigrants – A continent on the move', May 2000.

Europe Documents. 'Impact of currency fluctuations on the internal market', November 1995.

Europe Documents. 'The stability pact for Europe proposed by German Finance Minister Theo Waigel', November 1995.

Europe Documents. 'Convergence and structural funds: Commission gives its view on ideas put forward by France', August 1996.

Europe Documents. 'Concluding summary of the European Commission Report on the situation of Member States in relation to 'Maastricht Criteria', November 1996.

Europe Documents. 'The historic report of the ECOFIN council and the EMI that define the stability pact, the new exchange rate mechanism and the legal status of the Euro', December 1996.

Europe Documents. 'First European Commission analysis and guidelines on future role of euro and international monetary system', May 1997.

Europe Documents. 'Guidelines by social or social democrat ministers of the fifteen on the management of single currency and economic and monetary union', November 1998.

Europe Documents. 'Provisions endorsed by the Vienna Summit on external representation of the euro zone and coordination of economic policies', December 1998.

Europe Documents. 'European Commission suggestions for preparing for the introduction of the euro notes and coins at the start of 2002', September 1999.

European Central Bank. 'Euro area monetary arrogates and their role in the eurosystem's monetary policy strategy', February 1999.

European Commission. Delors Report: *Economic and monetary union in the European Community*, Brussels, 1989.

European Commission. 'Financial services: Implementing the framework for financial markets: action plan', 1999.

European Commission. 'A review of regulatory capital requirements for EU credit institutions and investment firms', November 2000.

European Monetary Institute. 'The European Monetary System (EMS): The record'. Frankfurt.

European Monetary Institute. 'Role and Functions of the European Monetary Institute', Frankfurt, February, 1996.

Federation Bancaire de L'Union Europeene. 'Survey on the introduction of the single currency'.

Financial Times. 'Shape of currency crisis to come', January 1997.

Financial Times. 'A fallback plan for EMU', May 1997.

Financial Times. 'Preparing for EMU', May 1997.

Financial Times. 'Europe takes its new currency to the marketplace', September 1997.

Financial Times. 'EMU and the banking system', October 1997.

Financial Times. 'The euro-creature', October 1997.

Financial Times. 'Moment of fusion', October 1997.

Financial Times. 'UK will not join EMU before 2002', October 1997.

Financial Times. 'American eyes on EMU', October 1997.

Financial Times. 'Masters of the grand gesture', November 1997.

Financial Times. 'Some EMU surprises', February 1998.

Financial Times. 'International capital markets', April 1998.

Financial Times. 'Return to Keynes', October 1998.

Financial Times. 'The European economy', Quarterly Guide, May 1999.

Financial Times. 'Euro falls after Prodi's speech confuses markets', June 1999.

Financial Times. 'World economy and finance', Parts 1 and 2, September 1999.

Financial Times. 'Euro-zone economy', December 1999.

Hughes Hallet, A. and Scott, A. 'The fiscal policy dilemmas of monetary union, in P. Coffey (ed.), *Main Economic Policy Areas of the EC after 1992*, Kluwer Academic Press, Dordrecht and Boston, 1993.

INDEX